# DOSTOEVSKY'S *THE IDIOT*

## *A Critical Companion*

Edited by Liza Knapp

Northwestern University Press

The American Association of Teachers of

Slavic and East European Languages

Northwestern University Press

Evanston, Illinois 60208-4210



Published 1998.



Printed in the United States of America

ISBN 0-8101-1533-6

**Library of Congress Cataloging-in-Publication Data**

Dostoevsky's The Idiot : a critical companion / edited by

Liza Knapp.

p. cm. — (Northwestern/AATSEEL critical

companions to Russian literature)

Romanized record.

ISBN 0-8101-1533-6 (pbk.)

1. Dostoyevsky, Fyodor, 1821–1881. Idiot. I. Knapp,

Liza. II. Series.

PG3325.I3 1998

891.73'3—dc21 98-26139

CIP

The paper used in this publication meets the minimum requirements of the American National Standard for Information Sciences—Permanence of Paper for Printed Library Materials, ANSI Z39.48-1984.

# Contents

# Acknowledgments, with Notes on References, Transliteration, and Translation

I am grateful to all of the contributors, to Barry Scherr, and to Susan Harris of Northwestern University Press for their goodwill in this project. My special thanks to Ellendea Proffer of Ardis and to David Lowe for generously making it possible to use the translations of Dostoevsky's letters.

The following texts (in revised form) appear here by permission, which I acknowledge with gratitude:

David M. Bethea, "*The Idiot:* Historicism Arrives at the Station," in *The Shape of Apocalypse in Modern Russian Fiction* (Princeton: Princeton University Press, 1989). Copyright © 1989 by Princeton University Press. Reprinted by permission of Princeton University Press.

Robin Feuer Miller, "The Notebooks for *The Idiot*," in *Dostoevsky and "The Idiot": Author, Narrator, and Reader* (Cambridge: Harvard University Press, 1981). Copyright © 1981 by the President and Fellows of Harvard University.

Nina Pelikan Straus, "Flights from *The Idiot*'s Womanhood," in *Dostoevsky and the Woman Question: Rereadings at the End of a Century* (New York: St. Martin's; Basingstoke, Engl.: Macmillan). Copyright © 1964 by Nina Pelikan Straus. Reprinted by permission of St. Martin's Press, Incorporated, and Macmillan Ltd.

Fyodor Dostoevsky, *Complete Letters*, ed. and trans. David A. Lowe, vol. 2, *1860–1867:* vol. 3, *1868–1871* (Ann Arbor, Mich.: Ardis, 1989–1990) [selections]. Reprinted by permission of Ardis Publishers.

The essays by Miller and Straus give complete bibliographic references on first mention in their notes. I have maintained this apparatus here and followed it in my own essays. Bethea's essay uses shorthand references to the "Works Cited" section in his chapter (excluding references to well-known literary works). Because each essay has its own set of references, there is inevitably overlap between the individual studies and the final Select Bibliography. At the same time, the individual contributions contain some references that do not appear in the Select Bibliography, which lists only studies treating *The Idiot.*

All references to Dostoevsky's works and letters in this volume are to the *Polnoe sobranie sochinenii v tridsati tomakh*, ed. V. G. Bazanov et al. (Leningrad: Nauka, 1972–90). The reference "8:123," for example, refers to page 123 of volume 8. Volumes 28–30, which contain Dostoevsky's letters, are each divided into two books. Thus, "28.2:136" refers to page 136 of book 2 of volume 28. The dates of Dostoevsky's letters are also included in the citations.

It might help to recall that the Russian calendar at this point lagged behind the Western calendar by twelve days. When two dates are given (for example, July 9/21), the first is the Russian date, the second a translation of that date into the Western calendar.

The Select Bibliography uses the Library of Congress transliteration system. My contributions use a more popular mode of rendering Russian names. In the reprinted essays, the usage of the author has been maintained.

Translations of letters included in the Primary Sources are those of David Lowe. Translations of other material in the Primary Sources are my own.

# I INTRODUCTION

# Introduction to *The Idiot*
# Part 1: Where, When, and How *The Idiot* Was Written

LIZA KNAPP

## 1. Escape from Petersburg

On Holy Friday 1867, Fyodor Dostoevsky and his young wife, Anna, left Russia for what they thought would be a few months. They did not return until July 1871. In setting off for Europe, Dostoevsky left behind him in Saint Petersburg heavy debts and complicated family obligations. Dostoevsky's first wife, Marya Dmitrievna, had died of consumption in April 1864, leaving Dostoevsky in charge of her teenage son (by her first husband) Pavel (Pasha) Isaev (b. 1848). Dostoevsky's beloved brother Mikhail had died a few months later, in June 1864. At this point, Dostoevsky took on responsibility for his brother's family. Out of loyalty, he also undertook to pay back debts his brother left behind.

Dostoevsky had met Anna Grigoryevna Snitkina on October 4/16, 1866, when she began to serve as his stenographer. He needed to finish the manuscript of *The Gambler* by the end of October; otherwise, he would have had to forfeit the rights to (and profit from) all his works for the next nine years. (So desperate had Dostoevsky been for money that, for the sake of an advance, he had agreed to these conditions, set by the infamous publisher Stellovsky.) Dostoevsky frantically sought some way of meeting the deadline. At the suggestion of a friend, he decided to try working with a stenographer. To Dostoevsky's great relief, this new method of composition by dictation worked efficiently. He spent his birthday (October 30) making final corrections to the manuscript he had finished dictating the day before and delivered the manuscript the next day. Dostoevsky then invited Anna Grigoryevna to help him finish *Crime and Punishment.* Soon thereafter, he proposed to her. They were married in February 1867.

By all accounts their marriage developed into a happy one and it provided Dostoevsky with the stable family life he had longed for. Initially, however, the new couple found their life in Saint Petersburg trying, or rather, Anna Grigoryevna especially did. Dostoevsky's creditors were hounding them and debtors' prison threatened. Dostoevsky's extended family continued to make demands on him. They did not cotton to his new wife and they behaved toward her in ways which Anna Grigoryevna found distressing and demeaning, but which her husband seemed not to notice. Hoping to save the marriage by removing herself and her husband from the trying situation in Saint Petersburg, Anna pushed for the trip abroad. She pawned her dowry to raise the money necessary for them to get away.

Of course, Dostoevsky's Saint Petersburg relatives' requests for money and Dostoevsky's concern about them never ceased. But now transactions with them took place by mail. Dostoevsky and his wife were left very much on their own together for the whole period of their exile, and they developed a strong sense of mutual dependence and love. They had little social contact except for occasional encounters with old Russian acquaintances who were also abroad and a few visits from Anna's mother and brother. They kept in touch with friends and family by letter. Dostoevsky followed current events in Russia, to the extent possible, by reading Russian periodicals available in the West and by asking his correspondents, especially Apollon Maikov, for news.

The Dostoevskys moved from Germany (Dresden, Baden-Baden) to Switzerland (Basel, Geneva, Vevey), to Italy (Milan, Florence) during the first two years and then found themselves staying in Dresden until their return to Russia. All along the way, they expressed their longing to go home, and yet financial, literary, and familial obstacles of one sort or another seemed to conspire to keep them in Europe.

## 2. Gambling and Epilepsy

The time Dostoevsky and his wife spent abroad, especially in the early stages, was punctuated by attacks of Dostoevsky's gambling and epilepsy, both of which caused great suffering and hardship to the couple.

As on his previous trips abroad, Dostoevsky could not resist the roulette table. Oppressed by financial need and dreading working on his new novel (*The Idiot*), Dostoevsky would make "one last attempt" after another to gamble their way out of their financial troubles. In the letters to his wife that he wrote when he would leave her and go off gambling, Dostoevsky would swear to reform; he would heap praise on her for being angelically forbearing and abuse on himself for being unworthy. Dostoevsky would also give a thaler-by-thaler account of the trip. He would describe his foolproof "system" for winning. Then would come the pleas to send him train fare back to her.

In the aftermath of his gambling, Dostoevsky became even more desperate for money. He was constantly asking his friends, and even the occasional enemy, for loans, although he was ashamed to tell them that he had gambled away his last money. The hocking and redeeming of the Dostoevskys' few possessions was a periodic event. Eventually, Dostoevsky found that the only hope for their future was to buckle down and write the novel, which had been promised to Katkov for his journal the *Russian Messenger;* the advances and payments were what the Dostoevskys lived on.

Sigmund Freud considered Dostoevsky's gambling to be a manifestation of his innate pathological desire for self-punishment.[1] Dostoevsky's wife regarded his gambling as "a disease" for which she feared there was no cure. Eventually Dostoevsky cured himself: he gambled for what was to be the last time in Wiesbaden on April 16/28, 1871.[2] He signs the letter written to his wife that night

"Yours entirely *from this day on,* Fyodor Dostoevsky" (emphasis added).[3]

During their life abroad, Dostoevsky's epileptic attacks, from which he suffered until the end of his life, continued, although by some accounts less frequently than in the period prior to their departure. (Part of the rationale for their trip abroad had been hope that removal from Saint Petersburg would be beneficial to Dostoevsky's health.) As James Rice's discussion of the frequency of Dostoevsky's attacks reveals,[4] what Dostoevsky would mention in letters did not always coincide with the recorded facts. (Dostoevsky kept a log of his attacks and his wife's diary refers to them.)

Dostoevsky passed epilepsy on to the hero of *The Idiot.* The attack Myshkin suffers in part 2 is generally thought to be clinically realistic and to match what Dostoevsky himself experienced. Many critics have noted the important ways in which epilepsy has been incorporated into the novel, both its thematics and its poetics.

The thematic aspect relates to the suspension of time.[5] According to Myshkin, during an epileptic fit the epileptic undergoes an experience of "there being time no more"; the experience is described in language associated with the apocalypse in the Revelation of Saint John, one of Dostoevsky's favorite texts. The epileptic, feeling released from the laws ordinarily binding him on earth, experiences a "synthesis," which for Dostoevsky was a taste of heaven. As critics have noticed, epilepsy, known as the holy disease, may have been suffered by Jesus. Although one can only guess at how epilepsy influenced Dostoevsky's poetics, it may be that Dostoevsky developed his particular brand of realism, with its "fantastic" quality, in response to epilepsy. Surely, Dostoevsky had some affinity for this kind of sensation and was drawn to it in his writing.

While the "aura" during an attack was sometimes beatific, Dostoevsky suffered greatly as a result of this disease. Anna Grigoryevna describes the constant dread of these attacks, their onset, the physical torment, and the effects that lasted for days: weakness, disorientation, debilitation, gloom, and grouchiness. Especially poignant are her descriptions of the fear of death that these attacks brought on.

After an attack Dostoevsky would be afraid of dying and not want to fall asleep unless she was at his side. Dostoevsky himself repeatedly associates an almost mystical sadness with his epilepsy.[6] Although Myshkin's epilepsy and the "mode of being" associated with it in the novel are often thought of as beatific, one should keep in mind that while epilepsy may have given Dostoevsky a taste of heaven, it did not do so without making parts of his life on earth hell.

## 3. An Encounter with Turgenev: The Telescope and *Madame Bovary*

Before he began to work in earnest on the novel, Dostoevsky paid a visit to Ivan Turgenev (1818–83) in Baden-Baden in July 1867.[7] Since the 1840s, relations between the two authors had undergone ups and downs. After a period of unfriendliness, the two authors had had a rapprochement in the 1860s when Dostoevsky expressed his appreciation for Turgenev's *Fathers and Sons* and Turgenev agreed to publish a piece in Dostoevsky's journal. But, in August 1865, a desperate Dostoevsky, gambling furiously, had borrowed money from Turgenev (he asked for one hundred thalers; Turgenev gave him fifty). Dostoevsky had promised to pay him back soon, but never had.

After he arrived in Baden-Baden in 1867, Dostoevsky had been dodging Turgenev. When Ivan Goncharov, whom Dostoevsky had met at a gaming hall, mentioned that Turgenev had caught sight of him, Dostoevsky decided that he could avoid Turgenev no longer. With his unpaid debt eating away at him, Dostoevsky felt it would be cowardly not to go and see Turgenev. (For Dostoevsky's lively description of his visit, see his letter to Maikov of August 16/28, 1867, given in Primary Sources). Everything about Turgenev, from his way of offering his cheek to be kissed to his politics, bothered Dostoevsky.

As his letter to Maikov reveals, Dostoevsky used this particular encounter with Turgenev to formulate, a bit histrionically, some of his most heartfelt ideas about the whole tradition of Russian Westernizing liberals, the father of whom for Dostoevsky was the influential literary critic Vissarion Belinsky (1811–48). Belinsky, in fact, was the subject of an article Dostoevsky was working on at that time. Belinsky was associated in Dostoevsky's mind with Turgenev: Turgenev and Dostoevsky had been young writers championed during the same period by Belinsky. Dostoevsky's relations with Belinsky soured before Belinsky's death (Belinsky accused Dostoevsky of squandering his talent). Turgenev, however, had remained on good terms with him and had even dedicated his *Fathers and Sons* to the memory of Belinsky.

As his letter to Maikov shows, Dostoevsky disliked the way "all these trashy little liberals and progressives, primarily still of Belinsky's school, find their greatest pleasure and satisfaction in criticizing Russia."[8] Dostoevsky also objected to how the liberals boast of their atheism and "spit on" what Dostoevsky terms "the loftiest divine beauty": Christ. Here Dostoevsky continues the debate over Christ that he had begun with Belinsky in the 1840s. In fact, *The Idiot* may be seen as Dostoevsky's ultimate (or penultimate) answer to what he saw as the liberals' tendency to spit on Christ.[9]

Dostoevsky would go on to lampoon Turgenev in his depiction of the "famous author" Karmazinov in *The Devils*, the novel Dostoevsky wrote after *The Idiot*. Within *The Idiot*, Dostoevsky also takes a shot at Turgenev by blaming him for the nihilist movement. But this encounter with Turgenev may have had still more profound influence on the novel:

During their visit, each author offered the other some advice. Dostoevsky (as he proudly related) told Turgenev to go get a telescope, the better to see Russia with. (In Dostoevsky's view, the expatriate Turgenev was out of touch with the Russia he wrote about.) Dostoevsky may well have envisioned *The Idiot* as just what people like Turgenev needed in order to see what Russia was truly like.

Turgenev's advice to Dostoevsky was to read *Madame Bovary*, which, according to Anna Grigoryevna's diary report, Turgenev billed as the best thing written anywhere in the last ten years. Turgenev presumably did not heed Dostoevsky's advice to get a telescope, but Dostoevsky heeded Turgenev's. He and his wife bought the book four days later. (The fact that Dostoevsky followed Turgenev's advice attests to his respect for Turgenev's literary instincts. This respect, as Joseph Frank has pointed out, survived all their other disagreements.) Dostoevsky signals the importance of *Madame Bovary* in *The Idiot*, when we find that this was Nastasya Filippovna's reading during her last days.[10]

Thus, the encounter with Turgenev – an encounter that Dostoevsky had hoped to avoid – may have played a role in what *The Idiot* became. In reaction to Turgenev and all he represented to Dostoevsky, Dostoevsky wanted to make his novel as "Russian" as possible (to make it into the telescope to see Russia that Turgenev so sorely needed). And, thanks to Turgenev's tip, *Madame Bovary* acquired in *The Idiot* a Russian cousin, predating its more famous Russian cousin, *Anna Karenina*. (I follow here Osip Mandelshtam's use of the term "cousin" to describe the relation between Anna Karenina and Emma Bovary.)

## 4. A Dedication to Sonya Ivanova

Dostoevsky had decided even before the novel was written that he would dedicate it to his niece Sonya Ivanova. She was the twenty-one-year-old daughter of his sister Vera and her husband A. P. Ivanov. During the last months of his first wife's life, Dostoevsky had brought her to Moscow so that Ivanov, a doctor, could care for her. During this period, Dostoevsky got to know Sonya, whose childhood he had spent in exile. Writing in 1866 to Anna Korvin-Krukovskaya (whom Dostoevsky had once courted and who is thought to have inspired the character of Aglaya Epanchin in *The Idiot*), Dostoevsky praised his niece, saying, "What a marvelous, bright, profound, and sincere soul."[11] His devotion to Sonya was such that not only did he dedicate the book to her, but he had early on persuaded his wife that if the child they awaited was a girl, she should be named after Sonya.[12]

Dostoevsky corresponded with Sonya while he was abroad, somewhat sporadically but enthusiastically. His letters contain news of his life abroad and of the novel dedicated to her. One of these letters contains his claim (now famous) that in this novel he was attempting to depict a "positively beautiful man," the likes of which had not yet been put to paper, Christ having been the only model thus far.[13]

With his niece, Dostoevsky tried on the role he was later to adopt with many of the readers who turned to him for advice during the publication of *Diary of a Writer*. Dostoevsky's letters to his niece are particularly valuable for the insights they give into his attitude toward the choices which she, as a young woman, faced in her life. Sonya Ivanova had been under pressure from her family to marry, for their convenience rather than for love. She turned to her uncle for moral support after refusing. Dostoevsky fully supported her decision not to submit to this marriage. Dostoevsky encouraged her, instead of marrying a man she did not love, to find a profession, to study. He cites the example of Nadezhda Suslova (the sister of his former lover, Polina Suslova), who had just completed her studies in Zurich to become a doctor of medicine. In a comment interesting given the importance of the "woman question" to *The Idiot*, Dostoevsky tells his niece: "You should know that the woman question, and especially that of the Russian woman, will definitely make several great and wonderful strides even within your lifetime."[14] Although Dostoevsky distanced himself from "nihilists," he nevertheless embraced the idea of women being educated and being able to earn money in a non-demeaning way. Without these opportunities, as Dostoevsky showed in *Crime and Punishment*, women may feel they are compelled to sell themselves to men, whether as prostitutes (Sonya Marmeladov) or as wives of men they do not love (Dunya Raskolnikov).

Perhaps his own wife was a positive model of what Dostoevsky envisioned. She had pursued her training as a stenographer with great energy and determination. Forced to interrupt her course of study when her father died, Anna Grigoryevna later managed to finish learning stenography and make a living. While she and Dostoevsky were abroad awaiting their first child, Anna Grigoryevna (no doubt frustrated by her husband's handling of their finances) records in her diary her hope of getting a job as stenographer for the newly reformed court system on their return to Russia: "If there were a shortage of men, they might hire a woman." And the pregnant Anna mused about how good it would be to have the money; her earnings would be "a dowry for Sonya" or something for Misha (the names they had in mind for the baby that was to be born).[15] Dostoevsky and his wife suggested to Sonya Ivanova that she consider stenography as a profession and invited her to come stay with them in Saint Petersburg on their return and study with Anna Grigoryevna's former teacher. It was crucial to Dostoevsky that his niece be able to earn a living.

Dostoevsky adamantly wanted to "save" Sonya from the violation or "the swinishness" of a loveless marriage.[16] Dostoevsky's ruminations on his niece's fate, on the choices she faced, on the parental pressure to marry and her own resistance, are reflected in the novel he dedicated to her. To marry or not to marry is one of the major issues debated, in one way or another, throughout the novel. As has been suggested by Robin Feuer Miller,[17] the presentation early in the novel of the "three marriageable maidens" (the Epanchin daughters) evokes something of the aura of a Jane Austen novel, but with something definitely "askew." And by the end of *The Idiot*, readers find that Dostoevsky is a far cry from Jane Austen.

Initially, the novel seems to promise something positive for its women: the Epanchin daughters have been allowed to eat, paint, and read to their heart's content; they have not, at least until the recent plan for Alexandra to marry Totsky, been under pressure to marry. Even Nastasya Filippovna, orphaned and seduced at a young age, appears ready for the first time in her life to take charge of her fate and belong to nobody but herself.

## 5. From Notebooks to Part 1

At various points during his career, Dostoevsky declared his envy of writers like Tolstoy and Turgenev who had the luxury of working and reworking drafts. As Jacques Catteau has noted, Dostoevsky's complaints, especially as reported by his wife in her *Reminiscences*, have led many to the conclusion that, with more money and more time, Dostoevsky would have written "better" novels, meaning novels with a more conventional "aesthetic standard." On the other hand, as Catteau points out, Dostoevsky, whether he and others liked it or not, was writing in a new and innovative form, "enthralled and passionate" in Dostoevsky's own words. According to Catteau, Dostoevsky was "extremely sensitive to criticism" and did not quite dare to defend his new poetics openly. Thus he may himself have contributed to the tendency to regard his works as suffering from a lack of proper revision.[18]

Dostoevsky divided the labor of writing a novel between the "poet" and the "artist." Dostoevsky's "poet" thought of the idea or summoned up from his heartfelt experience impressions and then his "artist" gave form to this raw material (which Dostoevsky likened to a gem, with the artist then functioning as jeweler).[19] In the early stages of writing a novel, Dostoevsky would make notes for himself about ideas, characters, situations, working and reworking them, almost as if they were puzzles. (At one point, Dostoevsky wrote "Eureka!" on finding a solution to a compositional problem.) Eventually he would begin to dictate the novel in fairly finished form to his wife, who would take it down in stenography and then transcribe what he had dictated. He would then make revisions (probably minimal) and she would make a clean copy. Dostoevsky increasingly grew to depend on this method of writing.

Dostoevsky began writing notes for *The Idiot* in earnest a few days after completing his article on Belinsky on September 14. It would take Dostoevsky three months to come up with the plan he stuck with. During this period, he made various notes about characters and situations that bear little direct resemblance to what he ended up with. He scrapped plan after plan and reworked, in various arrangements, the relations between the various characters and also the natures of his characters.[20]

Notable is the fact that the Idiot, when he first appears in the notebooks, is far from being the "positively beautiful man" that

Dostoevsky sought to depict in *The Idiot* as we know it: the original Idiot is mean, spiteful, and proud. The notebooks also show Dostoevsky trying to get the family groupings right and figuring out where the Idiot should stand in relation to the question of family. Dostoevsky proposes various scenarios, debating about whether his hero should be "illegitimate" or "legitimate" but without a mother. Either way, the Idiot was to be something of an outsider, who, in the novel, seeks to clarify his position in regard to family. The notebooks also show that Dostoevsky envisioned his hero as a "sphinx" and, later, as "Christ."

The general plan for *The Idiot* was that Dostoevsky was to send off monthly installments. What we know as part 1 of the novel appeared in two successive months, for example. Dostoevsky, like other nineteenth-century Russian writers, wrote for serial publication in the so-called thick journals. (Intended to serve as the main cultural vehicle for all Russian culture, thick journals published material of all sorts – fiction, poetry, memoirs, science, politics, philosophy. The Dostoevsky brothers themselves had published two such journals.) This arrangement meant that Dostoevsky had to write in chunks that would be effective in that format, and end the installment for a given month in a way that would keep the readers coming back for more. Further, because of his particularly desperate finances, Dostoevsky hoped that the serial publication of *The Idiot* would be quickly followed by a separate edition and felt himself under extra pressure to make the novel good enough to convince a publisher that a separate edition would sell.

## 6. Part 1 of *The Idiot* and December 22, 1849

The very title of the novel defines Myshkin as an idiot, although Dostoevsky kept what was to be understood by this term a mystery, to be unraveled, as Robin Feuer Miller suggests, by each reader. In the opening scenes of the novel, all who meet him find something odd about him: his lack of experience with women, his populism, his preoccupation with death, and so forth. He is identified as a "holy fool" by Rogozhin early in the novel, and by Dostoevsky himself in his notebooks to the novel.[21]

The figure of the holy fool goes back to Saint Paul's Epistle to the Corinthians (1 Cor. 4:10: "We are fools for Christ's sake, but you are wise in Christ"). The holy fool is associated with saintliness, a lack of worldliness (or otherworldliness), marginality to society. And, because the notion derives from Saint Paul (who also establishes condemnation to death as a metaphor for human mortality in general), the holy fool is associated with death and, specifically, with condemnation to death. The fool is marginal to this life in more than one way.

The tradition of the holy fool is a rich one in Russia. One of Dostoevsky's immediate literary sources could be Grisha in Leo Tolstoy's *Childhood.* Grisha, a pilgrim who visits the Irtenev household, functions as a memento mori; he challenges the status quo, the social structure, and ultimately all systems, including language. Further, Grisha rejects the notion that one human being should judge and punish another: he voices his opinion that there is no need for Irtenev, the narrator's father, to punish his serf for failing to control one of the dogs. Grisha speaks in a manner that is incomprehensible to the narrator's father (who voices his opinion that holy fools should all be locked up) but is comprehensible to his mother (who welcomes holy fools). Much as Tolstoy's narrative creates a rift between those who reject and those who embrace holy fools, with the child narrator left to choose sides, Dostoevsky forces all who encounter his idiot, the heroes and heroines within the plot and the reader of the text, to respond to him in some way, and in so doing, take a stand on ultimate questions of life and death.

Dostoevsky's readers have always been quick to see in Myshkin certain autobiographical elements.[22] Additionally, it has been noted that Dostoevsky seems to make a cameo appearance in the novel as Myshkin's acquaintance in the insane asylum who was condemned to death and reprieved at the last moment. Dostoevsky uses this story to show how the reprieved man's experience granted him a (metaphorical) resurrection, a new love for life. This experience has been internalized by Myshkin himself, who treats all whom he meets with a kind of love born of contact with death.

On December 22, 1849, Dostoevsky and a number of acquaintances were taken from the Peter-and-Paul Fortress (where they had been imprisoned) to Semenovsky Square, read death sentences, prepared for execution by firing squad, and allowed to confess and kiss the cross. Dostoevsky and his cohorts had participated in a group that had discussed social change in Russia and read banned books. For the crime of their participation in the "Petrashevsky Circle" (named after their leader, at whose house they met), they were accused of plotting revolution and were sentenced to death.[23]

As they prepared to die, Dostoevsky reportedly said (in French) to his friend among the group, Speshnev, "We will be with Christ (Nous serons avec le Christ)," to which Speshnev replied (in Russian), "Yes, a bit of dust."[24] Dostoevsky is also reported to have gone around noting parallels between what they were going through and Victor Hugo's *Last Day of a Condemned Man*, the first-person narrative that lasts right up to the moment when the protagonist is guillotined.

After the first group of three – Petrashevsky, Grigoryev, and Mombelli, considered the three most guilty and therefore to be first executed – were blindfolded and ready to be shot, a messenger of Tsar Nicholas I rode up and read them a reprieve, which commuted their sentences to various terms of prison and exile. (Dostoevsky would spend five years, from 1850 to 1854, in at a prison labor camp in Tobolsk.) Later that day, back in prison at the Peter-and-Paul Fortress in Saint Petersburg, before beginning the trip to Siberia, Dostoevsky wrote to his brother of the experience, quoting loosely by memory from Hugo's work and heralding his own rebirth and new love for life. Having been that close to death, Dostoevsky felt that he had undergone a kind of rebirth.

When Dostoevsky emerged years later from what he referred to as the "house of the dead" (prison camp), he again likened his experience to a "resurrection." Throughout the rest of his life, Dostoevsky drew in various ways on his experience on December 22, 1849.

Having been "face-to-face" with death had, he felt, given him a new understanding of life. He imparts some of his understanding to his "holy fool" Myshkin. On the other hand, one of the Petrashevsky group, Nikolai Petrovich Grigoryev, who had been among the three already blindfolded when the reprieve was read, never recovered from this mock execution and the penal servitude that followed. He went mad. Being "face-to-face" with death and then "alive again" can make someone into a holy fool or it can bring on madness. Dostoevsky in *The Idiot* explores both of these possibilities in his portrayal of Myshkin.

## 7. Fatherhood and the Sting of the Grave

Amid the pressures of writing *The Idiot*, in the face of their desperate finances, living in isolation, worried about Dostoevsky's health (physical and mental), the Dostoevskys looked forward quite joyously to the birth of their first child. When Dostoevsky went off gambling in October 1867, his letters to his wife contain affectionate references to "Misha" and/or "Sonya." In one letter, Dostoevsky opens by announcing that he has "lost everything" and continues to describe pawning his ring and coat, but then he cheerily asserts that he will find some way of covering "the expenses for our future guest and little angel."[25]

In her diary, Anna Grigoryevna reports Dostoevsky's solicitous anticipation. She tells of how the Swiss midwife asked them which of Dostoevsky's friends lived in her street; she had caught sight of Dostoevsky so often near her house that she assumed he must be visiting a neighbor of hers. It then came out that Dostoevsky had taken to walking to her house during his daily walks; he wanted to be thoroughly familiar with the route before the time came for him to summon her to assist at the birth.[26] Dostoevsky was proverbially bad at finding his way in strange cities.

When his wife's labor began, Dostoevsky was asleep, recovering from an epileptic attack. His wife, reluctant to wake him, underwent the first hours of her labor while he slept. The next morning she finally awakened him and he went for the midwife. Dostoevsky gave her to understand that she was not showing the requisite concern and alacrity, to which she muttered, "Ô ces russes, ces russes!" But never, said this Swiss midwife to Anna Grigoryevna later, did a father show such feelings at the birth of his child, and she exclaimed, "Ô ces russes, ces russes!" some more. Dostoevsky's wife suggests that Dostoevsky modeled Shatov's reactions to his wife's labor, described in *The Devils*, on Dostoevsky's own.

Sonya (Sophia) was born on February 22/March 5, 1868. Writing especially to his friend Maikov (and Sonya's godfather to be) Dostoevsky revealed his feelings about fatherhood: "I have been feeling, for almost a month now, terribly much that is new and that until now has been unfamiliar to me, from exactly that moment that I first saw my Sonya, up to that moment when, through joint efforts, we just bathed her in a basin. Yes, an angelic soul has in fact flown in to be with us. But I won't describe my feelings to you. They are growing and developing with every day."[27] A bemused and very proud Dostoevsky describes how much his daughter resembles him: "She already even has exactly my facial expression, my whole face, including the wrinkles on the brow – she lies there and looks as though she's writing a novel!" With his Saint Petersburg relatives, he was more guarded.

But, in the beginning of May, Sonya took ill and died of pneumonia a week later. How did this death affect Dostoevsky? Dostoevsky's wife's memoirs tell of their shared sorrow and despair, and especially of her concern for her husband: "Deeply shaken and saddened by the loss, I was terribly afraid for my poor husband: his despair was stormy, he wept and cried like a woman; standing in front of the cold corpse of his loved one, he covered her pale face and hands with warm kisses. I never ever saw such stormy despair."[28]

To Maikov, a grieving Dostoevsky wrote: "Where is Sonya? Where is that little human being for whom, I make bold to say, I would undergo suffering on the cross so that she might live?"[29] He continues a month later: "I will never forget and will never stop suffering! Even if we have another child, I don't understand how I will love him; where I will find love; I need Sonya. I cannot understand that she is no more and that I will never see her."[30]

When his first wife died in 1864, Dostoevsky put the question to himself in his diary, "Masha is lying on the table. Will I see her again?" and tried to console himself by envisioning eternal life.[31] And even just a few months before his daughter's death, Dostoevsky had comforted his relatives after the sudden death of A. P. Ivanov, the father of his niece Sonya, to whom *The Idiot* was dedicated. Dostoevsky assured the grieving family that they would "see" Ivanov again and admonished them not to give way to "atheism." But when his own Sonya died, Dostoevsky seems to have felt the sting of death and the victory of the grave more powerfully than ever before.

How did this death affect *The Idiot?* In order to answer this question, it may be helpful to look ahead to *The Brothers Karamazov*, a novel that responds in overt ways to the death in 1878 of another of the Dostoevskys' children, their three-year-old Aleksei. In this instance, Dostoevsky named the hero Aleksei after his dead son, and, as Robert Belknap has suggested, wrote the novel "to create a rich identity for the namesake of his dead son."[32] Furthermore, within the novel, consolation is offered for the death of children: Zosima counsels a grieving mother that with time her tears will turn to joy and asserts that Job *can* love his new children after his first ones have been murdered. The young Ilyushechka's death gives meaning to the boys who will remember him and "see him again." And the novel's epigraph ("Verily, verily, I say unto you, except a corn of wheat fall into the ground and die, it abideth alone: but if it die, it bringeth forth much fruit") suggests the fruitfulness of death.

Robin Feuer Miller has written that "the theme of the lost child is as important to Dostoevsky's entire literary canon as it is to that of Dickens. The outpouring of grief for a dead, injured, or suffering child constitutes the groundswell of [*The Brothers Karamazov*]."[33] If Dostoevsky poured his own grief into the parts of *The Idiot* written after Sonya's death (which occurred when he was in the midst of part 2), he kept it beneath the surface of the novel, perhaps ultimately adding to the cathartic "groundswell" of grief that pours out in *The*

*Brothers Karamazov*. Although it is impossible to say exactly how the death of Sonya figures in *The Idiot*, the fact that death appears increasingly as an inexorable and cruel force as the novel progresses may have been influenced by Dostoevsky's own despair. Where are the reprieves from death of the sort that Myshkin's Swiss tales, told to the Epanchins in part 1, led the reader to expect?

But perhaps the most disturbing change in the latter part of the novel is the emergence of Ippolit Terentiev, a youth dying of consumption, as a key figure. Joseph Frank calls him "the first in Dostoevsky's remarkable gallery of metaphysical rebels." Frank continues: "For Ippolit is revolting not against the iniquities of a social order but, anticipating Kirillov and Ivan Karamazov, against a world in which death, and hence immitigable human suffering, is an inescapable reality."[34] (Recall, in connection with the theme of dying children in particular, that Dostoevsky's most famous "metaphysical rebel" Ivan Karamazov adamantly refuses to accept the suffering and death of innocent children, and he rebels against Zosima's message of Job-like reconciliation.) In his confession, Ippolit calls into question Christ's resurrection. If, as Holbein's painting of the dead Christ suggests to Ippolit, men and women hope in vain for eternal life, then the whole universe becomes a dead machine that swallows life.[35]

As Joseph Frank has reminded Dostoevsky's readers, Ippolit's interpretation of the Holbein painting is not the only one provided in the novel.[36] Earlier, in part 2 (in a section written *before* Sonya's death), Myshkin had responded to the same painting. While he admits that such a painting could cause one to lose faith, he goes on to tell Rogozhin several stories intended to document the faith and religious feeling of the Russian people. In one of these stories, a woman compares God's joy at the prayer of a sinner to a mother's joy at her baby's first smile (8:183–84).

Thus, the novel provides an alternative to Ippolit's bleak view of a world devoid of faith in Myshkin's image of the uncanny faith of the Russian people. Indeed, Dostoevsky adheres throughout the novel to his "idea." What seems to have changed, in response to Sonya's death perhaps, is the sheer force with which death and human destruction are felt at the end of the novel and the introduction of the metaphysical rebel. For many readers, this metaphysical revolt has become the essence of Dostoevsky's works. Here again, however, Myshkin counters this revolt. When asked by a dying Ippolit how best to die, Myshkin gives what Joseph Frank calls "a moving and beautiful reply":[37] "Pass by us and forgive us our happiness!" (8:433). These words, said quietly by Myshkin within the novel, contain the essence of the message of reconciliation and consolation that Dostoevsky subsequently elaborates upon in *The Brothers Karamazov.* The "corns of wheat" dying in *The Idiot* would bear fruit in *The Brothers Karamazov.*

## 8. Italy and Dostoevsky's "Fantastic Prince"

Soon after the death of Sonya, the Dostoevskys moved from Geneva to nearby Vevey and then to Italy in September 1868. Reluctant as they were to leave behind Sonya's grave, they were relieved to be gone from Switzerland. The peasants of Italy they met during their travels reminded them of Russian peasants; they provided a welcome antidote to the Swiss "bourgeois" about whom the Dostoevskys complained. They settled in Milan first and eventually in Florence, where they enjoyed the museums and sights. To Dostoevsky's relief, Anna Grigoryevna's spirits began to improve bit by bit. Work on the novel progressed; Dostoevsky finished it by the end of 1868.

As his work on the novel drew to a close, Dostoevsky grew more and more concerned about how the novel was being received back in Russia. He worried that the public did not like the novel and began to criticize the novel himself. His comments have sometimes been taken as proof that he regarded his novel as a failure. However, as with most of Dostoevsky's statements, it may be misleading to take them out of context.

All along, Dostoevsky depended largely on his friend Maikov for information. Writing to Dostoevsky shortly after the publication of the first section of the novel, Maikov begins: "I know, I know, I know, dear Fyodor Mikhailovich, I know that you are burning with impatience to know, how is the novel doing?"[38] Maikov reported that the novel was making a splash. In his next letter, written after he read the next installment (up to the end of Nastasya Filippovna's birthday party), Maikov voiced praise for the Idiot himself, deeming him to be "the most realistic character." "Does that seem strange to you?" Maikov adds. He then goes on say that all the other characters "live in a fantastic world, they all are illuminated by a strong, particular, but fantastic glow. You read it avidly but at the same time it does not seem believable."[39] Maikov here expresses hesitation about the "fantastic" aspect of his friend's novel. It was not the first time that Dostoevsky's works had been rejected as being "fantastic." Belinsky had objected to "the fantastic coloring" of Dostoevsky's *The Double* (1846), declaring "the fantastic in our day has its place only in madhouses, and not in literature, and it is in the purview of doctors, not of poets."[40]

Dostoevsky, of course, refused to heed Belinsky's advice. In *The Idiot* Dostoevsky once again tears down the boundaries that Belinsky wanted to maintain between literature and the madhouse. No doubt, much about *The Idiot* would have struck Belinsky as being fantastic, and this may well have been Dostoevsky's intention as he wrote the novel: to embrace the very aspects of his own thematics and aesthetics that Belinsky objected to in *The Double.* Dostoevsky, as he settled down to write *The Idiot* after his article on Belinsky, may still have been settling scores with Belinsky.

One of Dostoevsky's tactics when criticized was to take the criticism (you are calling my writing fantastic and you mean it as a slur) and make it into a cherished virtue (agreed, my writing is fantastic, and that is what makes it good). Whether in response to Maikov or the ghost of Belinsky, as he wrote *The Idiot* Dostoevsky increasingly identified his vision with the "fantastic."[41] When Dostoevsky's old friend, the critic Nikolai Strakhov, praised Myshkin, Dostoevsky wrote back begging for more opinions and then set about trying to explain what he wished to do in the novel. "I have my own special view of reality (in art), and what the majority calls almost fantastic and exceptional sometimes constitutes the very essence of the real. The ordinariness of phenomena and a banal view of them are not yet realism, in my opinion, but even the contrary."[42] Dostoevsky goes on to defend his "fantastic *Idiot*" who partakes of some transcendental reality. In the same paragraph, Dostoevsky says critical things about how the novel came out: "In the novel a lot was written in haste, much is dragged out and not successful, but there are some successful things too. I'm not defending my novel, but my idea."

Readers and critics have tended to voice criticisms about the novel similar to those Dostoevsky expressed. What Dostoevsky says may be an accurate judgment of the novel or it may have been something that Dostoevsky did not fully believe. Dostoevsky was desperate for this novel to succeed, for financial reasons (so that a separate edition would be published, so that he would be paid more per page for the serial publication of his next novel) and also for the sake of his pride and all he had put into the novel, which was written under difficult conditions.

As time went on, Dostoevsky was more willing to defend not just the "idea" of the novel but the novel itself. In 1877, for example, he responds to a reader who claimed to like *The Idiot* best of Dostoevsky's novels: "All those who speak to me of [*The Idiot*] in terms of its being the best of my works have something special in the cast of their minds that always touches me and pleases me."[43] Those who consider *The Idiot* to be their favorite of Dostoevsky's novels are likely to be those who welcome the "fantastic" – understood in Dostoevsky's own sense of the term, as pertaining to a higher form of reality that embraces both life and death – in literature.

## 9. After *The Idiot*

After Dostoevsky finished *The Idiot*, he and his wife moved on from Florence to Dresden, where they settled until their return to Russia. In Dresden, Anna Grigoryevna gave birth to their daughter

Lyubov in September 1869. Dostoevsky finished *The Eternal Husband* and began work on *The Devils.*

The Dostoevskys arrived back in Saint Petersburg during the summer of 1871, shortly before the birth of their son Fyodor. Upon return to Russia, Dostoevsky lived a much more settled life than before. The Dostoevsky family eventually divided its time between Saint Petersburg and the village of Staraya Russa. Dostoevsky made trips to Germany for his health. (During one of these trips, he visited Sonya's grave in Geneva.)

Dostoevsky's exile from Russia renewed his emotional ties to his homeland and his dedication to the depiction of Russian life. Upon his return, he sought, more than ever before perhaps, to understand the full diversity of Russian life: women and men, young and old, common folk and intellectuals. Throughout the rest of his Russian life, he prided himself on not turning away from the chaos he saw around him. And, even while he was being lionized, he continued to take an active interest in his public. He would write to, or talk with, strangers who appealed to him for advice. He engaged in literary, social, religious, and political debates, as shown in his *Diary of a Writer.* He came to consider himself at this time the chronicler of the new Russian society.

Surfacing in his work of this later period (*The Adolescent* [1875], *The Brothers Karamazov* [1879–80]), were his hopes for the resurgence of the Russian family and his faith in the "Godbearing" Russian people. The hopes developed during the period of exile and they were articulated in *The Idiot,* but along with uncertainty and doubt, as if the seeds of hope needed Russian soil to bear fruit.

## NOTES

1. "Dostoevsky and Parricide," in *Dostoevsky. A Collection of Essays,* ed. René Wellek (Englewood Cliffs, N.J.: Prentice-Hall, 1962), 98–111.

2. F. M. Dostoevsky, *Polnoe sobranie sochinenii,* 29.1:299; April 16/28, 1871.

3. There has been debate about whether Dostoevsky stopped gambling because of his inner resolve or simply because the casinos in Germany were shut down during his trips abroad in 1874, 1875, 1876, and 1879. But, as his wife points out in her memoirs, had he been drawn to the roulette table, the distance to Monte Carlo and its casinos would not have been an obstacle.

4. James Rice, *Dostoevsky and the Healing Art: An Essay in Literary and Medical History* (Ann Arbor, Mich.: Ardis, 1985).

5. See Natalie Nikolaevna Minihan, "O vliianii Evangeliia na zamysel i na osnovnye literaturnye istochniki romana 'Idiot,'" Ph.D. diss., Brown University, 1989, chap. 3, sect. 1–4.

6. See Rice, *The Healing Art.*

7. See Joseph Frank, *Dostoevsky: The Miraculous Years, 1865–1871* (Princeton: Princeton University Press, 1995), chap. 11.

8. 28.2:210; August 16/28, 1867. The full text of this letter is found in the Primary Sources.

9. For more on this, see my essay in this volume, "Myshkin Through a Murky Glass, Guessingly."

10. For discussion of some of the many ways in which *The Idiot* responds to *Madame Bovary*, see Introduction, Part 2, below.

11. 28.2:158; April–May 1866.

12. Anna Grigoryevna gives different versions of how the Dostoevskys arrived at this choice: in her *Reminiscences,* she says that her husband had wanted to name the baby Anna after her but that she refused and that "by mutual agreement" they decided on Sonya. The stenographic version of Anna's diary (for June 11/23, 1867) records Dostoevsky rejecting the name Anna and Anna Grigoryevna then concurring and Dostoevsky first suggesting Sonya. When Anna Grigoryevna herself transcribed the diary for publication, she excised the part where Dostoevsky suggested the names Sonya and Misha. These changes, minor as they are, nevertheless show that these redactions were prepared with great care and that the changes aimed at putting Dostoevsky in a better light – in this case by having him want initially to have the baby named after his wife.

13. 28.2:251; January 1/13, 1868 (see Primary Sources).

14. 28.2:252; January 1/13, 1868 (see Primary Sources).

15. Entry of July 26/August 7, 1867, A. G. Dostoevskaia, *Dnevnik 1867 goda*, ed. S. V. Zhitomirskaia (Moscow: Nauka, 1993).

16. While Dostoevsky was rabidly opposed to his niece marrying a man she did not love, he just as fervently wanted her to marry – choosing "with a

free heart and according to her convictions" – for he could not imagine her happy unless married and he insisted that she "was meant to be happy (without fail!)."

17. Robin Feuer Miller, *Dostoevsky and "The Idiot." Author, Narrator, and Reader* (Cambridge: Harvard University Press, 1981), 98–100.

18. See Jacques Catteau, *Dostoyevsky and the Process of Literary Creation*, trans. Audrey Littlewood (Cambridge: Cambridge University Press, 1989), 146–53.

19. Described at length by Catteau, *Process.*

20. See the analysis of the notebooks in the essay by Robin Feuer Miller included in this volume.

21. For discussion of the holy fool in *The Idiot*, see Walter Nigg, *Der christliche Narr* (Zurich: Artemis, 1956); for the argument that the concept is central to all of Dostoevsky's oeuvre, see Harriet Murav, *Holy Foolishness: Dostoevsky's Novels and the Poetics of Cultural Critique* (Stanford: Stanford University Press, 1992).

22. The autobiographical view of Myshkin (among others) is stated by Konstantin Mochulsky, in *Dostoevsky: His Life and Work*, trans. and introd. Michael A. Minihan (Princeton: Princeton University Press, 1967), chap. 15.

23. For background, see my *Dostoevsky as Reformer: The Petrashevsky Case* (Ann Arbor, Mich.: Ardis, 1987), or Joseph Frank, *Dostoevsky: The Seeds of Revolt, 1821–1849* (Princeton: Princeton University Press, 1976).

24. F. N. L'vov, "Zapiska o dele petrashevtsev," *Literaturnoe nasledstvo* (Moscow: AN SSSR), 63:188.

25. 28.2:236; November 6/18, 1867.

26. A. G. Dostoevskaia, *Vospominaniia A. G. Dostoevskoi*, ed. L. P. Grossman (Moscow and Leningrad: Gosdarstvennoe izd., 1925; reprint [n.p.], Gregory Lounz Books, 1969), 116–19.

27. 28.2:277; March 21–22 /April 2–3, 1868 (see Primary Sources).

28. Dostoevskaia, *Vospominaniia*, 121.

29. 28.2:297; May 18/30, 1868 (see Primary Sources).

30. 28.2:302; June 22/July 4, 1868.

31. See additionally my study of Myshkin as well as David Bethea's (both essays in this volume). The full text is given in Primary Sources.

32. Robert Belknap, *The Genesis of "Brothers Karamazov": The Aesthetic Ideology and Psychology of Making a Text* (Evanston: Northwestern University Press, 1990), 54. Belknap suggests a similarity between Dostoevsky and Shakespeare: "It has been suggested that *Hamlet* is the longest of Shake-

speare's plays because Shakespeare became involved in creating a rich identity for the namesake of his own son Hamnet, who died soon before he wrote the play. *The Brothers Karamazov* is Dostoevsky's longest work in part, perhaps, because Dostoevsky found it hard to stop making a life for Aleksei Karamazov."

33. Robin Feuer Miller, *The Brothers Karamazov: Worlds of the Novel*, Twayne's Masterwork Studies 83 (New York: Twayne, 1992), 39.

34. Frank, *Miraculous Years*, 331.

35. In describing Dostoevsky's response to Sonya's death in her memoirs, composed many years later, Anna Grigoryevna describes their despair at parting with their "priceless babe" and Dostoevsky's complaints about "cruel fate" having taken from him "such a dear being"; the "greatest and sole human happiness" is, according to Dostoevsky, "to have one's own child." Readers of *The Idiot* may hear an echo of Dostoevsky's despair in Ippolit's comments that looking at Holbein's Christ makes the universe seem like a beast or machine that destroyed "the great and priceless being – the very being that alone was worth all nature and all the laws of nature, worth all the earth, which perhaps was even created solely so that this being could appear" (8:339). The similarities between these passages suggest that for Anna Grigoryevna (or for the editors of her memoirs) Ippolit embodies some of the despair Dostoevsky felt over Sonya's death.

36. Frank, *Miraculous Years*, 327–28, 332–33.

37. Ibid., 333.

38. N. T. Ashimbaeva, "A. N. Maikov. Pis'ma k F. M. Dostoevskomu. 1867–1878," *Pamiatniki kul'tury. Novye otkrytiia. 1982* (Leningrad: Nauka, 1984), 65 (February 26[?], 1868).

39. Ashimbaeva, "Maikov. Pis'ma," 67 (March 14/26, 1868).

40. As quoted in Dostoevsky, *Polnoe sobranie sochinenii*, 1:492.

41. On the fantastic, see Robert Louis Jackson, "Some Considerations on 'The Dream of a Ridiculous Man' and 'Bobok,' from the Aesthetic Point of View," in his *The Art of Dostoevsky: Deliriums and Nocturnes* (Princeton, N.J.: Princeton University Press, 1981), 288–303, and in his *Dostoevsky's Quest for Form: A Study of His Philosophy of Art* (New Haven: Yale University Press, 1966), 71–91.

42. 29.1:19; February 26/March 10, 1869.

43. 29.2:139; February 14, 1877.

# Introduction to *The Idiot* Part 2: The Novel

LIZA KNAPP

## 1. Heroes, Heroines, and Their Relations

The major characters of *The Idiot* are discussed below with respect to the meaning of their names and their family affiliation. In this novel, Dostoevsky appears to emphasize his characters' identities – who they are. (Plot – what the characters end up doing – becomes less crucial.) The names a person acquires at birth and the family she is born into seem to give that person a ready-made identity or, rather, a set of expectations about life. These are expectations, not fixed determinations.

Dostoevsky was a master at playing on the expectations his characters' names and their family structures create. Dostoevsky's name-play often adds a symbolic level to the reader's understanding of a given character's identity. When Dostoevsky gives a character a meaningful name, he does so in order to evoke a set of questions about this character, not to define him or create an allegory or fixed correspondence. On a broader level, Dostoevsky rejected the notion of the "genetic" family, based entirely on blood and name, in favor of the "accidental" family, a structure where chance and love bind.[1] In this sphere as well, Dostoevsky creates a tension between what seems predetermined and what is not.

The meanings and associations that inhere in the names of the major characters of the novel are discussed below.[2] The characters are grouped by family, but, given that Dostoevsky deals in "accidental" family units, the groupings become fluid.

The case of Prince Lev Nikolaevich Myshkin is especially complex. As a "prince" he belongs to an old aristocratic line, but in his case one that now has little wealth or power. His last name is said in the novel to be found in Nikolai Karamzin's *History of Russia*, a fact that lends the aura of historical authority. And yet its Russian root is the same as that for "mouse." Hence it is associated with meekness and lack of power. His first name, Lev, means "lion." Lev combined with Myshkin makes an oxymoronic menagerie of lion and mouse – suggesting a fable with a moral, on the order of Aesop's "The Lion and the Mouse." His patronymic Nikolaevich (son of Nikolai, meaning "victory over the people" in Greek) further suggests that he was born with heroic expectations. But as an orphan, Lev Nikolaevich Myshkin was left on his own to interpret his legacy without the biological parents to whom he owes the names.

The combination "Lev Nikolaevich" also belongs to Lev Nikolaevich Tolstoy, whose *War and Peace* had already started to be published in serial form. As Dostoevsky wrote his major novels, he was quite aware of Tolstoy's presence as a writer. It has been the fate of the two authors to be compared constantly to one another. Dostoevsky was forever gauging himself against Tolstoy and, of course, trying to outdo him. The fact that Nikolai Strakhov, Dostoevsky's old friend, later became increasingly devoted to Tolstoy served to divide rather than bring together the two writers.

Myshkin is an orphan and an "idiot" (the original Greek word ἰδιώτης ranging in meaning from private person – someone who stands apart from social structures – to an ill-informed man). Yet in the course of the novel, he discovers and develops various kinds of familial relationships with many of the families or individuals in the novel. As the orphaned outsider Myshkin affiliates himself with various families, we see Dostoevsky challenging the notion that family is exclusively a genetic unit.

After the death of his parents, Myshkin had been under the guardianship of Nikolai Andreevich Pavlishchev (evoking Russian *pavlin*, "peacock"). Pavlishchev eventually entrusted Myshkin to the medical care of the Swiss doctor Schneider (from German *schneiden*, "to cut"). To what extent are these men responsible for Myshkin? Are they surrogate fathers? Do they fail Myshkin? What does fatherhood mean? Dostoevsky seems to be searching for new definitions here.

When a relative of his mother's dies, Myshkin inherits money. Again Dostoevsky asks what "family" means – Myshkin gets money from a distant relative he never knew simply because of a genetic relation. Further, Dostoevsky dramatizes the undeniable role that financial interdependence plays in binding families together. (Certainly money was central in Dostoevsky's relations with various family members.) The subplot involving "Pavlishchev's Son" further highlights the question of paternity (or relatedness in general) and what it means: a group of young nihilists try to con Myshkin out of part of his inheritance when one of them, Antip Burdovsky, claims (falsely, it turns out) to be the illegitimate son of Pavlishchev. ("Burdovsky," incidentally, has the same root as the Russian word for the slops that pigs eat. It suggests swinishness and, possibly, in an ironic twist, Dostoevsky's beloved parable of the Prodigal Son: the son, having demanded his inheritance of his father, squanders it and ends up sharing the swine's food, before returning, repentant, to his father.) The rationale for Burdovsky's claim is that Myshkin was getting money from Pavlishchev in the past that, by natural rights, should have gone to Pavlishchev's biological son. Now that Myshkin has money, he is duty-bound to reimburse Pavlishchev's biological son. The irony here is that these nihilists are touting family values simply in an attempt to take advantage of Myshkin and to make money.

Myshkin is distantly related to Lizaveta Prokofyevna Epanchin, who was a princess Myshkin (that is, from an old aristocratic family) before her marriage to Ivan Fyodorovich Epanchin, who advanced from humble origins to the rank of general. They have three unmarried daughters: Alexandra, Adelaida, and Aglaya. The Epanchin parents have just recently abandoned their system of not pushing their daughters into marriage as they realize that Alexandra has "suddenly and almost unexpectedly" turned twenty-five. Aglaya, later in the novel, rebels against being married off.

The Epanchin daughters' names all begin with the letter *A* and have Greek etymologies. The three sisters have been likened to the

Three Graces. "Alexandra" comes from the Greek for "defend," "Adelaida" comes from the Greek for "obscure" (she is a painter who ends up marrying Prince Shch. – for whom a cipher-like initial takes the place of a name, a detail that makes him a good match for "obscure" Adelaida). "Aglaya" comes from the Greek, meaning "radiance." The symbolism of light becomes important later in the novel when Myshkin's love for her brings him the promise of a "new, radiant life." But, by the end of the novel, she has associated herself with the forces of darkness rather than life by cutting herself off from her family, marrying a Pole, and becoming a Catholic – in the Dostoevskian system these actions suggest that she has turned away from the light and is not living up to the promise of her name. A possible link has been suggested between her name and Blanche (from the French for "white"), for whose sake Marguerite forfeits her happiness in *La Dame aux camélias* (by Dumas the Younger).

When Myshkin first arrives with his bundle on the Epanchins' doorstep, the General wants to send him away. In his initial conversation with Myshkin, he reveals his fears that Myshkin has come to sponge off of his relatives. Myshkin, however, disarms him. Eventually Epanchin relents and introduces him to the women of the family, his blood relations, who feel naturally drawn to him. Here Dostoevsky seems in fact to be suggesting that affinities are sometimes genetically determined.

The Epanchin family is often cited as one of the few families in Dostoevsky's fiction where the nuclear family is intact (two parents and their shared offspring live under the same roof) and relatively happy. We are told that Epanchin never regretted his early marriage, that he "respected his wife and sometimes feared her to such an extent that he even loved her." If examined more carefully, this intact family may not be so perfect even at the beginning of the novel: Epanchin, for example, buys Nastasya Filippovna expensive pearls for her birthday (which she returns, telling him: "Take these pearls and give them to your wife"), and he has developed a scheme for marrying Alexandra off to Totsky.

Afanasy Ivanovich Totsky is a womanizer in his fifties. He has been, since the death of her parents, the guardian – and surrogate father – of Nastasya Filippovna Barashkov. (Her mother died in a fire; her shaken father died soon thereafter; her sister died of whooping cough while under Totsky's care.) Totsky kept her living with various caretakers and eventually a Swiss governess in a country place called Otradnoe (a name shared with the Rostovs' beloved estate in *War and Peace*). The name of that estate, approximately "felicity" in Russian, evokes a pastoral idyll. But here when Nastasya was still quite young, Totsky seduced her. Thus the Totsky-Barashkov "accidental" grouping becomes a perversion of family and demonstrates the possibly disastrous outcome of the demise of a genetic family.

When the action of the novel begins, Totsky is trying to marry Nastasya Filippovna to Gavrily (Ganya) Ivolgin, Epanchin's secretary, so that he, Totsky, can marry Alexandra Epanchin without being encumbered by Nastasya Filippovna. This plan to marry off Nastasya Filippovna is presented from Totsky's point of view as an attempt to regenerate and "resurrect" this fallen woman through "love and family" life (8:40–41). Here again, family values are touted, but with false motives.

Nastasya Filippovna would rather free herself from all connections to Totsky, who has been supporting her. Here again we see the interaction of family relations and financial dependence. On her birthday she declares: "I am the nameday girl and on my own for the first time in my whole life."[3] She declares that she will let Myshkin decide her fate, refuses to marry Ganya Ivolgin, and then runs off with Rogozhin.

Perhaps Dostoevsky intended Nastasya Filippovna's birthday celebration, the culmination of the first part of the novel, to contrast with the nameday celebration at the Rostovs' that occurs early in *War and Peace*, in a section Dostoevsky would have read before he wrote his opening to *The Idiot.* Tolstoy had used his party scene to show his Rostovs in all their glory; for Dostoevsky, these Rostovs are the "genetic" family par excellence. Even their name in Russian evokes the notion of biological growth. The celebration in *War and*

*Peace* honors two generations of Rostov women named Natalya (meaning "birth"). It celebrates generational continuity and clan loyalty. On any number of levels, Dostoevsky opposes Nastasya Filippovna's birthday celebration to the nameday celebration for the two Natalya Rostovs, using the contrast to suggest, among other things, the very different set of familial circumstances from which these two heroines, Natasha Rostov and Nastasya Filippovna, spring.

All three of Nastasya Filippovna Barashkov's names have rich symbolism. Her last name, "Barashkov," comes from the Russian word for "lamb" and possibly evokes all of the Gospel sheep and Old Testament sacrificial lambs. Her patronymic, from the Greek for "lover of horses," evokes the horses of Revelation, which become a subject of discussion between her and Lebedev and others in the novel. Her first name, in its long form "Anastasiia," comes from the Greek word for "resurrection." (Its meaning is thus opposed to that of Natalya, meaning "birth.") The name "Anastasiia" is linked to the idea of the resurrection of the dead, which also becomes a topic of debate later in the novel. (Ippolit argues that looking at Holbein's painting of the dead Christ, it is impossible to believe that Christ was resurrected.) As a fallen woman, Nastasya is metaphorically "dead." When Myshkin comes offering the hope of rehabilitation and regeneration, Dostoevsky presents this in the text and in the notebooks as a "resurrection." Thus he suggests that the drama of Nastasya is whether or not the potential in her name will be realized. As it happens, she ends up murdered rather than resurrected or rehabilitated through Myshkin's love. The scene at which Rogozhin and Myshkin hold vigil over her murdered body evokes the death of Christ where the Marys held vigil. Jesus' shroud has been replaced by sturdy American oilcloth, and the ointment the Marys brought with them has been replaced by the "Zhdanov liquid" that Rogozhin uses, along with the oilcloth, to counter the smell of decay. "How can you call *this* [the Anastasiia under the oilcloth] Resurrection?" is the question this tableau poses.

Parfyon Semyonovich Rogozhin, like Nastasya Filippovna, has a richly evocative name. His first name comes from the Greek word meaning "virgin." This name would seem not to fit, since Rogozhin represents a dark erotic force. Again, as with the first name "Anastasiia," the name goes counter to the reality but still evokes some sense of an ideal image of the person that has been violated. The last name "Rogozhin" comes from *rogozha*, the Russian word for "bast" or "bast mat," by metaphorical extension, something a bit shoddy. Curiously, the word is used in a proverb that invokes another family of *The Idiot:* "ne k rozhe rogozha, ne k litsu epancha" (a mat's not for the mug, a cloak's not for the face).[4] Dostoevsky may also have based the name "Rogozhin" on the name of a cemetery in Moscow associated with the Old Believers.

Rogozhin's family is from the merchant class and linked to Russian sectarianism.[5] Rogozhin's father has died, leaving him money; again money and heritage are interconnected. Rogozhin's family lives in a creepy old house in Saint Petersburg that is windowless, with thick walls. There in her separate quarters Rogozhin's mother reads the *Chet'i-Minei*, a compendium of devotional literature, including saints' lives, arranged according to the calendar. In Rogozhin's quarters, Myshkin and Ippolit view the copy of Hans Holbein's Dead Christ. It is there that Myshkin notices a garden knife Rogozhin is using to cut the pages of a book.

Rogozhin and Myshkin become "brothers" when they exchange crosses, an act that blurs the boundary between victimizer and victim. Rogozhin also at one point makes an attempt to murder Myshkin, stopped only when Myshkin has an epileptic attack. Yet Myshkin's devotion to his "brother" Rogozhin continues, surviving the attempted murder, the rivalry for Nastasya Filippovna, and even the murder of Nastasya Filippovna. At the price of his own sanity, perhaps, Myshkin stays with Rogozhin, stroking his cheek and caring for him after Nastasya Filippovna's death.

Myshkin met Gavrily (Ganya) Ivolgin, the older son of the Ivolgin family, at the Epanchins and comes to them as their boarder, thus entering their family life. By showing the Ivolgins forced by finances to take in boarders, Dostoevsky again shows the boundaries of the family being redefined in response to external factors. Myshkin joins

Ferdyshchenko (whose name hints at German *Pferd*, "horse") as a boarder. General Ivolgin, the head of this household, has gone to seed and remains obsessed with Napoleon, whom he claims to have served in his childhood during the siege of Moscow. A "Napoleon complex" may have been part of his patrimony to his son Ganya: when Ganya is first introduced at the Epanchins, he is said to have a "small, Napoleonic beard" (8:21). But the "Napoleonic beard" in question was a beard like that of Napoleon III, Napoleon's nephew who was the emperor of France at the time of the novel. Thus Ganya's Napoleonicism is a shoddier or diminished version of his father's. And Dostoevsky is suggesting that here, contrary to Darwin's theory, the sons (and nephews) are not an improvement over the fathers.

Ganya, describing to Myshkin his scheme to get rich, shares his dream of how in the future people will say, "Behold, Ivolgin, King of the Jews," in imitation of the inscription on Jesus' cross. In addition, Dostoevsky draws here on Heinrich Heine's depiction of James Rothschild as the "King of the Jews." Alexander Herzen, in his *Past and Thoughts*, likewise had used the term "King of the Jews" for Rothschild in the context of a discussion of how money brings power and independence.[6] Dostoevsky thus presents Ganya as involved in an imitation of the wrong "King of the Jews." (Myshkin, on the other hand, imitates the correct King of the Jews.)

Dostoevsky uses Ganya as an example of an "ordinary" person who wants desperately to be extraordinary. Ganya, along with his sister Varya (short for "Varvara," from Greek, "foreigner, barbarian") and the man she marries, Ivan Petrovich Ptitsyn (Russian *ptitsa*, "bird"), are the subject of the long discourse on "ordinary" people with which part 4 of the novel begins.

The adolescent Kolya (short for "Nikolai") Ivolgin develops a close relationship with Myshkin. He nurses Myshkin after his epileptic attack, defends and protects Myshkin from the group of young nihilists, and seems to act under the influence of Myshkin when he helps the dying Ippolit.

Myshkin is first introduced to Ippolit Terentiev, a boy dying of consumption, when General Ivolgin takes Myshkin to visit Ippolit's mother, Ivolgin's mistress. Ippolit later turns up as part of the band of nihilists who try to extract money from Myshkin. He reads his "Confession" at Prince Myshkin's birthday party at the Lebedev dacha. Ippolit eventually moves out to Pavlovsk, where he is cared for by Mrs. Ivolgin and Kolya.

The name "Ippolit," meaning "looser of horses," may relate to the Horses of the Apocalypse that are discussed in the novel.[7] The fact that he and Nastasya Filippovna both have names containing the Greek root meaning "horse" links these two characters. Both show an active interest in the Apocalypse. Both are dead by the end of the novel.

Dostoevsky's Ippolit may be related to Flaubert's Hippolyte in *Madame Bovary*.[8] Hippolyte is the clubfooted youth whom Charles Bovary operates on, at Emma's urging. This newfangled operation was to have made Charles a famous doctor, bringing glory to their banal life. Charles, however, bungles the operation, making it necessary to amputate the whole leg. Both Hippolyte in *Madame Bovary* and Ippolit in *The Idiot*, living in their prematurely defective young bodies, must forgive (or envy) the happiness of other people, whose healthy bodies allow them perhaps to forget the mortality of their own flesh.

One of Dostoevsky's more "transparent" names is Kislorodov (from Russian *kislorod*, "oxygen"), Ippolit's materialist friend who informs him with scientific certainty that he will die.

The Lebedevs are another family who become increasingly important to the ideology and symbolism of the novel. Their last name is from the Russian word for "swan." It evokes the idea of a swan song, in keeping with Lukian Timofeich Lebedev's role as herald of the Apocalypse. He interprets the Apocalypse and declares the "railroad age" and all it represents to be the sign of the coming end. He rejects modernism in all its manifestations and yearns for a "binding idea" (more simply, faith that would inspire human life).

This family has suffered the recent death of Lebedev's wife. The grieving and drinking widower Lukian Timofeich is devoted to her memory. The now motherless children are a son, Konstantin, and a grown daughter, Vera ("faith" in Russian), who always appears carrying Lyubov (meaning "love"), her baby sister, to whom she becomes a surrogate mother. Also living in the Lebedev household is the son of Lebedev's dead sister. His name is Vladimir Doktorenko. In response to the death of Lebedev's sister, this family has welcomed into its midst Doktorenko (despite their obvious antipathy for his nihilist politics and manners). After the death of Lebedev's wife and sister, roles in the Lebedev family have been redefined (sister becomes mother, nephew becomes son). In the Lebedevs, Dostoevsky provides us with another example of a family forced by circumstances to constitute itself anew. It becomes a positive version of the "accidental family" that Dostoevsky felt was so crucial to the survival of Russian society.

Joseph Frank suggests that there is a similarity between Dostoevsky's attitude toward his stepson, Pasha (Pavel Isaev), and Lebedev's attitude toward his nephew Doktorenko: the common denominator is loyalty to and tolerance of the young men, entrusted to them by a dying loved one, despite an increasing antipathy toward the lives these young men lead.[9]

When Lebedev introduces his nephew to Myshkin, he says: "And so this is the actual murderer of the Zhemarin family." When Myshkin is befuddled, Lebedev elaborates: "That is, allegorically speaking, this is the future second murderer of the Zhemarin family, if there ever is such a thing" (8:161). (Frank points out that Dostoevsky saw in Pasha the makings of Raskolnikov or Gorsky, the man who murdered the Zhemarins.)[10] According to the news reports of this murder, the youth Gorsky, a Polish Catholic by birth, murdered in cold blood six members of the Zhemarin household, where he tutored one of the children. He had fashioned a special murder weapon for the crime. During his trial, Gorsky admitted to being an atheist. For Dostoevsky this murder was further evidence that nihilist and atheist ideology lead to crime. As his remark about Pasha suggests, Dostoevsky in fact saw a connection between Raskolnikov and Gorsky, although probably Dostoevsky would have considered

Gorsky, with his Polish Catholic heritage, not as redeemable as Raskolnikov. The Zhemarin murder crops up at various points in the novel. Myshkin distinguishes between the cold-blooded, calculating murderer of the Zhemarins and a murderer such as Rogozhin or the Russian peasant who coveted his friend's watch and, no longer able to control himself, crossed himself, asked God's forgiveness in the name of Christ, knifed his friend, and took the watch (8:183).

The Lebedev family becomes peripherally more involved in the central drama of the novel because Myshkin moves into their dacha in Pavlovsk after his epileptic attack in part 2. (In this way Myshkin enters the life of yet another family.) There are hints of some sympathy developing between Vera Lebedev and Myshkin. Some readers have suggested that Myshkin, caught between Aglaya and Nastasya Filippovna, overlooks Vera.

At the end of the novel, an attachment, by letter, develops between Vera and Evgeny Pavlovich Radomsky (whose name evokes the Polish city of Radom). Radomsky has been dubbed the raisonneur of the novel.

## 2. The Texts in the Novel

Below are discussed some of the literary works and one painting that figure in *The Idiot*.[11] Although all authors do this to some extent, Dostoevsky has been particularly known and studied for the ways in which he "copies, imitates, quotes, uses, parodies, or reacts in other ways" to various materials.[12]

In many of the cases discussed below, the texts actually appear as props in the novel. For example, Lebedev quotes "To be or not to be . . . "; a copy of Holbein's Dead Christ hangs on Rogozhin's wall. In *The Idiot*, Dostoevsky explores how his heroes read and shows that some of them are at risk of developing "le bovarysme." Dostoevsky and his reading public may not yet have known the term, but they did know the disease. (And Dostoevsky had just finished reading *Madame Bovary*, the first case history.) "Le bovarysme" consists of "imitating hero[in]es of novels," even to the point of destroying one's life.[13] "Le bovarysme" and *imitatio Christi* are very different, but they share the imitation of a model. Each of these very different types of imitation, of course, can be practiced in many different ways and to varying degrees. What is important is how the imitation differs from the original.

### HOLBEIN'S *CHRIST IN THE TOMB* (1521)

Dostoevsky first read a description of Hans Holbein's (1497–1543) painting *Christ in the Tomb* in Nikolai Karamzin's *Letters of a Russian Traveler*, where Karamzin notes that in Holbein's Christ "there is nothing divine, but as a dead man he is portrayed extremely naturalistically." Karamzin reports that the work was painted from an actual corpse.

Dostoevsky saw this painting in Basel on August 11/23, 1867, just before settling in Geneva. His wife describes their visit to the museum in both her diary and her reminiscences (composed years after), with some differences in the story she tells. For example, in her (later) reminiscences, she reports that she was worried that Dostoevsky would have an epileptic attack from seeing the picture; earlier in her diary, she had reported being worried that Dostoevsky would be fined for standing up on a chair in order to see the painting better ("because they give you fines for everything here").

In her diary description, she notes that, whereas Christ is ordinarily painted with his face expressing suffering, the body usually "is not at all tortured or distorted, as in reality. Here [in Holbein's painting], however, he is presented with an emaciated body, the bones and ribs visible, the hands and feet pierced with wounds, swollen and quite blue, the way they are on a corpse that has already begun to decay. The face also was horribly tortured, with half-closed eyes, but that already see nothing and express nothing. The nose, mouth, and chin had turned blue; all in all it resembled an actual corpse to such a degree that I really thought I was not going to be able to convince myself to stay in the same room with it. Maybe it was strikingly true, but, it was not at all aesthetic and really it aroused in me only repulsion and a certain horror; Fedya was quite taken with the picture, however."[14] In Anna Grigoryevna's expectation that there *should* be an aesthetic component to art, rather than just a depiction of naturalistic reality, she echoes some of the aesthetic views expressed in Dostoevsky's writings.[15]

Within *The Idiot*, this painting serves as the antithesis to the Gospels (another important subtext). Whereas the Gospels proclaim the "good news" that Christ is risen, this painting depicts the bad news that Christ did not rise. As is the case with whoever hears the Gospels, the viewer can choose how to respond to the "news" the painting proclaims. A copy of this painting hangs in Rogozhin's house, where Myshkin and Ippolit both see it. Ippolit takes its news as truth.

### HUGO'S *THE LAST DAY OF A MAN CONDEMNED TO DEATH* (1829)

When Dostoevsky faced his own death on December 22, 1849, he compared his experience to that described in Victor Hugo's novel *Le Dernier jour d'un condamné à mort* (The last day of a man condemned to death). This gripping work is part treatise against capital punishment, part epistemological and narrative experiment: it is the "diary" of a man describing his last hours up until his head is chopped off by the guillotine. In Myshkin's descriptions of the execution he witnessed in France, echoes of Hugo's work can be seen. In general, Dostoevsky considered Hugo (especially as the author of this work) to be one of his precursors in developing an innovative type of realism that embraces a fantastic realm.

### HUGO'S *NOTRE DAME DE PARIS* (1830)

Victor Hugo's *Notre Dame de Paris* was published in Russian translation in the Dostoevsky brothers' journal in 1862. In introducing the novel, Dostoevsky identifies Victor Hugo as the first to embody "the fundamental idea of all of the art of the nineteenth century." That idea, according to Dostoevsky, is "a Christian and highly moral" one, consisting of "the restoration of a ruined man" and of "the justification of the pariahs of society, humiliated and rejected by all" (20:28–29). Dostoevsky refers to *Notre Dame*'s protagonist Quasimodo in the notebooks to *The Idiot*. No overt references to *Notre*

*Dame* have been discerned within *The Idiot*, but its presence is felt nonetheless. One of the questions Hugo poses in his novel is whether the faith that built cathedrals such as Notre Dame is possible in the modern world, which began, according to Hugo, with the invention of the printing press. (Further, in the plot of the novel, one of his characters asks whether it is possible for a mother whose child has died to still have faith in God; this theme was of personal concern to Dostoevsky, who had lost his daughter.)

Fundamental to Hugo's novel is the Cathedral of Notre Dame itself. Dostoevsky extends Hugo's vision by exploring the ways in which indeed in a post–printing press world, faith is challenged: as already seen, focal to *The Idiot* is the copy of Holbein's *Christ in the Tomb* that hangs in Rogozhin's house. This painting (a symbol of how faith is undermined in the modern age) is symbolically juxtaposed to the Cathedral of Notre Dame (a symbol of the faith of the Middle Ages) in multiple ways: one is the work of an individual, graphically depicting a dead male God; the other is the collective work of thousands, symbolically honoring a living female intermediary between man and God.

ROUSSEAU'S *CONFESSIONS* (1782–89)

The whole *petit jeu* played at Nastasya Filippovna's birthday party, whereby confession becomes a game and is devoid of all repentance, is meant to recall Jean-Jacques Rousseau's *Confessions*, where Rousseau engages in sordid confessions but seems to feel little remorse for all he has done. Ferdyshchenko, when he takes his turn at the *petit jeu*, tells a story of a theft he committed but for which a servant girl was blamed; the incident is a borrowing from Rousseau's *Confessions*.[16]

TYUTCHEV'S "SILENTIUM" (1830)

Fyodor Tyutchev was the superior of Dostoevsky's close friend Maikov in the censorship department at the time Dostoevsky wrote *The Idiot*. In a famous line of this influential poem of eighteen lines, the poet declares "the word spoken out" to be "a lie." The soul is "a whole world" unto itself; therefore there is no point in attempting to reach out to another. The poet gives the advice to "be silent" in the face of the impossibility of expressing in words what is in the heart and in the face of the impossibility of another ever understanding.

Echoes of this poem may be found in Ippolit's declarations before he reads his confession that "in every brilliant or new human idea, or simply even in every serious human idea, arising in somebody's head, there always remains something that simply cannot be communicated to other people, even if you were to write whole volumes and explicate it for thirty-five years" (8:328). The possible applications of this poem to Dostoevsky's thinking are very rich.

### DUMAS'S *THE LADY WITH CAMELLIAS*

*La Dame aux camélias* was a novel (1848), rewritten as a play (1852), by Alexandre Dumas the Younger. This work comes up directly in the *petit jeu* played at Nastasya Filippovna's birthday party, where each player is invited to relate the worst thing he has done in his life. Totsky tells a story that involves camellias, which were the rage because of the popularity of the novel. In Dumas's novel, Marguérite Gautier is asked by her lover to sacrifice her happiness with him and renounce him so that his sister, Blanche, can make a socially acceptable marriage that could not take place if her brother were associated with a "fallen" woman like Marguérite. Nastasya Filippovna is being asked, similarly, to remove herself so that Totsky can marry Alexandra. Later on, Nastasya Filippovna must again get out of the way if Myshkin is to marry Aglaya (who plays the role of Blanche).

### THE NEW TESTAMENT

While he was on his way to prison in Siberia in 1849, Dostoevsky was given a copy of the New Testament by the Decembrist wives, who had followed their exiled husbands and settled there a quarter of a century before. He kept this copy throughout the rest of his life and marked passages as he read. Dostoevsky's marginalia from his copy of the New Testament have been published in English translation, providing clues as to how Dostoevsky responded to what he read.[17]

The Gospels function as an important subtext throughout *The Idiot*, especially since Myshkin was modeled, in some way or another, on Christ.[18] Radomsky accuses Myshkin of being even more lenient on Nastasya Filippovna than Christ was in forgiving the woman taken in adultery.

Relevant to the discussion of the crucifixion in Ippolit's confession are the passages discussing the Resurrection of Jesus. The discussion in Saint Paul, the locus classicus for the holy fool (notably 1 Cor. 4:9–10), is relevant to Myshkin, termed a holy fool early in the novel. The Revelation of Saint John is also the subject of much discussion, with Lebedev and Nastasya Filippovna interpreting it.

### RENAN'S *LIFE OF JESUS* (1863)

In *Vie de Jésus* Ernest Renan attempted to apply "cold analysis" to his subject matter. In general, Renan denied Christ's divinity and set forth rational, scientific explanations for what have been perceived as miracles. Although there are crucial differences between Dostoevsky's Jesus and Renan's (divinity, for example), it is still probable that some traits of Renan's Jesus worked their way into the depiction of Myshkin.[19] This work is frequently mentioned in Dostoevsky's writings.

*The Idiot* could be regarded as the reverse of *Vie de Jésus:* Renan depicts Jesus in Jesus' own time and setting but from a modern, scientific perspective, while Dostoevsky depicts a Jesus-like man in a contemporary, modern time and setting, but from a New Testament perspective.

### PUSHKIN'S "THE POOR KNIGHT" (1835)

Alexander Pushkin's poem is read in the novel by Aglaya to poke fun at Myshkin. Apparently Aglaya identifies Myshkin with the poor knight. Of interest here is not so much the extent to which Myshkin does or does not fit, but that the poem poses certain questions relevant to Myshkin and the enigma of who he is.

This poem is known in two versions. Aglaya reads the version that omits a stanza in which the "poor knight" travels to Geneva, where he sees Mary, the Mother of God, at the cross. This stanza explains that the knight devotes himself to the Virgin Mary, eschewing earthly women. This particular stanza was the subject of discussion in an 1866 article in *The Contemporary* that Dostoevsky may have read (9:403). The author of the article took the view that ideal devotion, such as that fitting for the Virgin Mary, is inappropriate when applied to fleshly women.

Aglaya alters the poem she reads: blasphemously, she substitutes Nastasya Filippovna's initials NFB for AMD – standing for "Ave, Mater Dei" (Hail, Mother of God). By modifying the poem, she tries to make it apply more directly to Myshkin and tease him about his devotion to Nastasya Filippovna. When Aglaya substitutes initials, she creates questions, among them the question of how much Aglaya herself understands of this whole process. The poem is like one of the "meaningful" names Dostoevsky applies to his characters. Though the reader may yearn for a neat allegorical interpretation, Aglaya's play with initials creates a kind of chaos out of which some new and perhaps very partial truth emerges about the situation and/or character at hand.

SHAKESPEARE'S *HAMLET* (1600)

When Myshkin arrives on his birthday back at the Lebedev dacha, Lebedev, Ippolit, and many others greet him. Myshkin is informed by Lebedev that they have been discussing "To be or not to be" (8:305). (This opening to Hamlet's most famous speech is also quoted in the notebooks [9:380].) Lebedev says, "It's a contemporary topic, very contemporary! Questions and answers." Ippolit, who reads his confession, which is supposed to culminate in his own suicide, would like to imitate Hamlet and become a tragic hero.

DICKENS'S *PICKWICK PAPERS* (1837)

Mentions of Pickwick both in his letter to his niece (Letter 332, January 1/13, 1868, in Primary Sources) and in the notebooks for the novel reveal that Dostoevsky regarded Pickwick as one of the few literary incarnations of "positively good men." But Pickwick, like Don Quixote, aroused sympathy in the reader because he was comical. And Dostoevsky wanted Myshkin to be more innocent than comical.

Still, some aspects of Pickwick have been traced in the unfunny Myshkin, notably his "deficient sense of reality."[20]

GOGOL'S *GETTING MARRIED* (1842)

Podkolyosin, the hero of Nikolai Gogol's play *Getting Married* (or, *Marriage*), is discussed at length in the digression with which part 4 opens. The narrator is remarking about the difficulties of presenting "ordinary" people in an interesting way. At issue is the typicality of the hero of Gogol's play, who jumps out of the window at his wedding. The narrator admits that, while few grooms actually jump out of the window (and in this regard, his "typicality" has been exaggerated), many people still identify with him and did even before Podkolyosin existed. Here, as elsewhere, Dostoevsky is schooling his readers *not* to seek a perfect fit and to pay attention to differences as well as similarities.

The subject matter of Gogol's play is in fact quite relevant. Myshkin is a somewhat unlikely groom, like Gogol's groom in that respect; furthermore, like Gogol's play, *The Idiot* is about getting married – or rather planning on getting married and then not getting married (there are lots of marriages that fall through at various points along the way to the altar); the ultimate example is when Nastasya Filippovna flees at the very last moment.

FLAUBERT'S *MADAME BOVARY* (1857)

*Madame Bovary* appears directly in *The Idiot* as Nastasya Filippovna's reading material in the last days of her life. (On how Dostoevsky came to read this book, see my "Introduction to *The Idiot*, Part I.") Nastasya Filippovna, accused of having been damaged by too much reading (a trait she shares with Aglaya) proves to be the ultimate victim of "le bovarysme," for she dies after/from reading *Madame Bovary*. She accepts death, in imitation of Emma.

The scene from *Madame Bovary* in which Charles, Homais, and the priest hold vigil over Emma's corpse anticipates the scene in *The Idiot* in which Rogozhin and Myshkin hold vigil over Nastasya Filippovna's corpse.[21] Furthermore, iron, associated in *The Idiot* with the Apocalypse and the "railroad/iron road age,"[22] is likewise a recurrent, sinister motif in *Madame Bovary*. When Emma, in a crucial scene, becomes lost in thought outside the convent where she spent some time as a girl, she is brought back from her reverie by the sound of iron clanging. On another occasion, at a restaurant with Léon, Emma's maternal thoughts are interrupted as "a cart full of long strips of iron passed, casting against the walls of the houses a deafening metallic vibration." Iron is also associated with French hell (*enfer*). And Flaubert at one point likens language to a *laminoir*, a machine that flattens metal; within the novel even a curling iron takes on sinister associations by emitting a disturbing smell.

Thus iron is a symbol of industrialization and modernity in *Madame Bovary*, as it is also in *The Idiot*. But the symbol could also be a borrowing from *Don Quixote* (discussed below), an acknowledged subtext of both *Madame Bovary* and *The Idiot*. On a more profound level, the three texts could be said to share an interest in the possibility of nonrational knowledge.[23]

### CERVANTES' *DON QUIXOTE* (1605)

In his letter to his niece in which he describes the idea of *The Idiot* as being "to depict a positively beautiful man," Dostoevsky cites Don Quixote as an example of a previous attempt. But Dostoevsky argued that he wanted to avoid the comicality of Don Quixote, used to evoke sympathy in the reader.

Don Quixote, made topical in Russian literature by Turgenev's essay "Hamlet and Don Quixote," was one of Dostoevsky's beloved heroes. In a detailed discussion in his *Diary of a Writer* for September 1877, Dostoevsky lauds Don Quixote's positive qualities, but then goes on to note that "not seldom (alas, so often)" all these good qualities fail to achieve any results, because, despite all the gifts, one gift is lacking: "the genius" for guiding and directing all this power onto a course of action that is "not fantastic and mad" but "a true path, for the benefit of mankind."

Aglaya, on receiving a letter from Myshkin, written from the heart of Russia, places it in a book, her copy of *Don Quixote*. Aglaya marvels at how fitting this book was for a letter from Myshkin. And indeed, Myshkin has many of the same qualities and behaves like Don Quixote. For example, Don Quixote treats some prostitutes he meets as maidens, restoring to them a measure of dignity, for which they mock him. The dynamic between Myshkin and Nastasya Filippovna is a tragic imitation of the comic scene from *Don Quixote*.

It will be remembered that Don Quixote declared his quest and dream to bring back the Age of Gold to replace the Age of Iron in which he found himself living. These associations come into play when Lebedev announces that the railroad – or rather, that which the railroad stands for as an image – was a sign of an age that lacks a binding idea, a sign of the Apocalypse.[24]

## 3. The Setting of the Novel: Saint Petersburg, Pavlovsk, the Heart of Russia

The action of the novel is mostly divided between Saint Petersburg, the great imperial capital city built by Peter the Great, and Pavlovsk, one of its satellites, where the Epanchins, the Lebedevs, and Ivolgins spend the summer months in dachas. Switzerland figures in Myshkin's tales of his past and in the very end of the novel, which finds Myshkin back in his Swiss asylum. In the mysterious six-month hiatus between part 1 and part 2, Myshkin was in Moscow and elsewhere in the heart of Russia, getting to know the Russian people, as well as Nastasya Filippovna and Rogozhin.

Parts 1 and 2 both begin with Prince Myshkin arriving by train in Saint Petersburg. There is a long tradition of Russian literature, including that of Pushkin and Gogol, that comments on Saint Petersburg, on the drama of the individual man confronting the legacy of Peter (modernity, Westernization). When Myshkin returns in part 2 to Saint Petersburg during White Nights, after having been in the heart and bowels of Russia, perhaps he better understands the violation of the Russian way of life that Saint Petersburg represents. Peter's city threatens the individual in his pursuit of happiness: Evgeny, the hero of Pushkin's *Bronze Horseman*, meekly pursues happiness in the form of his beloved, only to end up mad, pursued through a flooded city by the Bronze Horseman himself. As Sidney Monas suggests in his discussion of *The Idiot* as a "Petersburg tale,"[25] Myshkin the idiot becomes another victim of Saint Petersburg. Possibly one can see in the novel Dostoevsky's veiled criticism of the tsarist regime. The novel also contains Dostoevsky's criticism of social change, of the new generation of opportunists.

Pavlovsk, with its trees and hedgehogs, provides a contrast to the urban Saint Petersburg. (Dostoevsky was familiar with Pavlovsk; Dostoevsky's brother's family and Maikov's family spent summer months there.) And yet it turns out to be not simply the setting of a pastoral idyll. The social atmosphere of Pavlovsk seems more vicious and petty than that of Petersburg society. Gossip develops great momentum in the artificial atmosphere of the summer resort.

Pavlovsk was also the terminus of the first railroad in Russia. Because concerts were often held in stations[26] – Dostoevsky and his wife also, during their stay in Germany, attended concerts at various German train stations – the railroad is curiously linked to music. The Dionysian combination of trains and music that comes out at the end of the novel later becomes a modernist theme, further explored by Osip Mandelshtam (in his "Concert at the Train Station").[27]

Although the uniqueness of Dostoevsky's novelistic realm is often emphasized, it should always be remembered that Dostoevsky consistently responds to and develops the various cultural associations of the raw material – names, places, and texts – that he uses. Although his novels may sometimes seem unconventional, Dostoevsky actively engages traditions. This introduction has been intended as an overview of some of the associations and traditions Dostoevsky works with in *The Idiot.*

The critical essays that follow explore different aspects of the novel and have been chosen not only for the information they offer but for the way in which they suggest to the reader new approaches to the novel. Robin Feuer Miller's essay on the notebooks of the novel documents and interprets how *The Idiot* evolved in Dostoevsky's mind. David Bethea's essay shows the intricate relationship between narrative and Dostoevsky's perception of time and history, with particular attention to the theme of apocalypse. Nina Pelikan Straus reads the novel through the prism of feminist theory and challenges readers to approach the novel actively and critically. Liza Knapp's essay suggests ways in which, far from being the "failure" many have held it to be, *The Idiot* embodies Dostoevsky's most sacred beliefs.

## NOTES

1. Gary Rosenshield also sees chaos in the family to be one of the manifestations of chaos in this novel. "All the families in *Idiot* – noble and commoner alike – are in disarray, although, to be sure, every disintegrating family is disintegrating in its own way." "Chaos, Apocalypse, the Laws of Nature: Autonomy and 'Unity' in Dostoevskii's *Idiot,*" *Slavic Review* 50 (1991): 880.

2. In addition to the notes to the edition of Dostoevsky's works (F. M. Dostoevskii, *Polnoe sobranie sochinenii v tridtsati tomakh* (*Pss*), ed. V. G. Bazanov et al. [Leningrad: Nauka, 1972–90]), I have drawn on the following: Charles E. Passage, *Character Names in Dostoevsky's Fiction* (Ann Arbor, Mich.: Ardis, 1982), and Ervin C. Brody, "Meaning and Symbolism in the Names of Dostoevsky's *Crime and Punishment* and *The Idiot,*" *Names: Journal of the American Name Society* 27 (1979): 117–40.

3. Although it is actually her birthday, Nastasya applies the term to a woman celebrating her nameday, the day honoring the saint whose name she bears. For Orthodox Russians, nameday celebrations were more important than birthday celebrations. Russian has no word for "birthday girl," hence it was natural for Nastasya to borrow the ready-made term for "nameday girl."

However, given the meaning of her name (resurrection), this term reminds us that Nastasya's birthday is potentially a rebirth-day or resurrection day for her. At least that is what she is attempting to make it.

4. Vladimir Dal', *Tolkovyi slovar' zhivogo velikorusskogo iazyka Vladimira Dalia*, 4th ed., ed. I. A. Baudouin de Courtenay (Saint Petersburg and Moscow: M. O. Vol'f, 1912), s.v. "rogozha."

5. William Comer, "Rogozhin and the 'Castrates': Russian Religious Traditions in Dostoevsky's *The Idiot*," *Slavic and East European Journal* 40 (1996): 85–99.

6. For further discussion, see the commentary in 9:399–400.

7. See David M. Bethea's essay, this volume.

8. I am grateful to Anne Hruska for this suggestion.

9. Joseph Frank, *Dostoevsky: The Miraculous Years, 1865–1871* (Princeton, N.J.: Princeton University Press, 1995), 295.

10. Ibid., 295.

11. For information about the subtexts of the novel, I have drawn on the commentary for the novel (9:334–469) in *Pss.* Victor Terras includes discussion of "The Literary Subtext" in "*The Idiot.*" *An Interpretation* (Boston: Twayne, 1990), 36–40.

12. For discussion of how Dostoevsky transformed his reading into his own works, see Robert Belknap, *The Genesis of "The Brothers Karamazov": The Aesthetics, Ideology, and Psychology of Making a Text* (Evanston: Northwestern University Press, 1990). The list of ways in which Dostoevsky uses the texts of others in his own is taken from page 1 of Belknap's book.

13. On "le bovarysme," see I. I. Lapshin, *Estetika Dostoevskogo* (Berlin: Obelisk, 1923), 55.

14. A. G. Dostoevskaia, *Dnevnik 1867 goda*, ed. S. V. Zhitomirskaia (Moscow: Nauka, 1993), 234.

15. For discussion of Dostoevsky's understanding of this painting, see Robert Louis Jackson, *Dostoevsky's Quest for Form: A Study of His Philosophy of Art* (New Haven: Yale University Press, 1966), 65–70. For commentary on the painting, see Julia Kristeva, "Holbein's Dead Christ," *Zone 3* (1989): 238–69.

16. For a full discussion of the role of Rousseau's *Confessions* in the *petit jeu* and novel, see Robin Feuer Miller, *Dostoevsky and "The Idiot." Author, Narrator, and Reader* (Cambridge: Harvard University Press, 1981), 178–82.

17. Geir Kjetsaa, *Dostoevsky and His New Testament* (Oslo: Solum, 1984).

18. See my "Myshkin Through a Murky Glass, Guessingly" in this volume.

19. G. G. Ermilova, *Taina kniazia Myshkina: O romane Dostoevskogo "Idiot"* (Ivanovo: Ivanovskii gosudarstvennyi universitet, 1993); Natalie Nikolaevna Minihan, "O vliianii Evangeliia na zamysel i na osnovnye literaturnye istochniki romana 'Idiot,'" (Ph.D. diss., Brown University, 1989).

20. For discussion of multiple sources in Dickens for characters in *The Idiot*, see N. M. Lary, *Dostoevsky and Dickens: A Study of Literary Influence* (London: Routledge and Kegan Paul, 1973), 51–105. For a briefer discussion, see Michael Futrell, "Dostoevskii and Dickens," in *Dostoevskii and Britain*, ed. W. J. Leatherbarrow (Oxford: Berg, 1995), 83–122.

21. Miller, *Dostoevsky and "The Idiot,"* 157–58.

22. See Bethea's essay, this volume.

23. Anthony J. Cascardi, *The Bounds of Reason: Cervantes, Dostoevsky, Flaubert* (New York: Columbia University Press, 1986).

24. See especially Bethea's essay, this volume.

25. On Petersburg and *The Idiot*, see Sidney Monas, "Across the Threshold: *The Idiot* as a Petersburg Tale," in *New Essays on Dostoyevsky*, ed. Malcolm Jones and Garth Terry (Cambridge: Cambridge University Press, 1983), 67–93.

26. See Stephen Baehr, "The Troika and the Train: Dialogues between Tradition and Technology in Nineteenth-Century Russian Literature," in *Issues in Russian Literature before 1917: Proceedings from the III International Congress on Soviet and East European Studies*, ed. Douglas Clayton (Columbus, Ohio: Slavica, 1989), 85–106.

27. O. Ronen, *An Approach to Mandel'štam* (Jerusalem: Magnes, 1983).

# II CRITICISM

# The Notebooks for *The Idiot*

ROBIN FEUER MILLER

*The whole secret of fiction and the drama – in the constructional part – lies in the adjustment of things unusual to things eternal and universal. The writer who knows exactly how exceptional, and how non-exceptional, his events should be made, possesses the key to the art.*
—*Thomas Hardy, notebook entry, February 23, 1893*

*I carried off his papers and spent a whole day looking through them . . . among them was one rather thick volume of finely written manuscript, unfinished, perhaps thrown aside and forgotten by the writer . . . some strange and terrible reminiscences jotted down irregularly, spasmodically, as though by some overpowering impulse. I read these fragments over several times, and was almost convinced they were written in a state of insanity.*
—*"Dostoevsky" describing Goryanchikov's manuscript,* The House of the Dead

In *The Idiot*, unlike his other novels, Dostoevsky did not finally settle the basic problems of characterization until he actually began to write the final draft for publication. Of the three notebooks for *The Idiot*, the first two thus reflect his preliminary struggles to establish the personality of the Idiot and his general position in the midst of the other characters and to fix upon a definite narrative strategy for his novel. These two notebooks are a testing ground for various ideas and plans that bear no direct, step-by-step relation to the final version.

The third notebook is qualitatively different. Dostoevsky worked on it only after part 1 (chapters 1–16) had already been published. This notebook reflects a different stage of creativity: rather than embodying the search for an idea, it illustrates the struggle to find the best way to express themes already decided upon and to plan the further stages of a work whose beginning had already been published. The first notebooks seek to establish a form; the last notebook has less freedom for change. Certain rules have already been established, and the author must maneuver within these self-imposed confines.

Ironically, neither the first two notebooks nor the third one gives us a typical creative notebook in which the novelist settles upon basic attributes in his novel and begins to work them out. Between the writing of the first two notebooks and the writing of part 1 of the novel there is a crucial gap. In that interval Dostoevsky destroyed what he had written so far, largely reversed his ideas, and began again. He wrote to Maikov on December 31, 1867/January 12, 1868, "All summer and autumn I was putting together various ideas [*mysli*] (some were most ingenious), but some experience always let me foresee either the falseness or the difficulty or the weakness of a particular idea. Finally, I stopped at one and began to work. I had written a lot, but on December 4, foreign style, I threw it all to the devil. . . . Then . . . I began to torment myself over the invention of a *new novel*" (28.2:239). In the creative process extending from the initial idea to the true beginning of a work, we have only the extreme boundaries on either side with which to work; the initial conception does not resemble the final product and is, in fact, often opposite to it.

Despite the amount of destroyed material, the gap between the initial conception and the final product is bridged somewhat by Dostoevsky's correspondence of the period. Moreover, a critic gifted with his well-developed faculty of hindsight can pluck out significant strands from the early notebooks and show how they are rewoven into the fabric of the novel. He can also identify certain broad movements that begin in the notebooks and carry on through the novel. The reversals, most significantly those in the character of the Idiot, do not take place entirely unheralded. The notes themselves contain intimations of the surprising switch from a hypocritical, proud, and vengeful Idiot to the Myshkin of the novel. (The actual manuscript of the novel, as dictated to Anna Grigoryevna, does not exist. It was probably destroyed before the Dostoevskys' return to Russia.)[1]

Throughout these notes, Dostoevsky's comments about style and structure, though infrequent, have implications for any study of the novel itself. It is equally important, however, to trace the movement of the notebooks as a whole, to follow the sequence of Dostoevsky's own sets of priorities. Where does the consideration of narrative fit into Dostoevsky's general scheme? When does it become a serious concern? When does it lack importance? Dostoevsky himself had asserted the old truth of the inseparability of form and content, but a discussion of narrative method in its emergent stages must be placed in a larger context.

We have already seen that Dostoevsky found especially agonizing the earliest stages of planning a novel. Anna Grigoryevna said of his labors during the fall of 1867 when he was planning *The Idiot*, "Fyodor Mikhailovich was faced with the most important part of the work that was especially difficult for him, namely the consideration, the creation [*tvorenie*], the making [*sozdanie*] of the plan of the novel. The writing of the novel itself came to him comparatively easily, but the making of a plan presented great difficulties for him. The whole trouble was in the richness of the fantasy and in the dissatisfaction of the author with that form in which he wanted to express the idea that was placed at the basis of the novel."[2] Dostoevsky sought the form that would best embody his idea, but, as these notebooks show, that search for form led to changes in the idea as well.

Although Dostoevsky typically separated the poet who has an "idea" from the artist who gives creative shape to that idea, he consistently emphasized the overlapping of functions between these two aspects of the author. Moreover, he assigned to the artist (as differentiated from the poet) a task far greater than that of technical experimentation. In the early notes for *A Raw Youth* he writes, "In order to write a novel, one must acquire, first of all, one or several strong impressions actually experienced by the author's heart. This is the poet's job. From this impression there are developed a theme, a plan, a harmonious whole. This is already the artist's job, although artist and poet help each other in one thing as well as the other, in both instances."[3] That is, it is the artist who endows the poet's idea with wholeness and harmony. The artist's technical experimentation, by forming the poet's idea, gives it its first existence. And indeed, from his earliest works, such as *Poor Folk* or *The Double*, it is commonplace to discover that Dostoevsky's technique (or style, or form) is inseparable from the idea of the work.

Only in one letter to Maikov, on May 15/27, 1869, does Dostoevsky seriously minimize the function of the artist as opposed to the poet:

> I will make an important digression: a poem, in my opinion, is like a natural precious stone, a diamond, in the soul of the poet, quite ready [complete], in all its essences; and here is the first task of the poet, as a *maker and creator*, the first part of his creation. If you wish – he is not the creator; life is – the powerful essence of life, the living and essential God, putting his strength in many distinct creations at various places, and most of all in the great heart and in the strong poet, so that if the poet himself is not a creator – (and one must agree with this . . . because certainly a creative work comes suddenly, as a complete whole, finished and ready, out of the soul of a poet) – if he himself is not a creator, then at least his soul is that very mine which gives birth to the diamond and without which it would not be found anywhere. Then follows the *second* task of the poet, no longer so deep and mysterious, but only that of the artist: that is, having received the diamond, to finish [*obdelat'*] and mount [*opravit'*] it. Here the poet is almost like a jeweler. (29.1:39)

In this passage Dostoevsky seems to have been carried away by the neatness of his own metaphor. In practice, he assigned the artist a far greater role than that of a mere jeweler; the borders between the poet and the artist were never so sharply defined. Moreover, in this letter, whose somewhat "romantic extravagance" has been aptly pointed out by Robert Jackson,[4] Dostoevsky has partially embraced the notion of the poet as a mere vessel for divine inspiration.

Edward Wasiolek has maintained that for Dostoevsky *The Idiot* was the result of "arduous and painful and exasperating technical experimentation." He has warned that we "cannot go to *The Idiot* with theories of the organic fitness of every part, of the necessity of every positioning. . . . Structure, I hazard, is never as exquisite as our current theories would have it, at least not in this novel . . . the notes show convincingly not only that Dostoevsky was trying out many routes, but that more than one route could have taken him to the same destination."[5] To agree with Wasiolek wholeheartedly in his sensible and prudent statement would mean an end of this study of *The Idiot.* But, even while granting the lack of an "organic fitness" of every part and the absence of "exquisite" structure, one can still make a forceful case that had Dostoevsky followed a different route, he would have arrived at a different destination. A comparative study of Myshkin in *The Idiot* and Alyosha in *The Brothers Karamazov* bears witness to this.[6] The central idea behind each of these characters is the same: they are both positively (that is, completely) beautiful men seeking to do good in the world. But they follow exceedingly different courses of action and arrive at opposite destinations. Thus questions of structure and the interrelation of the parts of a novel reenter through the back door. For example, Myshkin's resurrection of poor Marie through the children's love occurs at the beginning of this novel; in the ensuing tangle of events its significance gradually becomes blurred. Alyosha's momentary resurrection of Ilyusha ends that novel, and the reader joins the children in a moment of thrilling optimism.

---

The first two notebooks for *The Idiot* (nos. 3 and 11 by Sakulin's count, and nos. 3 and 4 in the 1974 edition) extend from September 14, 1867, to November 30, 1867. There is no break between these two notebooks; Dostoevsky simply made notes first in one book, then in the next. The first notebook already contained some notes written while he was working on *Crime and Punishment;* the second notebook is interlaced in the middle with notes for *The Eternal*

*Husband* and part of *The Possessed.* Fortunately Dostoevsky's entries are dated, so that a consecutive reading of the notes remains possible, and editors of each of the versions of these notes have arranged the material by dates, with some minor variations in the positioning of certain paragraphs. The third notebook (no. 10 in Sakulin, no. 5 in the 1974 edition) is interspersed with notes for "About Kartuzov" (a preliminary sketch for Captain Lebyadkin in *The Possessed*) and ideas for new works. This third notebook extends from March 7, 1868, to November 11, 1868, and contains notes for the rest of the novel. Dostoevsky wrote *The Idiot* while abroad with his new wife. He began the notes for the novel on September 14, 1867, in Geneva, where he stayed until the end of May 1868; continued them in Vevey from June until the beginning of September 1868; in Milan until the middle of November; and he finished the novel in Florence, where he stayed through January 1869 (9:338).

The first two notebooks are largely notes for an unwritten novel; the image of Myshkin as a completely or positively beautiful man, which dominates *The Idiot*, does not ever fully appear and is only hinted at toward the end of these notes. The remarkable development in these pages of the early version of the vengeful Idiot into the meek and good Myshkin demonstrates a quintessentially Dostoevskian development: the projected, though unrealized, plans for the transformation of the Idiot's personality reflect Dostoevsky's own conviction that true goodness arises out of the abyss of human evil and suffering. In the novel, however, no character undergoes such a far-reaching development. Most of the outlined plans for action in the first two notebooks are linear ones – where development and permanent changes in the characters occur – whereas the overall shape of the novel itself, in contrast to the notes, is a zigzag or a circle, the lines of which are constantly being retraced. One development is usually canceled out in the next scene by a reverse oscillation; heroes and heroines do not really change – they vacillate. At the center of the web of relationships and events stands the Idiot. Thus the novel's final structure, a sequence of oscillations, grew instead out of an opposite structure, a developmental one, planned for it in its early notebooks. The change in idea had led to a corresponding change in form. The portrayal of an Idiot who was evil but who finally repented would have given the novel a linear shape; on the other hand, a constant character, in this case a good man, creates waves around himself that intersect to make a circular pattern. This Idiot's constancy caused those around him to fluctuate within themselves and to clash with one another. (Even though the notebooks contain projected plans for the development of characters, the actual structure of the first two notebooks themselves is as circular as that of the final novel. Here too one plan for development cancels out the next; the final effect of the notebooks as a whole resembles the oscillations of Nastasya Filippovna in the novel.)

In the first two notebooks Dostoevsky sought to establish the broadest structural contours of his novel. From entry to entry he juggled repeatedly with the composition of the members of the families, trying to decide upon their intra- and interrelationships. Establishing the composition and the number of important families constituted a major task in the early notebooks. Most important, he experimented with the Idiot's position within the family as an illegitimate or legitimate son, nephew, and so on, and put him now in one family, now in another. At the same time Dostoevsky also sought to find the Idiot's role in that family; he tried to outline the shape of the Idiot's personality.

Bel'chikov and Sakulin as well as Wasiolek have divided their editions of these first two notebooks into a series of plans. Their rule for division has mainly been dictated by the changes in the familial structures throughout the notes. This division into plans is useful insofar as it quickly and correctly emphasizes the extreme importance Dostoevsky himself placed on the establishment of the structure of family relationships and interrelationships in the novel. We can see that Dostoevsky's novel began as a family novel, that the family was at the heart of its initial conception. In the long run, however, the division into plans, though initially helpful, is finally misleading, for it imposes an arbitrary order on the notes. The 1974 Soviet edition of the notes is more informative than the other two in that it does not follow this division into plans but sets the notes out as they were written, entry by entry.[7]

Throughout the many conceptual changes, certain constants remain from the earliest plans until the final version of the novel. The Heroine, the model for Nastasya Filippovna, is present from the beginning, as are, to a lesser degree, the related and mutually dependent themes of the ordinary versus the "original" man and of the power of money. Other plot fragments reappear repeatedly throughout: the burned finger, the arrival of the Idiot and the meeting with his brother (who later becomes Rogozhin) in a railway coach, an evening party at the General's house, the Idiot's handwriting, the lost wallet, and a preoccupation with severed heads. These fragments give no genuine clues to understanding how Dostoevsky built his novel. But because they provide the elemental stuff out of which Dostoevsky is able to spin some of his most powerful and scandalous scenes, they are able to show that the germs of certain heightened moments were present in the author's mind even before a particular scene had a reason for being as a function of an already existing plot and its characters.

Most of the plot material in the first two notebooks never recurs in the novel. For example, Dostoevsky was eagerly following the course of the case of Olga Umetsky during the fall of 1867.[8] Olga Umetsky, a girl beaten and maltreated by her parents, had several times attempted arson on her family's estate but had always then warned them of the fire. Nevertheless she was charged with having set the fires, and her parents were charged with having abused their child. Although Dostoevsky had originally intended this case to be a cornerstone in the plot, *The Idiot* contains only a shadowy reference to it in the fact that Nastasya Filippovna's parental estate had burned down many years before the story actually begins.[9] Dostoevsky's interest in this case as one of the first to be tried under the new jury system in Russia carries over into the novel, which contains numerous references to other trials by jury.

Despite the fact that the actual details of the plot in the notebooks differ from the final version, certain broad structural outlines remain throughout. Dostoevsky's preoccupation with the composition of and interrelationships among families provides the most fruitful thread to follow through the backtrackings and jottings that constitute the maze of the early notebooks. The changing patterns of family relationships reflect the alterations in the Idiot's character as well.

In the first entry, dated September 14, 1867, there are three families: a family of impoverished gentry, the Uncle's family, and the fiancé's family. The family of gentry is the initial conception of the Ivolgin family in the novel and contains a father, a mother, two sons (the elder, "the handsome son," and the younger, "the Idiot"), a daughter Masha, and a foster daughter, Mignon, who partly anticipates Nastasya Filippovna. Nastasya is also foreshadowed, however, by the Heroine, who is also called "the beauty," and Hero, who is a cousin in Masha's fiancé's family.[10] Dostoevsky's earliest plans were for an intense family drama; three prototypes of main characters in the novel, the Idiot, Ganya, and Nastasya crowd together within the confines of a single family unit. All relationships among characters are double-bonded by familial ties. The theme of incest exists from the beginning; the father of the first family tries to rape his foster daughter, Mignon.

This family structure holds through the second entry on October 4/16. In both entries Dostoevsky emphasizes the tense relationship between the Idiot and his mother. In the first entry his mother detests him; in the second, he scornfully pushes her away. Toward the middle of the second entry Dostoevsky introduces a second general's family (9:154). This family's high opinion of itself vaguely foreshadows the Epanchin family. Dostoevsky's addition of yet another family with a willful mother provides a hazy prefiguring of General Epanchin's wife. By the next entry, dated October 17, this structure has broken down. A pattern of vacillation begins and continues throughout these notes. Dostoevsky tentatively distances the Idiot by suggesting that he may be a stepson or a natural (illegitimate) son, not of the impoverished General but of the Uncle (9:155). The Heroine enters the General's family as a ward or governess. By

October 18, the Uncle has acquired yet another son: the Idiot is his natural son, the second son is legitimate. Deciding upon the Idiot's familial ties becomes necessary for the expression of the main idea about him.

In a later entry the same day the Idiot is simply the son of the Uncle (9:160). On October 22, Dostoevsky notes that he must work out the relations between the two brothers (9:162). They are to meet for the first time on a railway car: 'The Natural Son. He was traveling with the Son. They have become acquainted. The Natural Son knows that this is the Son. The Son has heard that there is a Natural Son. . . . The Son: 'Yes, but he doesn't seem stupid to me. It's true, he's strange. He's quite a *iurodivyi* [fool, in the sense of God's fool, that is an idiot believed to possess the gift of prophesy]'" (9:163). Although he later at times wandered away from it in the notes, by this ninth entry Dostoevsky had found a formulation that was to resurface as the beginning of his novel, where Myshkin and Rogozhin meet on the train. In these earliest notes, then, the Idiot has moved out of the central family into the Uncle's family. He has become successively a stepson and a natural son. Dostoevsky further distances him by having him *arrive* on the scene and by having him meet his brother for the first time. Family ties have slackened rapidly in Dostoevsky's structural scheme.

The son's labeling of the Idiot as a *iurodivyi* counterbalances the frequent assumption of critics that the early drafts of the novel show an Idiot completely unlike the Myshkin of the novel. Although this characterization does not occur again until the last entries of the first two notebooks, its early presence suggests that Dostoevsky's final notion of the Idiot did not spring full-blown in December 1867, but was a possibility in his mind all along. Indeed, as we shall see, other intimations of the final meek Idiot appear amid the early notes, which depict him, for the most part, as a predominantly vengeful and proud character.

In the tenth entry, October 27, Dostoevsky transplants the Idiot back into the General's family, where the Heroine has remained as a ward. Olga Umetsky is still part of the family as well (9:165). At the head of this entry Dostoevsky has written "Ganya" in calligraphic lettering.[11]

The Idiot has reentered the tight structure of the family, so that the son's and the Idiot's shared passion for the Heroine carries a shade of incest. Throughout all these early entries, however, the Uncle, who is also a suitor of the Heroine, plays a central role; at times he overshadows the Idiot. In the tenth entry Dostoevsky assigns them equal significance: "*Memento.* The main point of the novel: the Uncle and the Idiot, two characters."[12]

On October 29, Dostoevsky again slightly distanced the Idiot from the family; he becomes a natural son of the General. Everyone is terribly kind and affectionate to him but unjust at the same time. This arouses hatred in the Idiot (9:169). Later on the page, Dostoevsky reemphasizes the Idiot's abrupt, bewildering arrival on the scene. "From whence has the Idiot come? (They all make him understand that he has fallen on their shoulders). . . . The heirs of his godmother sent him from somewhere or other with a letter" (9:169).

In entry 12, October 30, the Idiot becomes the child from a prior marriage of the General; Ganya's mother hates the Idiot, while Ganya himself resembles the Idiot of the final version. "Pure, beautiful, virtuous, strict, very nervous, and a deeply Christian, compassionate lovingness. . . . He lives by feeling. He lives powerfully and passionately. In a word, a Christian nature" (9:170). He forgives the spiteful and sneering Idiot. Dostoevsky's idea of portraying a beautiful, Christian character has found its first fleeting expression in this plan for Ganya. (Ironically, in the third notebook Ganya often becomes like the Idiot of the first two notebooks. Their symbiotic relationship, so powerful in the notebooks, disappears in the novel. There Ganya never fully develops as a character.)

Dostoevsky commences another entry later the same day: "The novel begins with family difficulties and with the arrival of the Idiot" (9:172). The notion that the Idiot, though still part of the General's family, must arrive as a newcomer seems to have taken firm hold. Two days later, on November 1, Dostoevsky begins his entry by shifting the Idiot to the Uncle's family:

> No good. The main thought about the Idiot does not emerge. It is necessary: that the Idiot – is the son of the Uncle. THE IDIOT IS THE SON OF THE UNCLE. (9:174)

Dostoevsky's mounting frustration in his struggle to settle upon characters and a plot for the novel thus became focused on the problem of deciding upon the Idiot's kinship relationship with everyone else. Dostoevsky repeatedly tries to solve his difficulties with expressing "the main thought about the Idiot" by reshuffling family groupings. Here the solution is to remove the Idiot from the General's family and to place him once again in the family of the Uncle. Yet even here Dostoevsky has the Idiot exert power in much the same way as Myshkin subsequently does in the novel – through his simple, childlike honesty. "The Idiot captivates everyone with his childlike naïveté" (9:174).

Nevertheless the Uncle continues to vie for the central role in the novel; on November 2, Dostoevsky writes, "N.B. The figure of the Uncle over everything. *This is the main thing*" (9:175). Interestingly, the Uncle, who plays a major role throughout the first two notebooks, disappears in the novel, although some vestiges of him reappear in General Epanchin and Totsky. But plans for the Uncle's central role do not solve any of Dostoevsky's problems with the figure of the Idiot; still fussing about the family structure, Dostoevsky asks himself, "Why not arrange it so that the Mother of the Idiot is alive?" (9:176). He plans to have the Idiot seek her out and find her living in squalor in Saint Petersburg. Dostoevsky's intensifying struggles obsessively repeat themselves in juggling the Idiot's position. Once again the Idiot becomes legitimate, "*The Idiot* – a legitimate son of the Uncle and the blood brother to the Son, but he has been an outcast since childhood and has never seen the Son" (9:177).

Later the same day, Dostoevsky begins his next entry with the now familiar emphasis on family structure as the root of the problem:

> 2 November. Hurry.
> He is a legitimate, but unacknowledged son of the Uncle. An Idiot. (9:177)

Now the Idiot has been married off into the Umetsky family and sent to Switzerland. Amid a maze of plot intrigues the sentence "*He is a legitimate son*" appears again (9:178). It is as though Dostoevsky felt that the repetition of this phrase would somehow anchor his work and hold its fragments together. In this same entry relationships are then suddenly reshuffled: "The Heroine is a princess . . . but he is simply a Ptitsyn. (Is he a Ptitsyn?). . . . Umetskaya is not his sister" (9:179). Then, several pages later, "Either a Ptitsyn or a legitimate son? (a final decision)" (9:182). The oscillations grow more pronounced, "MAYBE IT WOULD BE MUCH BETTER TO MAKE HIM A LEGITIMATE SON" (9:184). We are witnessing one-half of an intense internal argument taking place within Dostoevsky. All the heavy, argumentative assertions of the Idiot's legitimacy are in firm reply to some unexpressed alternative solution. Dostoevsky is fighting against an intuition that he should remove the Idiot farther away from any family by making him illegitimate.

It is difficult for a reader of the notebooks to understand why, out of all the thousands of potential problems tormenting Dostoevsky in his attempts to set the foundations for this novel, the question of the Idiot's position in the family should assume such terrific proportions. The next entry for November 3 provides a clue: "THE FUNDAMENTAL QUESTION: In which way will the figure of the Idiot express the idea more interestingly, more romantically, and more graphically? By legitimacy or illegitimacy?" (9:187). Dostoevsky then sets up a plan for each alternative. Legitimacy would give the Idiot more pride; he could demonstrate that even without wealth or the help of other people, he could still triumph. If he were illegitimate, he could at first harbor dreams of the Heroine, of a career, and of high society, and then suddenly encounter the vivid possibility of attaining them all. Dostoevsky weighs the interest value of pride and domination against that of dreams and the sudden accessibility of those dreams. It is significant that Dostoevsky sees *both* possibilities as alternative ways of expressing the same idea (*mysl'*). Thus, the problem of the Idiot's legitimacy or illegitimacy boils down to the achievement of an aim that we have already seen is crucial for Dostoevsky: Which way would be more interesting?

Neither alternative has yet outweighed the merits of the other. The vacillations continue:

> BETTER THAT HE IS LEGITIMATE (WITHOUT A MOTHER) . . .
> Illegitimate is better: everything will be explained . . .
> Illegitimate: a terribly proud and tragic character.
> N.B. *But why not thus:* legitimate, but rejected, he has rejected himself. A majestic role. (9:188–89)

Dostoevsky hammers persistently at the possibilities for each alternative. This November 3 entry reads like an ugly fugue between two monotonous voices, neither of which achieves any resolution.

Part of this debate over questions of the Idiot's legitimacy and the role of the Uncle is simply the exorcism or suppression of the complex of ideas that emerges later, in *A Raw Youth.* There the Uncle figure develops into Versilov and the natural son becomes the Raw Youth. Some parts of the early notes for *A Raw Youth* could belong in the notebooks for *The Idiot:* "Stepson and stepfather. An artistic nature. . . . Better if he is his natural Father. . . . BUT WHAT IS MOST IMPORTANT, retain throughout the entire narrative a tone of his unchallenged superiority over the Youth and everybody else . . . let the reader feel all along that, at the end of the novel, he is tormented by an idea."[13] Dostoevsky, for all his seemingly profuse outpourings of ideas for entire novels and fragments of plot and character detail, was extremely economical: he rarely let a good thought go to waste.

Dostoevsky's preoccupation with the legitimacy or illegitimacy of his hero may reveal a partial influence of Tolstoy's *War and Peace,* where Pierre Bezukhov, just returned from Switzerland, is established as an illegitimate son. Myshkin, like Pierre, has just returned from Switzerland. Both men receive an inheritance that suddenly changes their expectations. Each has an overriding sense of his mission in the world. They share minor personality traits as well. Myshkin, in part 1 of the novel, enters General Epanchin's office through the wrong door, yet he still quickly wins over both the

General and the General's wife by his candid, cheerful modesty. At the beginning of *War and Peace* the narrator describes Pierre at Anna Pavlovna's soirée: "All his absentmindedness and inability to enter a room and converse in it was, however, redeemed by his kindly, simple and modest expression. Anna Pavlovna turned to him and, with a Christian mildness that expressed forgiveness of his indiscretion, nodded and said: 'I hope to see you again.'"[14]

There are other hints of Tolstoy's influence on *The Idiot.* The Idiot is Prince Lev Nikolaevich Myshkin. The name and patronymic are Tolstoy's own, and Myshkin, or "mousekin," is a kind of antonym to Lev (lion) and even to Tolstoy (stout, heavy). Later, in the third notebook, Dostoevsky writes, "The chain and hope. To do a little" (9:241), and later, "The chain, he speaks of the chain. Make the shackles clank. To do a little" (9:269–70). The editors of the 1974 edition of the notes cite Tolstoy's influence here. (This is especially interesting because the notion of the chain becomes so crucial to *The Brothers Karamazov.*) They write that the chain as a symbol of the immortality of good deeds most probably derives from *War and Peace:* "In trying to convince Andrei Bolkonsky to become a mason, so that he might serve goodness, Pierre Bezukhov says ' . . . enter our brotherhood . . . and you will at once feel yourself to be . . . *part of that vast, invisible chain,* whose source is hidden in the heavens. . . . Don't I feel . . . that I form *one link,* one step, between the lower and higher beings. . . . I feel that I cannot disappear, because nothing in the world disappears, but that I shall always exist and that I have always existed'" (9:465).[15] The editors then cite Dostoevsky's letter to A. N. Maikov of February 18/March 1, 1868, in which he says that he has read the first half of Tolstoy's novel.[16]

In the first two notebooks for *The Idiot,* the tangle of frustrations about family structure and the position of the Idiot within a family has unraveled into the question of the Idiot's legitimacy. Dostoevsky's debate over this matter, which to the reader seems like an unproductive and endless repetition of alternatives without any hint of progress, bears fruit: the resolution of the question of legitimacy bears as much upon the Idiot's personality as it does upon his place in the family structure. The issue of the Idiot's legitimacy becomes at once a private and a public question that shapes both his personality and the ultimate structure of the family; his place in the family has gradually condensed into a more inherently interesting problem: the determination of his character.

---

By following this particular thread, we have seen the unerring but unconscious path of Dostoevsky's mind throughout these entries. Elizabeth Dalton, who has found that these notebooks resemble "primary process thinking," has asserted that "the author is simply recording rapidly whatever comes into his mind without much attempt at order or coherence."[17] Although her observation may well reflect the actual creative process in Dostoevsky's mind as he jotted down ideas and outlines, the end result – the notes themselves – exhibits, if only in its regularity of oscillation, a discernible structural coherence. Some instinct compelled him to cover the same ground over and over again while seeming merely to repeat himself. When in the following entries Dostoevsky seems to have simply abandoned the question of the Idiot's legitimacy, he has not done so at all. He has found a more essential way of asking the question he has really been asking all along: What is the Idiot's place? Where does he fit? Who is he? That has been the real issue since the beginning.

The search for the novel's structure forces Dostoevsky to state his ideas in their most elemental form. On November 4 he no longer asks himself whether the Idiot is legitimate or illegitimate. "*An enigma.* Who is he? A terrible villain or a mysterious ideal?" (9:195). The Idiot's position in the family no longer defines him; Dostoevsky has moved into a more metaphysical realm. Nevertheless, he still halfheartedly experiments with family relations until he finally arrives at his solution, "*There are no relatives*" (9:204). The most important concern has become the crystallization of the Idiot's personality. On November 21, Dostoevsky notes: "NECESSARY: to set forth the character of the Idiot in a masterly way" (9:208). Throughout this entry the Idiot reveals his character indirectly, through the stories he tells. Dostoevsky again reminds himself, "The character of the Idiot" (9:208).

On 6 November, while planning the Idiot's arrival upon the scene in a railway car, Dostoevsky writes:

> The Idiot. Everything is based on vengeance. A humiliated being . . .
> He is a *Prince.* A Prince. *Iurodivyi.* (He is with the children)?! (9:200)

This formulation, so crucial for the entire novel, predictably appears as a fragment amid mounds of unrelated material. Nor does the characterization even hold. Within the same entry the Idiot returns to his former role of the envious, proud seducer. But the crucial passages discussing the Idiot's place in the family appeared in the same fragmented way – amid pages of material that were never brought into the novel. The critic's hindsight does not give him any power to discern a rule that determines which material will be picked up again and which will be finally rejected, but it can enable him to gaze upon an intricate, maze-like tableau that presents a convincing picture of the fact that, for the artist, there is a path through that maze, after some barriers are pushed aside to disclose it.

The appellation *iurodivyi* holds; throughout the next page Dostoevsky repeatedly calls the Idiot *iurodivyi* (9:201). From here the determination of the character of the Idiot takes precedence over the efforts to place him in a family situation. (Dostoevsky's deadline for sending in part 1 was rapidly approaching.) "THE CHARACTER OF THE IDIOT. There are oddities. Quiet. Sometimes, he says nothing" (9:201). He reads to the children about future bliss. Dostoevsky emphasizes the Idiot's relations with the children, "THE MAIN THING. *The character of his relations toward children. Very weak health*" (9:202).

The final entry for the early notebooks, dated November 11/30, bears even less resemblance to the novel than do most of the preceding notes. The material is mostly about the children and the Umetsky family. The Idiot does not occupy much of Dostoevsky's attention here, although his conception of the Idiot has consciously and irrevocably changed. Dostoevsky reveals that he himself now thinks of the Idiot as having changed from one kind of character to another when he writes, "N.B. The nephew, the character of the former Idiot. A tirade about the King of the Jews" (9:212). Still preoccupied with shaping the Idiot's new personality, he notes, "*About the Idiot there are only stories*" (9:213). (This idea becomes increasingly important in the third notebook.) "The Idiot's character" (9:214). "N.B. Until the slap itself, everyone laughed at the Idiot and he was in terrible disregard. He is always silent" (9:215). This final entry closes with the vow, "Make a detailed arrangement of the plan and *begin* in the evening" (9:215).

Dostoevsky's painstaking arrangements and rearrangements of the family structures in the early notes led him inexorably, though in a pattern of seeming oscillation, to distance his central character from any family role. As the Idiot withdrew from the family, Dostoevsky, in the last several entries, instead emphasized the Idiot's illness as well as the fact that he was "with the children." In the final version of the novel, Dostoevsky gives his hero only the vaguest of biographies. In fact in the novel Myshkin knows little about his past; a man whom he encounters at General Epanchin's evening party seems to know as much about Myshkin's life history as he does himself. (This stranger, it turns out, had met Myshkin briefly when he was a child.) Thus, the Idiot is isolated; the reader and the other characters know only stories about his past, stories he and others tell. His own memory is often hazy. He becomes, as it were, part of each family in the novel, while really belonging to none. This, rather than having him be in any one family, best expresses the "idea" behind the Idiot. Dostoevsky's instinct had led him to the solution.

Bakhtin has pointed out that the internal monologues of many of Dostoevsky's characters, most notably those of Golyadkin, Raskolnikov, and the underground man, can be read as dialogues between doubles.[18] Dostoevsky's notebooks reveal that this mode of thought was far more than a literary device employed to create a polyphonic effect. The entire fabric of the notebooks can be unraveled into such dialogues in much the same way that a paragraph from *The Double*, *Crime and Punishment*, or *Notes from the Underground* can be. Yet there is an important distinction to be made: in his notebooks Dostoevsky often explored variant ways of expressing a single idea; in the end, however, he always decided firmly upon a single way. His characters' internal monologues, on the other hand, usually remained unfinalized.

Other, perhaps more interesting, questions for the reader, such as why the Idiot is called an idiot or what his childhood was like, do not receive the same insistent treatment, although Dostoevsky does touch upon them sporadically and tantalizingly. Throughout, the question of the Idiot's idiocy is mildly problematic. In the earlier drafts he has merely been dubbed an idiot by his mother, who hates him. The other characters do not understand why he has been called that. In the ninth entry on October 22, the Idiot is merely pretending to be an idiot; at the General's he shows triumphantly that he is not one at all. The son says of the Idiot, "Either he is very proud, so that he disdains everything, or he is very stupid, that is, sincere" (9:164). The son adds later, "He is simply not an Idiot" (9:164). On October 29 Dostoevsky writes, "The Idiot was always considered an Idiot" (9:169). But three days later, on November 1, the Idiot's mother is again declaring that the Idiot is merely pretending, dissembling (9:173). Then Dostoevsky writes, 'The Idiot is an idiot," though the Uncle later doubts that he is an idiot (9:174). The debate continues from time to time throughout the notes.

For a reader of the novel, the problem of Myshkin's idiocy and what it means looms large. Is his idiocy to be understood strictly as a link to the tradition of the Russian kenotic saint and *iurodivyi?* Is Myshkin the Idiot because he has fits, because he is childlike? Each reader must work out some understanding of what Myshkin's idiocy signifies to him. Clearly, this was Dostoevsky's intention in the novel. Yet he never refers to this problem in the notebooks. He himself vacillates over the depletion of the hero's idiocy; he notes the perplexity of the other characters, but he provides no substantial clue or formulation of what Myshkin's idiocy means.[19]

The word "idiot" in both Russian and English comes from the Greek *idiotes:* private person, a common man, an ignorant uninformed person. *Idios* means private, own, peculiar.[20] So idiot need not mean merely imbecile and fool; it can also signify a man who is private and somehow set apart. It can also carry the meaning of a private versus a public man. All these meanings reverberate throughout *The Idiot* at various times.

At scattered intervals throughout the early notes Dostoevsky posits a psychological explanation for why the Idiot is so proud and so full of hatred. He depicts the Idiot as having suffered a terrible spiritual wound in childhood. We have already seen that his mother hates him. In the first entry, Dostoevsky had noted: "N.B. In childhood he wept upon being scolded, but then he became stronger and *he scoffs at others.* There was an incident with a headmaster" (9:157). On October 29, Dostoevsky wrote again of his hero's difficult childhood, "He needed from childhood more beauty, more beautiful sensations, more encompassing love, *more bringing up.* But now: *a thirst for beauty and at the same time a 40% lack of faith in it,* or faith, but no love for the ideal. The devils also believe, and tremble'" (9:167).[21]

On November 2, another jotting seeks to link the Idiot's childhood to his character. "In his development and in his surrounding milieu he assimilated all these poisons and principles, which entered into his blood. A totally outraged heart has unlimited magnanimity and a need for love. *He did not have them,* and therefore he revenged himself and acted evilly toward those whom he wanted to love endlessly and for whom he wanted to shed his blood" (9:180). Dostoevsky's note to himself is difficult to follow, but the main point seems to be that the Idiot's acute suffering in childhood, though it had not destroyed his desire to love, had destroyed his ability to do so. Harder to explain is the peculiar assertion that the Idiot's childhood had been terrible, but not terrible enough for him to attain an unlimited magnanimity and need for love. Here the novelist has not explicated his idea for any reader; this abbreviated note remains, for the most part, indecipherable.

Dostoevsky's explanations of the Idiot's character in terms of his childhood resemble the attempts to fix him within a tight family structure; a typical hero in a nineteenth-century novel comes complete with memories of his childhood and family ties. Dostoevsky's movement away from the typical biographical explanations parallels his decision not to present the Idiot as a son in a family: in both aspects the writer has moved toward the creation of a more isolated, more enigmatic character. Of course one must also remember that these are sketches for the notebook Idiot who often differs greatly from his namesake in the novel. All of the psychologizing about the Idiot disappears in the novel, where Dostoevsky sticks to the narrative formula he had found toward the end of these notes, "About the Idiot there are only stories."

As early as October 22, 1867, Dostoevsky had already characterized the Idiot as a *iurodivyi*, so that side by side with the proud, dissembling Idiot who would eventually be regenerated through love, there already existed glimpses of a character who resembled the final version of the Idiot. The term *iurodivyi* provides a bridge between the character of the Idiot in the early notebooks and the almost opposite character of the Idiot in the novel: on the one hand a *iurodivyi* could be a shrewd, calculating, aggressive, and objectionable figure; on the other hand, because he had renounced the flesh "for Christ's sake," he was believed to have the gift of prophecy. James Billington has observed that this figure of the holy fool "reinforced the already marked tendency of Slavic Orthodoxy toward passion and prophecy rather than reason and discipline."[22] The notebook Idiot embodies the less attractive traits of that figure, while the novel Idiot displays more of the positive traits, but any Russian reader would be aware of the entire spectrum of associations invoked by the word, *iurodivyi*.

In the novel Myshkin mimics the *iurodivyi*'s effect on others more than he wishes to. The *iurodivyi* often feigned madness and immorality to cause a public scandal that served, in a roundabout way, to convert sinners; he also wished to provoke vilification against himself in order to struggle against his own pride, the worst fear of the ascetic.[23] The *iurodivyi* fought his own propensity for corruption this way, but he also had a public duty or quest. George Fedotov has described this quest as consisting of "service to the world in a special mission, not by word or beneficent action but through the power of the Spirit which works through the disguise of madness but is manifested in clairvoyance and prophecy" (*RRM* 320). Myshkin carries with him an aura of these qualities: he provokes extreme anger in men; he causes scandal; and he has a definite sense of being on a mission of service in the world. He has a fondness for making parabolic and prophetic statements.

Fedotov describes the life of a holy fool as a "perpetual oscillation between moral acts of saving men and immoral acts of insulting them," (*RRM* 320). This could also serve as an epigram for Myshkin: although Myshkin never sought consciously to insult the other characters he unwittingly does so repeatedly throughout the novel. The *iurodivyi* made an ethical attempt to deride the world of common sense by laying bare the gap between the order of the world and God's order (*RRM* 322). Myshkin too sought to bring the other characters back to the simpler moral and religious precepts of God's world; he advocated a return to a more primitive form of Christianity. Moreover, many holy fools were supposedly of foreign origin (*RRM* 327), and Myshkin, though his Russian ties become increasingly important, seems like a foreigner at the beginning of the novel.

Myshkin particularly resembles one such holy man, Michael of Klopsko. Like Myshkin, he had obscure origins, but in social rank he was almost a prince; this heightened the effect of his humility (*RRM* 336). The same may be said of Prince Myshkin. When Michael first appeared at Klopsko, the Abbot asked him, "Who are you, my son, a man or a Devil?" Michael replied, "Are you a man or a Devil?"[24] When Myshkin arrives on the Saint Petersburg scene people react to him with the same ambivalence, and he too immediately starts questioning and involving himself in the lives of others.

In the novel Myshkin also shares a kinship with the Russian kenotic saints, such as Theodosius, Sergius, and Tikhon. The Russian kenotic saints, who sought to make their lives an active example of Christ's humility, love, and service, were not, generally, proselytizing teachers. Saint Theodosius (d. 1074) of Kiev was the first representative of kenoticism; many of his beliefs were modeled on those of Saint Theodore the Studite (d. 826). In his ideal of community life and service to the world, he humbled himself not before the powerful but before the lowly.[25] Myshkin follows the same general lines of action.

Saint Sergius (d. 1392) was remarkable for his gentleness, for his "neighborly," simple, humble, and grave character (*RRM* 202). These are, of course, all qualities of Myshkin as well. Like Sergius, Myshkin enters upon his mission of service to the world after a period of isolation in the symbolic desert – in Myshkin's case, a Swiss hospital. Kenotic humility cannot be equated with obedience; all the Russian kenotic saints lived by their own ascetic law. Myshkin's humility is not synonymous with obedience either. Unlike these saints, however, Myshkin is a wealthy prince who does not renounce his property. In this respect he rather resembles the *iurodivyi*, who were sometimes even quite greedy. While the kenotic saint shunned earthly possessions, Myshkin is simply indifferent to them.

Saint Tikhon (d. 1783), who lived in the eighteenth century and was known as a Westernizing kenotic, suffered from a combination of nervous illness and melancholy that resembles Myshkin's. Moreover, Myshkin echoes him in the two foci of his spiritual life: the thought of death and the vision of the celestial world. Myshkin, like Tikhon, is preoccupied with the idea of the "double eternity" (*RRM* 184), that is, the eternity of death and the eternity of the other world. Tikhon, who is regarded as un-Russian in his continual concentration on the suffering of the crucified Savior, "had always before his eyes the icons, or rather pictures – portraying the various moments in the tragedy of Golgotha" (*RRM* 184). Myshkin too is obsessed with pictures of Christ's suffering and with the moments before and after death.

Myshkin's sensations during the moment before an epileptic fit resemble the spiritual state experienced in prayer described by another holy man of the fifteenth century, Nilus of Sorsk (d. 1508). "Of a sudden, the soul is infused with joys, and this incomparable feast paralyzes the tongue. The heart overflows with sweetness and while his delight endures, a man is drawn unwittingly from all sensible things. . . . One who has discovered this joy in God, not only knows no stirring passion but is forgetful of his very life since the love of God is sweeter than life."[26] For Myshkin the "incomparable feast" which overwhelms him is the "feast of life," but, like Nilus he experiences moments when his "soul is infused with joys" and he undergoes an acute perception of something beyond life.

The most typical characterizations of the Idiot in the early notes find their final fruition in the novel in the figures of Ganya, Rogozhin, and to some extent Ippolit. For example, on October 29, 1867, Dostoevsky writes of the Idiot:

> The finale of a great soul.
> Love – in three phases: revenge and self-love, passion, a loftier love. Man becomes purified. (9:168)

Then, in the later notes for part 2 of the novel (after part 1 had already been published), Dostoevsky writes on March 12, 1868:

> IN THE NOVEL THERE ARE THREE KINDS OF LOVE:
> 1) Passionate-spontaneous love – Rogozhin,
> 2) Love out of vanity – Ganya.
> 3) Christian love-the Prince. (9:220)

Dostoevsky, in the first notebooks, has parceled out to these other characters the stages of development planned for the Idiot. None of them undergoes any significant change or development in the course of the novel.[27]

On October 18, 1867, Dostoevsky conceived a plan for the Idiot's character, which he called Plan for Iago.

> FOR THE CHARACTER OF THE IDIOT – Iago. But he ends divinely. He renounces, and so on.
>
> N.B. He has slandered everyone; he has intrigued before everyone; he has attained everything; he has taken money and even a fiancée, and yet he renounces. (9:161)

Iago's primary role in *Othello* is to incite action, to ensnare other characters in their own webs. The Idiot becomes an inciter, a catalyst for action in the notes. Even when the Idiot acts as a peacemaker – as, for example, between the Uncle and the son – he still incites one against the other. In the novel the Idiot's boundless, though quiet, energy also often causes situations to become extreme. Myshkin seeks sincerely to spread peace and goodwill among the other characters. Yet the result is often better than his Iago counterpart could have hoped. His interference in the family fight at the Ivolgins' in part 1 of the novel, for example, serves to intensify all the existing tensions.

Later in the Plan for Iago entry, Dostoevsky described the Idiot's depression and weariness, his sense that he is separated from life and that events resemble a vaudeville. In the novel, Myshkin, at his weariest moments on the park bench in Pavlovsk, also perceives everyday life as something from which he alone has been excluded, a festival in which he cannot take part.

In entry twelve, October 30, the Idiot arrives from somewhere, enters into the family as a nonentity, and gains ascendancy over all of its members (9:170). Prince Myshkin of the novel, unwittingly and in good faith, achieves the same power over most of the other characters – such as the Ivolgins, the Epanchins, the Lebedevs. "The Idiot," writes Dostoevsky in the notes, "does not justify himself. His magnanimous deeds (they were, *invent*) are done by him without publicity, but he is nevertheless dissatisfied with himself; he judges and torments himself, because his pride is not pure but *vain*" (9:192). Nor does Myshkin seek to justify himself; at most, he is at times vaguely aware of his own "double thoughts." Thus, however different the early and the final versions of the Idiot may be, Myshkin bears more than slight resemblance to his energetic, demonic predecessor in the early notes. They share the qualities of the *iurodivyi* and of a catalytic, unsoliloquizing Iago figure.

---

Dostoevsky's frenzied attempts in these first two notebooks to establish the most general structural outline and to shape his characters did not leave him much time to worry about narrative manner. A few brief references and remarks, however, show in a kind of shorthand how he conceived the narrative method of his novel; these comments prove interesting later in the light of the third notebook. Twice in the first entry of the early notes Dostoevsky tells himself to "invent some terrible episodes." Later, having made a plan for the spiteful Idiot's eventual regeneration, Dostoevsky adds to himself: "(N.B. Trace the thread of his character – that will be entertaining.)" (9:156).

In the novel the characters do not change very much and Dostoevsky does not give any extended biographical details about his hero. Thus the final narrative is not usually explanatory. But here, in the early notes, Dostoevsky planned to follow the Idiot through successive and varied stages of development. Such a content demanded a different sort of narrative, as Dostoevsky tells himself: "But do it this way: . . . Show what kind of man has been oppressed" (9:156). Throughout these chaotic notes the attainment of some degree of clarity in the narrative becomes at times a primary stylistic goal – along with, of course, the constant desire to be entertaining. On October 30, Dostoevsky writes, "(Explain and delineate *more precisely* and *more clearly*)" (9:172).

Not surprisingly, one assertion can lead to its opposite. On the same page, Dostoevsky, while planning a series of violent events ("a fire, a finger [burned], a rape") which would show what the Idiot is capable of, chooses an opposite narrative manner, "N.B. Without explanation" (9:172). But the basic aim still seems to be "to explain," for on November 2, 1867, he reiterates the need for an explanatory narrative style, "Explanatory conversations for the whole novel and scenes with the brother and the Uncles – as before" (9:178). The explaining is to be done through "showing" rather than by "telling": "From this it follows that it is necessary to explain this passion and this burning love *in the course of the novel* by means of episodes" (9:183). Curiously, even at the time of writing these early notes, while the novel hulked before him as a shapeless, unwritten thing, Dostoevsky foresaw the defense he would later make for his work, "*For the epilogue:* I have written a fantastic novel, but never more real characters" (9:199).

Toward the end of the first two notebooks, in the last entries, Dostoevsky's primary narrative concern is that "I must be concise" (9:106). On November 11/30 he begins his final entry for the early notes, "*Part One.* The Idiot and Umetskaya, *the business has begun*, a concise story" (9:209). But conciseness for Dostoevsky does not necessarily mean clarity or explanation. ("About the Idiot there are only stories.")

It would be rash to attribute undue significance to the few unsystematic notations about narrative manner that Dostoevsky has made in the early notebooks. It is striking, however, that the early versions of the Idiot as a developing character loosely paralleled the author's search for an explanatory narrative. By the last entries, when Dostoevsky had already decided upon the *prince-iurodivyi* plan for the Idiot, the desire for an explanatory style gave way to a more generalized goal of conciseness. Conciseness refers to a narrative manner rather than content: to be concise does not necessarily include explanations; one can be enigmatic and still be concise. Dostoevsky's new emphasis on conciseness carried over into part 1 of the novel, where the events take place in a single day. There too we have "only stories" about the Idiot; he has arrived as a stranger.

Although much of the material in these notes never resurfaces in his published fiction, the first two notebooks contain intimations of elements that reappear in Dostoevsky's last three novels: *The Possessed*, *A Raw Youth*, and *The Brothers Karamazov*. Many of the notes are taken up with the Idiot's secret marriage to a humble girl in the Umetsky family, who is at times described as a *iurodivaia*. The Idiot courts the Heroine despite his secret marriage; she offers herself to him. The marriage is suddenly revealed, and in some of the notes the Idiot kills his wife. Perhaps, too, he married her while he was drunk. These themes cluster around Stavrogin in *The Possessed*. The Idiot's "Byronic despair" describes Stavrogin (9:190). The Heroine's letter to the Idiot resembles in imagery and tone Pyotr Verkhovensky's letter to Stavrogin. The Heroine writes: "Why you? Because you were there like some kind of sun; at that time everyone sought you out; everyone adored you, but I hated them all. . . . And you are the sun, you ridiculed me from our first meeting" (9:190). Pyotr says to Stavrogin, "Stavrogin, you are beautiful. Do you know that you are beautiful! . . . You are my idol! You injure no one, and everyone hates you. You treat everyone as an equal, and yet everyone is afraid of you – that's good. . . . You are the leader, you are the sun, and I am your worm" (10:323). The Heroine's letter immediately follows a plan for the death of the Idiot's secret wife; Pyotr's mad speech occurs on the eve of the murder of Maria Timofeevna, Stavrogin's secret wife.

The "Rothschild" theme, of a poor man slowly and deliberately amassing a fortune, reverberates through the notes for *The Idiot* and finds fruition in *A Raw Youth;* another theme in the notes, of the hero's suffering and blighted childhood, also finds it fullest expression in *A Raw Youth*. The editors of the 1974 edition of the notebooks for *The Idiot* stress the similarity of the relationship between the Idiot and the Uncle with that of Arkady and Versilov. *A Raw Youth* also continues the theme of illegitimacy explored in the early notes for *The Idiot* (9:345). Finally, the theme of a father's and son's rivalry for the same woman recurs in *A Raw Youth* and in *The Brothers Karamazov*. The Idiot of the early notebooks fragments into Dostoevsky's next four major heroes: Myshkin, Stavrogin, Arkady, and Alyosha.

The last entry of the second notebook is dated November 11/30. Presumably the next few days were spent in intense writing. Then, on December 4 Dostoevsky announced that he had "thrown it all to the Devil"; he began to rework his plans for the novel and started to write again on December 18.[28] Unfortunately these crucial notes no longer exist. Twenty-three days later Dostoevsky sent off part 1 of the novel to the *Russkii vestnik.* (He had sent off the first five chapters of part 1 by January 5.)[29] Between the last notebook entry and the first page of the novel, then, there is a large gap. It may be bridged at various points by minimizing rather than accentuating the differences between the early notes and the final version, thereby allowing us to see that the novel *did* in fact grow, in however mutant a form, out of the notes. Such a dramatic gap certainly lends itself also to psychological interpretation, and Dalton, who finds that the overall creative process in the notebooks resembles the formation of a dream, discovers an essential act of regression in the gap between the notes and the novel: "The notes record not only the movement toward expression of ideas . . . but also, paradoxically, the struggle to repress those ideas. Between the last plan and the beginning of the novel itself, an act of creative repression has taken place. The novel is a compromise formation."[30]

But it would be wrong to underestimate the importance of the vision that came to Dostoevsky during these days in December and about which he had written so movingly to his friend Maikov and to his niece Sonya Ivanova. The months of unsuccessful attempts to portray an idea resulted in a drastic recasting of that idea. On December 31, 1867/January 12, 1868, Dostoevsky wrote to Maikov, after a long silence, about his novel:

> And with me it's been this way: *I have been working and tormenting myself.* Do you know what it means *to compose?* . . . Having taken so much money from *Russkii vestnik* (alas! 4500 rubles) I, you see, had fully hoped at the beginning of the year that poetry wouldn't desert me, that the poetic idea would flash and develop artistically toward the end of the year, and that I would manage to satisfy everyone. It seemed all the more probable to me because always both in my head and in my soul many pregnant artistic ideas flash and are felt. But they only flash, and a full embodiment is neces-

sary, and such an embodiment always proceeds accidentally and suddenly. But one cannot predict exactly when it will arise; and only after that, having received in your heart a full image, can you set about the artistic embodiment of the image. . . . Well then, all summer and autumn I have been putting together various thoughts (some were most ingenious), but some experience always let me foresee either the falseness or the difficulty or the weakness of a particular idea. Finally, I stopped at one idea and began to work. I had written a lot, but on the 4th of December, foreign style, I threw it all to the Devil. I assure you that the novel could have been satisfactory; but it became incredibly repulsive to me precisely because it was satisfactory and not *positively* [*polozhitel'no*] *good.* I didn't need that. But what was I to do? It was already the 4th of December! . . .

I thought from the 4th till the 18th of December new style. . . . My head was turning into a windmill. Why I didn't go mad, I don't know. Finally, on the 18th of December I sat down to write a new novel; on the 5th of January (new style) I sent off to the editorship 5 chapters of the first part (nearly 5 sheets) with the assurance that on the 10th of January (new style) I would send the remaining *two chapters* of the first part. Yesterday on the 11th I sent these 2 chapters, and so I have sent off *the whole first part* – 6 or *6-1/2* printed sheets . . .

Now about the novel. . . . In essence I absolutely do not myself know what I have sent off. . . . For a long time already a certain thought has tormented me, but I was afraid to make a novel out of it, because the thought was too difficult and I was not ready for it, although the thought was completely tempting and I loved it. This idea is – to portray a wholly beautiful man [*izobrazit' vpolne prekrasnogo cheloveka*]. There can be, in my opinion, nothing more difficult than this, especially in our time. . . . This idea formerly has appeared for a moment in some artistic form [*obraz*], but indeed, only *in part,* and the whole is necessary. Only my despairing situation compelled me to take up this premature thought. I gambled as one does at roulette, "maybe it will develop under my pen." This is unforgivable.

In general, the plan has taken shape. Furthermore, there flash by me details which are very seductive to me and which inspire fervor in me. But the whole? The hero? . . . I am obliged to construct an image. Will it develop under my pen? . . . Of the 4 heroes . . . the fourth, that is the main one, the first hero, is extremely weak. Maybe he does not sit weakly in my heart, but he is terribly difficult. (28.2:239–41)

A day later, in his letter to Sonya Ivanova, Dostoevsky elaborated on his new plan:

I have destroyed much of what was written. . . . At that time, 3 weeks ago I applied myself to another novel and began to work day and night. The idea of the novel – my old and beloved, but nevertheless difficult, idea – is one which, for a long time, I dared not tackle, and if I have tackled it now, it was decidedly because I was in a desperate situation. The main thought of the novel is to portray a positively beautiful person [*izobrazit' polozhitel'no prekrasnogo cheloveka*]. There is nothing more difficult than this in the world, and especially at this time. All writers, not only ours, but even all Europeans, who but undertook this depiction of the *positively* beautiful man – always had to pass it up. Because this problem is immeasurable. The beautiful is an ideal, but an ideal that neither we nor civilized Europe has in the least perfected. On earth there is only one positively beautiful person – Christ, so that the appearance of this immeasurably, infinitely beautiful person is, of course, an infinite miracle in itself. . . . But I have gone on too long, I will mention only, that of the beautiful characters in Christian literature Don Quixote is the most finished. But he is beautiful only because at the same time he is also comic. Pickwick of Dickens (an infinitely weaker idea than Don Quixote, but nevertheless great) is also comic, and by that alone affects us. Compassion appears toward the beauty that is mocked and doesn't know its own worth – and consequently sympathy appears even in the reader. This awakening of compassion is the secret of humor, Jean Valjean is also a powerful attempt, but he excites sympathy

> by his terrible misfortune and by society's injustice toward him. I have nothing similar, nothing, decidedly, and therefore I am terribly afraid that it will be a positive failure. Some details perhaps aren't bad. I am afraid that it will be boring. It's a long novel. I wrote the *first part* entirely in 23 days. . . . It will decidedly not be effective. . . . My only wish is that it will awaken even a little curiosity in the reader, so that he will go on to the second part. . . . The novel is called *The Idiot.* (28.2:251, January 1/3, 1868)

The ideas expressed in these oft-quoted letters provided the cornerstone for the novel. The early notes were a preparation for that vision; in them one can discover the seeds of Dostoevsky's decision to portray a positively beautiful man. Throughout these two letters Dostoevsky treated his problem as a narrative one – that of portrayal (*izobrazit'*) rather than as a philosophical or ideological one. The idea "to portray a wholly beautiful man" was "old and cherished" but "difficult." The difficulty revolved around turning that idea into words, making others accept and love it.

---

The third notebook, written after the first sixteen chapters of the novel had already been published in the January and February (1868) issues of *Russkii vestnik*, also gives evidence of authorial indecision and contains brief, unfinished plans. But whereas the indecision of the first two notebooks revolved around the conception of the Idiot's character and the search for the idea of the novel, the problems in the third notebook often derive from the very stability of the Idiot's character and the subsequent need to focus events around him; that is, the problem of the artistic execution of the idea (what Dostoevsky called *khudozhestvennost'*). This last notebook touches more often upon questions of narrative strategy than do the first two, although there is still no systematic discussion of the problem.

For Dostoevsky the writing of part 2 of the novel (which he thought of as part 3, part 1 being the first six chapters and part 2 being chapters 7 to 16) proved excruciatingly difficult; it did not pour forth in a whole as had part 1. The notes for part 2 in the third notebook reflect Dostoevsky's loss of momentum. Although the first part of the novel foreshadowed the course of the narrative, the perspective of the work still remained unclear to Dostoevsky.[31] Part 2 was due to appear in *Russkii vestnik* in April 1868, but only the first two chapters of part 2 were published in April. The following three chapters appeared in May. Dostoevsky suffered over this piecemeal form of writing. In a letter to Maikov, he called it "shameful" (28.2:302; June 22/July 1868). On June 3 he sent off the next four chapters (6–9) of part 2, but only chapters 6 through 8 were published then. Chapter 9 evidently arrived too late. In July Dostoevsky finally completed part 2, through chapter 12.

The notes from March through July 1868, while Dostoevsky was trying to write part 2, reflect his uncertainty over the direction of the novel. In seeking to formulate the plot for part 2, Dostoevsky also continually outlined plans for the rest of the novel. Part 1 had ended noncommittally, with most of the major characters setting off to Moscow; upon their return anything could happen. In writing part 1 Dostoevsky needed to settle upon a definite characterization of the Idiot, but he had not yet had to commit himself to a certain plot. The notes for part 2 of the novel portray this search.

Predictably, in the third notebook Dostoevsky addresses himself often to the question of the manner in which the novel should be written. But when Dostoevsky writes about the structural organization and the narrative strategy of his novel, he does not formulate abstract or ideal statements about the craft of writing novels. Instead, he makes precise, practical prescriptions for getting this particular and troublesome novel under way and written. Thus notes about composition and narrative are often expressed as notes about the plot – How long is the Idiot in Moscow? Whom does he marry? – and about the roles of other more peripheral characters, like Ganya, Evgeny Pavlovich, and the children. We have already seen that proposed elaborate character development in the first two notebooks did not carry over into the novel and that stages of development in the

Idiot's personality were fragmented into separate characters in the novel. In the transformation of the third notebook into the novel further reductions occur: Ganya's role diminishes; the Idiot of the novel becomes less introspective than the Idiot of the third notebook, and the children's club, of which the Prince is head, disappears.

In the opening pages of these notes Dostoevsky is clearly at loose ends. "The Prince was away three weeks in Moscow" (9:216). (In the novel, he is away for six months.) Dostoevsky plans that the Prince will marry Nastasya Filippovna, "N. F. Is he married to her in secret or not, that's the question?" (9:216). "The Prince is married to N. F." (9:216). "Invent a role in the intrigues for Ganya, Ippolit, and others. For Vera" (9:218). Moreover, in these first pages of the third notebook, the Idiot, like his earlier version, experiences and expresses more turmoil and doubt than he exhibits in the novel. "N.B. At every moment (inwardly) he asks himself: Am I right or are they right?" (9:218). Ganya's role also resembles that of the earlier Idiot; he must make himself indispensable to everyone (9:219). Dostoevsky is frantically seeking a beginning for part 2, and by implication, an ending for the novel. "*Project:* Shouldn't I begin then with Ganya? Intrigues of Ganya, Varya, Ptitsyn, Rogozhin, and company. Lebedev and the others . . . PROJECTS. N.B. Shouldn't I end the novel with a confession, published publicly?" (9:220). After postulating a beginning for part 2 and an end for the novel (neither of which he finally used), Dostoevsky, on March 11, turns to a plan for his narrative strategy:

> N.B. The relations with the children, do it this way: at first, when the subject matter is about Aglaya, about Ganya, about N. F., about the intrigues, and so on, why not mention casually and almost enigmatically [*zagadochno*] about the relations of the Prince with the children, with Kolya, for example, and so on. Don't mention about the club, but why not present it suddenly, having introduced it with vague rumors, and present the Prince in its midst like a tsar, in the 5th or 6th part of the novel?
>
> N.B. Why not present the character of the Prince enigmatically *throughout the entire novel*, from time to time defining by

> means of details (more fantastically and more questioningly, arousing curiosity) and suddenly to elucidate his character at the end and, on the other hand,
>
> N.B. With all the other characters *from the very beginning* more defined and elucidated to the reader? (as, for example, Ganya?) (9:220)

The children's club and the final elucidation of Myshkin have disappeared, but the narrative manner proposed here carries over into the novel. Much of the narrative of the novel is at once casual and enigmatic, often maddeningly so. Vague rumors about the Prince abound; by an arbitrary presentation of details about the Prince, the narrator makes him more unreal and curious to his reader. On the other hand, other, minor characters, like Totsky, General Epanchin, Pavlishchev's nephew, the General's wife, Kolya, and General Ivolgin are clearly drawn throughout.

Dostoevsky's strategy of balancing enigma with explanation has taken root. On March 12 he writes:

> Detailed plan of 3rd part.
> 3 months later.
> Morning. Ganya, Ptitsyn. The sister is in the other apartment. . . . They are expecting something and someone. An enigmatic conversation. (An explanatory chapter. The scene at the garden.)
> OR
> *1st chapter* explanatory; scene at station. But the only main character – Ganya.
> *2nd chapter* . . . Enigmatic conversation. (9:224–25)

Later in this entry, Dostoevsky continues to conceive his plan in terms of how it will affect his readers; he deliberates over whether or not he will maintain the reader's interest through arousing his curiosity or through revealing what has been hidden.

> . . . the character of Rogozhin in the 3rd part is mysterious . . . (9:226)

2) Meanwhile, actually there are only rumors about the Prince's exploits, good deeds, about the children (so that in the end everything comes to light).
But however;
3) Something flashes by fits and starts even before the end. (N.B. Or else to develop things not so quickly??) . . .
The course of events? N.B. N.B. N.B.? The course of events. (9:227)

For Dostoevsky the creation of the texture and tones of the narrative was inseparable from elaborating the plot itself; thus, the need to create a balance between enigma and explanation partially shapes the course of events. Once Dostoevsky had conceived of the character of the Idiot and the most general idea of his novel, the business of setting the pace of the narrative was as crucial to the expression of the idea of the novel as was the development of the plot and was often indistinguishable from it.

Although most writers, to some degree, seek to balance an enigmatic with an explanatory narrative, to witness in the notes the way in which Dostoevsky makes choices that create this balance shows us that his novels, at their most heightened, passionate moments, often grew out of a deliberate, prearranged choice of narrative tone. Dostoevsky's decision to present the Prince "enigmatically, *throughout the entire novel*," means that the reader is to learn about him through stories and rumors, but shall also be permitted flashes of understanding. Another writer might have elaborated Myshkin as fully as possible. By reading an author's notes and thereby crossing into the realm of intentional fallacy, one can attain a glimpse of the rudiments of that author's style and of his own perception of how he forms that style.

Imperceptibly Dostoevsky's goal of balancing enigma with explanation turns into the attempt to weld these two seemingly opposite narrative styles into a single narration. He creates a kind of narrative oxymoron – a mode of "enigmatic explanation." He strives for a style that is both precise and mysterious, that seems to explain without really explaining. "My task: to write more briefly. So that it should be more catchy [*shchegol'ski*], sympathetic (briefly and always to the point), and entertaining. N.B. the mysterious relations of N. F. with Rogozhin in the 3rd and 4th parts" (9:231). Brevity and absence of digression masquerade as explanation, while an air of mystery really prevails. "N.B. Indispensable: They crowd around him and pester him from all sides as if to get money. The result: Only dark rumors about the adroitness of the Prince" (9:231). One must bear in mind that these notes reflect Dostoevsky's hopes for his novel; writing it was another matter.

The first two chapters of part 2, which Dostoevsky was working on at the same time he wrote these notes, continue the pattern by disguising the narrator's long-windedness and digressions as accurate reportage; there is a minimum of explanation. The opening pages of chapter 1 of part 2 quickly set the tone:

> It was said at the time that there might be other reasons for his hasty departure, but about this, and about the Prince's adventures in Moscow and generally about the entire period of his absence from Saint Petersburg, we can provide only scanty information. The Prince was away exactly six months and even those who had a reason to be interested in his fate could find out very little about him during that time. True, certain rumors did reach them at times, although very rarely; and they were for the most part strange ones and almost always mutually contradictory. . . .
>
> Little by little the rumors that had spread through the town became enshrouded in uncertainty. . . . This news turned out to be completely accurate as it was later shown. (8:149–51; 199–201)

Throughout the middle of March Dostoevsky continues with this precarious narrative manner that hovers between concealment and disclosure. "Indispensable – as much as possible to characterize the personality of the Prince (by his *facial expression* and his idiosyncrasies) in the 3rd part – especially on the occasion of his change of situation because of the inheritance and because of his three-month stay in Russia. . . . (Does he love Aglaya?)" (9:233). Showing becomes a way to avoid telling, but later, in the novel itself, this frequently arbitrary and strictly dramatic presentation of the Prince by a talkative narrator, who can also at will be privy to the thoughts of his character, creates problems for the reader. What is significant about these passages from the notebooks is that they show Dostoevsky *deliberately* undertaking such a narrative. One cannot argue therefore that the shifting perspectives and narrative distances in the novel arose through carelessness on the part of the author or by chance.

Indeed, in the third notebook Dostoevsky, perpetually concerned about the effect of his narrative on the reader, defines the narrative texture he hopes to create:

> Write more briefly: only the facts, without reasoning and without a description of feelings? . . .
> Write using only the facts.
> Say simply, that Ganya brought the Prince the 100,000. From that time there was a friendship (between them), so they say . . .
> Write in the sense of: *people say* . . .
> N.B. Recount the facts *lightly*, without special reasoning. (9:235–36)

Dostoevsky gauged the effect upon his readers of a light, seemingly casual recounting of the facts. The facts must prove to be entertaining as well as mysterious:

> N.B. The general's wife, getting angry, says the sentence, "And I will tell you frankly: *you yourself are in love with him.*" (N.B. that is why you are attacking him.)
> She speaks in such a way so that her meaning, even for the reader, must be quite *unexpected*, that is, even the reader must not be prepared for the fact that Aglaya is in love with the Prince. (9:238)

Yet at the same time Dostoevsky acknowledges that a light, seemingly factual narrative is not enough. At times a discursive, descriptive voice proves necessary:

> *Indispensable Note*
> (1) the effect of *Russia* on the Prince. How much and in what way he has changed. *In the description.* (9:237)

Oddly, this grouping of narrative methods has the effect of placing facts on the side of rumor and mystery rather than on the side of description and explanation. The *final* irony of the narrative in the novel is that the narrator's description and explanation prove to have been misleading in the end; the sparsely scattered facts and abundant mysteries are the stuff out of which the reader must form his understanding of the meaning.

At this point Dostoevsky seems to have settled provisionally upon the overall narrative manner for the novel. In the notes of late March he returns to the problem of portraying the Idiot in a way that will be convincing to the reader. "THE SYNTHESIS OF THE NOVEL. THE SOLUTION OF THE DIFFICULTY. How to make the personality of the hero more sympathetic to the reader?" (9:239). Several months earlier, in the two letters quoted above, Dostoevsky had defined in narrative terms "the main idea" that had been his cherished intention in this novel: to portray a positively beautiful man in Russia. The problem of how best to portray such a beautiful character still loomed large. The difficulty was how to establish an effective mechanism of communication between the novelist and the reader and how to make the hero's goodness interesting: "If Don Quixote and Pickwick, as virtuous characters, are sympathetic to the reader and succeed, it is because they are comic. If – the hero of the novel, the Prince, is not comic, he possesses another sympathetic feature: he is! Innocent!" (9:239). Dostoevsky here consciously rejected the comic mode as a means of depicting his hero. But a straightforward presentation of a virtuous character could be extremely boring. As an avid reader in his youth of Gothic and adventure novels, Dostoevsky knew how entertaining an air of mystery was. His many directives to himself to recount only the facts without explanation and to make use of rumor and enigma reflect his awareness that he had to counteract the potential dullness of a perfectly good man.

The Idiot is to be portrayed indirectly, by his facial expressions and idiosyncrasies. His innocence provides, as Dostoevsky noted, "another sympathetic feature." As opposed to the merely virtuous hero, an innocent man, like a comic one, has a great capacity for arousing interest, and Dostoevsky immediately begins to exploit these possibilities. He writes, "All the questions, both those of a personal nature for the Prince (in which the children play a passionate role) and *general* questions are decided by him, and in this there is much that is touching and naive, for in his most extremely *tragic* and *personal* moments the Prince is occupied with the solving of general problems. *N.B. Prepare many incidents and stories*" (9:240). The Prince becomes interesting or sympathetic through his naïveté, through his often tragic confusion of the personal with the general.

Increasingly, Dostoevsky in these plans turned away from an exploration of the Prince's psychology to a demonstration of how he affected the lives of others: "But wherever he only even touched [the lives of others] – everywhere he left a permanent trace. And thus, the infinity of the story in the novel (the wretched of all classes) along with the flow of the main theme. (N.B. N.B. N.B.! that main theme is the one to be polished and created.) He teaches the children through stories" (9:242). During March Dostoevsky had emphasized the Prince's self-doubt (9:218–19). By April, however, Dostoevsky no longer has the Prince asking himself whether he is right or they are right. Instead, "And why not present the Prince as a perpetual Sphinx? Some mistakes and comical traits of the Prince" (9:242). Dostoevsky had finally acknowledged to himself that his hero permanently perplexed him.

Since February he had published nothing; the decision to portray the Prince as a "perpetual Sphinx" thus reflected Dostoevsky's own difficulties with the Prince's character, but it also provided a way to get on with the work at hand. If the Prince were a perpetual sphinx, the author (or the narrator-chronicler), Dostoevsky realized, did not ever need to explain him. In a retreat from his previous intention, Dostoevsky here also plans to resort to comedy himself, as Cervantes and Dickens had done, by showing comical traits in the Prince. The decisions to present the Prince as a perpetual sphinx and to show his "comical traits" illustrate both the frustration Dostoevsky was experiencing in characterizing the Prince and the ways in which he hoped to overcome it: he planned to solve his difficulty through the use of mystery and comedy, that is, through the medium of narration. (These choices of narrative tone eventually, of course, contribute to shaping the plot of the novel as well. But it is interesting that Dostoevsky resolved these matters before he had decided firmly upon most of the details of the plot.)

Frustration mounts. After composing a crowded outline of events for part 2 (he calls it part 3), in which, in a jumbled foreshadowing of subsequent scenes that instead span the entire novel, there occurs yet another party at Nastasya Filippovna's, a children's journal, a forthcoming meeting between Nastasya and Aglaya, and episodes involving Ferdyshchenko and Pavlishchev, Dostoevsky writes:

> N.B. from me: this is too much for the third part.
> Secrets, mysteries, and subsequent plots.
> N.B. The problem of presenting N.F.
> N.B. The Prince as a sphinx.
> As a sphinx. He reveals himself without explanation by the author, except perhaps in the first chapter.
> If Ganya from the first has recounted what he knew about N.F. (to Aglaya) . . . and then the report of Lebedev (*earlier in the morning*) to the Prince, then the reader is sufficiently enlightened so that the role of a sphinx can be maintained. . . . (N.B. And Ganya too is a sphinx.) (9:248–49)

Dostoevsky has returned to balancing enigma and enlightenment for his readers; here enlightenment serves merely to maintain an enigma, to make the Prince's role of a sphinx believable to the reader, who must be enlightened only enough to be further confused about the hero. Even Ganya has become sphinxlike. Dostoevsky has asked earlier, "And Ganya? His role? . . . the role of Ganya: incessant betrayals and vacillations" (9:245–46). Like the Prince, Ganya has driven Dostoevsky to try to dismiss him as a sphinx.

Dostoevsky's repeated use of the word "sphinx" in the entries for April 9 and 10 reflected a mounting impatience with his inability to get on with his work, while at the same time it suggested a solution to the problem. A week before the sphinx image first appeared in the notes, Dostoevsky, in despair, admitted that for a month he "had not written a single line!" (*P* 2:97). At this moment of keen frustration a new formulation abruptly appears. It relates to nothing else, yet it provides the impetus for movement. On April 9 and 10 Dostoevsky twice jots down the epithet "Prince Christ" (9:246, 294). Just as in the earlier notebooks the notation "He is a Prince. A Prince. A *Iurodivyi* (He is with the children)" (9:200) appeared suddenly and seemed to give the notes new life, here the words "Prince Christ" appear in isolation and later take firm root.[32]

Later the same day Dostoevsky returned to the problem of narrating, of portraying:

> N.B. Write more sympathetically, and it will be good. The main problem: the character of the Idiot. Develop him. That is the idea [*mysl'*] of the novel. How he reflects Russia. Everything that would have been worked out in the Prince is extinguished in the grave. And that is why gradually showing *the Prince in action* will be sufficient.
>
> But! For this is needed the *plot of the novel* [*fabula romana*]. In order to set forth the character of the Idiot [more sympathetically] it is necessary to think up for him a field of action. (9:252)

Dostoevsky has come to a major realization: if the narrator-chronicler portrays the Idiot as a sphinx, he need not fill the pages with his hero's thoughts, dreams, hopes. Instead, the prince's character will be set forth through the action of the plot.

The characterization of the Idiot as a "Prince Christ," far from contradicting the notion of the Prince as a sphinx, complements and deepens that conception of him. The figure of Christ and the style of the Gospels, which portray Him through parables and stories rather than through authorial explanations, provide Dostoevsky with models for characterization and narration. The characterization of the Idiot as Prince Christ has evoked a narrative solution as well. (In a sense the narrative portrayals of Christ in the Gospels and Iago in *Othello* are similar: each figure remains a sphinx; their deeds cannot be absolutely interpreted because we are forbidden insight into their mental workings and see them only in action. Dostoevsky's passage from an image of Iago in the second notebook to one of Prince Christ in the third notebook therefore carries with it an underlying narrative logic.)

Dostoevsky then turns back to the task of structuring his narrative. He plans to insert some narratives to complement both the main story line and each other:

> (1) in general, HISTORIES and stories, that is, histories continuing throughout the whole novel must be harmoniously conceived and executed in a way parallel to the whole novel, and therefore
> (2) think them over and the *essential* story with the Aide-de-camp [becomes Radomsky], but the main thing, as far as possible, parallel stories. (9:252)

He then lists parallel stories involving Ferdyshchenko, Ivolgin, and Ippolit and ends with the words "Pr Christ" (9:253). The governing concern remains the creation of the Prince's field of action and the elucidation of his character through parables and stories.

Five days later, on April 15, Dostoevsky found an outline for a field of action that would carry him through the first chapters of part 2. The Prince returns in a confused state to Saint Petersburg after an absence of six months; he has sent a letter to Aglaya via Kolya; the General's wife pays the Prince a visit. "They need him at the Epanchins. . . . Ganya needs him. Kolya – Rogozhin needs him. . . . And the main thing, N. F., even Lebedev . . . needs him, and the Prince's heart glowed ('Here, it must be, is my occupation.')" (9:256). The plot has taken shape through the need that all the characters have for the Prince. Dostoevsky himself realizes this, "THE MAIN THING IS THAT THEY ALL NEED HIM" (9:257).

From here on the character of the notes written during the composition of part 2 changes: since Dostoevsky has discovered his basic narrative method, more of the material from the notes subsequently reappears in the novel. Even the end of the novel has begun to take shape. Throughout all the notes, plans for Rogozhin's eventual murder of Nastasya have existed. In the third notebook there have been plans for a meeting between Aglaya and Nastasya. But on April 15 and 16 Dostoevsky sketches in concrete details: in the scene between Aglaya and Nastasya, Aglaya is to act uncontrollably, and the Prince agrees to marry Nastasya (9:257). At the last moment Nastasya will run off with Rogozhin.

Getting even closer to the final text, Dostoevsky plans that during the engagement with Nastasya the Prince shall be thought, by general rumor, to be mad. "Everyone has deserted him, except for a few people" (9:258). On April 16 Dostoevsky writes: "IN THE 3RD PART THE SCANDAL ABOUT THE PRINCE MUST BE TOO GREAT. THE PUBLIC INSULT . . . the explanation of the Prince, the Aide-de-camp, almost a duel . . . in the 7th and 8th parts the picture of the ill and wandering Prince. . . . They take the Idiot abroad" (9:260). Here Dostoevsky has foreshadowed the shape and outcome of the eventual meeting between the two rivals, the public scandal in the park at Pavlovsk where Myshkin intercedes for Nastasya and almost becomes involved in a duel, and Nastasya's final departure with Rogozhin. Most important for the narrative structure of the novel, we see that Dostoevsky during the writing of part 2 of the novel had already planned the course of Myshkin's growing isolation from those around him. He is to be deserted by his friends and by the narrator as he grows more and more ill and lost.

This note offers a vital tool for assessing the narrative in the novel; it shows that Dostoevsky had intended the narrator and the other characters to become impatient with the hero. ("THE SCANDAL ABOUT THE PRINCE MUST BE TOO GREAT.") Thus in chapter 9 of part 4 in the novel, when the narrator himself seems to desert Myshkin and to agree with such critics of the Prince as Evgeny Pavlovich, Dostoevsky has not lost control over his material. He has not abdicated responsibility for a hero who has become too difficult to portray; he is having his narrator act according to plan.[33]

The last pages of notes for part 2 contain the working out of the scene in which Aglaya reads Pushkin's poem "The Poor Knight" to the group assembled at the Prince's rented cottage in Pavlovsk. The novelist has found his way at last and is willing to defend his narrative and defy his would-be critics. In an earlier entry for November 6, 1867, Dostoevsky had written, "For the epilogue: I have written a fantastic novel, but never more real characters" (9:199). On June 11, 1868, he confirms the feeling of rightness:

> N.B. The main thing
> After the scene between the two rivals:
>
> We admit, that we will be describing strange happenings. Because it is difficult to explain them, we will limit ourselves to the facts.
>
> We agree that nothing could have happened differently with the Idiot.
>
> So let us bring to an end the story of a character, who perhaps was not worth so much of the reader's attention – we agree with that.
>
> Reality above all else. It is true, perhaps, that we have another view of reality, 1000 souls, prophecies – a fantastic reality. Maybe in the Idiot is a man who is more real. However, we agree that they may say to us: "that's all so, you are right, but you have not been able to present the affair, to justify the facts, you are a bad artist." But here already, of course, there is nothing to be done. (9:276)

In this entry Dostoevsky has further outlined how he intends the narrator-chronicler to express himself near the end of the novel. He has previewed the narrator's distancing of himself from his hero at the very moment when the reader most desires an explanation. Part of this passage recurs in the novel as a cynical apology to the reader on the part of the narrator-chronicler (8:475–79, 589–94). The narrator-chronicler lays bare his device: because it was difficult to explain, I confined myself to recounting the facts. He shrugs off the criticism that in not explaining – that is, in not justifying the facts –

he has shown himself to be a bad artist. Thus, the narrator's unexpected and disturbing abdication of responsibility toward the hero and the events of the story (in chapter 9, part 4), which proves so surprising to a reader of the novel, has been, as these notes of June 11 indicate, the novelist's intent all along. If the reader finds the narrative to be enigmatic and baffling, he has merely experienced what the author intended.

---

The remaining notes are few; some ten pages of notes exist for the rest of the novel, parts 3 and 4. Dostoevsky worked on part 3 from August through part of October 1868 and finished part 4 by the first half of January 1869 (9:378). Despite uncertainties as to exactly how the plot would develop (in October, Dostoevsky still toys with the idea of the Prince marrying Aglaya), he has the novel securely under way. Dostoevsky wrote the third and fourth parts in half the time of the first two parts. By October 4, while writing the end of part 3, Dostoevsky had decided upon all the basic events of part 4, including the most climactic scene of the novel: the tour de force of Rogozhin's and Myshkin's vigil beside Nastasya's corpse.

> 2nd Half of the 4th Part
> N.F. – the fiancée of the Prince.
> Eccentricity. A scene in the temple alone.
> To Rogozhin in despair (he murders her). He summons the Prince.
> Rogozhin and the Prince beside the corpse. Finale. *Not bad.* (9:283)

This is the only moment in the notebooks where Dostoevsky allows himself a burst of pride and self-congratulation.

From here on the notes are brief, except for the November 7 entry, which further outlines the final scene by Nastasya's corpse (9:285–86). Dostoevsky was terribly proud of this final scene; on the same day he wrote to Maikov, "Now, when I see everything as if in a mirror – I am completely convinced that never in my literary life have I had a single poetic idea that was better and richer than the one which has been elucidated in part 4, in the detailed plan" (28.2:321; October 26/November 7, 1868). On the same day he also wrote to Sonya: "Finally, and the main thing for me is that the fourth part and its finale are the main part of my novel, that is, almost the whole novel was thought out and written for the sake of the denouement" (28.2:318; October 26/November 7, 1868).

In the entry for October 15 Dostoevsky outlines a scene between Nastasya and the Prince on their wedding morning and a scene between Aglaya and the Prince (9:284–85). In both, the word "Othello" appears in parentheses. This is perhaps an unconscious, but powerful symbol for the transformation of the Idiot that has taken place throughout these three notebooks. Iago has become Othello. The inciter of action and instigator of mistrust has become a man infinitely vulnerable to the acts of others, trustful, and uneasily roused to jealously. Othello's dying words (*Othello*, 5.2.341–44) aptly describe Myshkin's own tragedy:

> When you shall these unlucky deeds relate,
> Speak of me as I am; nothing extenuate,
> Nor set down aught in malice: then must you speak
> Of one that loved not wisely, but too well.

The editors of the 1974 edition of the notebooks note that Dostoevsky probably read P. I. Veinberg's 1864 translation of *Othello.* They show similarities of phrasing between this entry and the Russian translation of the play, especially in the passage in which Othello says of Desdemona that she loved him for his sufferings, and that he loved her for her compassion for them. Myshkin assures Nastasya that he loves her not only with compassion but with love (9:382). Like Desdemona's love for Othello, Aglaya's love for the Prince grew from the stories he told of his past experiences.

The notes for parts 3 and 4 contain no more narrative directives. Dostoevsky had discovered his narrative method while working on part 2 on the novel. Yet in his own assessment of the novel upon its completion, Dostoevsky was more ready to find fault with his *por-*

*trayal* of the Idiot, with his narrative in general, than with the idea behind it. In February 1869 he wrote to Sonya Ivanova, "Now it is finished at last! I have written the last chapters day and night, with terrible anguish . . . but I am not happy with the novel: it does not express even a tenth of what I wished to express. Although, nevertheless, I will not disclaim it, and I still love my idea even though it has not succeeded. But in any case the fact is that it is not effective for the public" (29.1:9–10; January 25/February 6, 1869). Several weeks later, in a letter to Strakhov, he wrote, "There is much in the novel that was written rapidly, much that is drawn out, much that didn't come off, but something did come off. I don't stand behind my novel, but I do stand behind the idea" (29.1:19; February 26/March 10, 1869).

Nevertheless, his choices of narrative method had been deliberate and the techniques he developed here reappear, with greater success, in *The Possessed* and *The Brothers Karamazov.*[34] Each is a virtuoso performance of the balancing and welding together of enigma and explanation. Ultimately, the narrator-chronicler provides the perfect device for realizing this aim: his explanations serve to create even larger mysteries. Dostoevsky, in these notes, had designed a narrative style and a plot that would allow the reader, often through the very act of disagreeing with the narrator's assessment of events, to participate in the moral action of the novel.

## NOTES

1. See *Polnoe sobranie sochinenii* (*Pss*), 9:339. Dostoevsky feared a search at the Russian border when they returned from their sojourn abroad. Anna Dostoevsky has written of the fate of this manuscript, "Sad as I was to part with the manuscripts, still I had to yield to Fyodor Mikhailovich's insistent arguments. We lit a fire in the fireplace and burned the papers. Thus perished the drafts of *The Idiot* and *The Eternal Husband.*" See Anna Dostoevsky, *Reminiscences,* trans. and ed. Beatrice Stillman (New York: Liveright, 1975), 167.

2. P. N. Sakulin and N. F. Bel'chikov, eds., *Iz arkhiva F. M. Dostoevskogo: Idiot, neizdannye materialy* (Moscow, 1931), 3; and *Pss,* 9:339. See also the

English edition of these notebooks: *The Notebooks for "The Idiot,"* ed. Edward Wasiolek, trans. Katherine Strelsky (Chicago: University of Chicago Press, 1967), 9.

3. Fyodor Dostoevsky, *The Notebooks for "A Raw Youth,"* ed. Edward Wasiolek, trans. Victor Terras (Chicago: University of Chicago Press, 1969), 31.

4. Robert Louis Jackson, *Dostoevsky's Quest for Form: A Study of His Philosophy of Art* (New Haven: Yale University Press, 1966), 166.

5. Dostoevsky, *The Notebooks for "The Idiot,"* 9.

6. For example, see Robin Feuer Miller, "Myshkin and Alyosha: The Genesis, Premature Birth, and Fruition of the Positively Beautiful Man" (M.A. thesis, Columbia University, 1974), 72–107.

7. As the 1974 editors explained, "This division [into plans] does not concur with the more fragmented and impulsive authorial articulation of the material; it insufficiently sets off important changes of an ideological and artistic order"; they find that Bel'chikov's and Sakulin's divisions provide only a provisional orientation to the material (9:340).

8. Anna Grigoryevna wrote that in the autumn of 1867 Dostoevsky was preoccupied with the Umetsky case and that he wished he were in Russia so that he might follow it more closely. See Sakulin and Bel'chikov, *Iz arkhiva*, 204. Dostoevsky read about the Umetsky case in the fall issues of *Golos* (The Voice) and *Moskva* (Moscow). He had already begun work on *The Idiot* before he heard of the case, but quickly incorporated it into the notes. Mignon, another early version of Nastasya Filippovna, became Olga Umetsky, the would-be arsonist whose parents had beaten her and their other children mercilessly yet were not severely punished. Olga was acquitted but the Russian public feared for her future after her parents' release from prison, and faith in Russia's newly established jury system was undermined (ibid., 205–8; 9:340).

9. Elizabeth Dalton finds that though the "painful and dangerous Umetsky material is emphatically repressed" in the novel, "the themes of the violated child and the sadistic father are nevertheless present." Dalton compares the effect of the Umetsky case in the genesis of the novel to the way in which "the day's residue works in the creation of a dream. . . . Before it could enter the novel it had to be buried and transformed: barred from direct expression . . . it undergoes that 'proliferation in the dark' of which Freud writes, helping to create the web of organic connections that make up the

emotional texture of the novel." *Unconscious Structure in "The Idiot": A Study in Literature and Psychoanalysis* (Princeton: Princeton University Press, 1979), 200. Yet Dostoevsky's preoccupation with the Umetsky case may derive partly from the fact that this case reflected and affirmed themes already present in his earlier published fiction.

10. The 1974 editors also suggest her kinship with Hero in Shakespeare's *Much Ado About Nothing* (9:352).

11. Wasiolek notes that Ganya and Ptitsyn are the only proper names retained in the published text that appear in the early notes (Dostoevsky, *The Notebooks for "The Idiot,"* 78). In fact toward the end of the second notebook in the entry for November 11/30, Kolya's name also appears.

12. *Pss* 9:167; Sakulin and Bel'chikov, *Iz arkhiva*, 39. Unfortunately the English version of the notes mistranslates the "Memento"; "the chief point of the novel is the Uncle and the son, these two characters" (Dostoevsky, *The Notebooks for "The Idiot,"* 81).

13. Dostoevsky, *The Notebooks for "A Raw Youth,"* 73–74.

14. L. N. Tolstoy, *Sobranie sochinenii v dvadtsati tomakh* (Moscow, 1961), 4:33.

15. Of course as Arthur O. Lovejoy has pointed out, the image of the great chain of being, in which everything had its place and every deed reverberated through the world, has long occupied a dominant position in men's conceptions of their universe. See *The Great Chain of Being: A Study of the History of an Idea* (Cambridge: Harvard University Press, 1934). Dostoevsky and Tolstoy were both drawing upon an idea that was "in the air."

16. 28.2.258–59; February 18/March 1, 1868. In this letter Dostoevsky praises *War and Peace;* he also, however, criticizes it for having too many petty psychological details. But Tolstoy had already begun to publish *War and Peace* in *Russkii vestnik* in 1865 (book 1, parts 1 and 2) under the title "1805." Dostoevsky had certainly read these early parts as they came out.

17. Dalton, *Unconscious Structure in "The Idiot,"* 187.

18. Mikhail Bakhtin, *Problems of Dostoevsky's Poetics*, trans. R. W. Rotsel (Ann Arbor, Mich.: Ardis, 1973), 150–228.

19. The 1974 editors stress in particular the sense of the word "idiot" as used in the Middle Ages; an idiot was thought to possess a deep spirituality; his wisdom stemmed from this rather than from any bookish knowledge (9:394).

20. The editors also emphasize this meaning of the word "idiot" (9:394).

21. Dostoevsky has quoted the General Epistle of James 2:19.

22. James H. Billington, *The Icon and the Axe: An Interpretive History of Russian Culture* (New York: Random House, 1966), 60.

23. George P. Fedotov, *The Russian Religious Mind* (Cambridge: Harvard University Press, 1966), 2:318–19. Cited in text as *RRM.*

24. Serge A. Zenkovsky, ed. and trans., *Medieval Russia's Epics, Chronicles, and Tales* (New York: Dutton, 1963), 249.

25. George P. Fedotov, *A Treasury of Russian Spirituality* (New York: Sheed and Ward, 1948), 13; and Donald Attwater, *The Penguin Dictionary of Saints* (Baltimore: Penguin Books, 1965), 306.

26. Helen lswolsky, *Christ in Russia* (London: Morrison and Gibb, 1962), 142.

27. Dalton has likened the rejections, transformations, and remoldings of these roles to a process "very like the repression, condensation, displacement, and secondary vision that go on in the formation of a dream. Moreover, by that law of conservation that operates in the unconscious, virtually none of the ideas in the notebooks is lost. The violent, sexual, incoherent material Dostoevsky consciously rejects turns up later in the novel, disguised and buried, but animating *The Idiot* with the power of repressed idea and impulse." Dalton, *Unconscious Structure in "The Idiot,"* 186.

28. Sakulin and Bel'chikov, *Iz arkhiva*, 203.

29. In the last entry of the second notebook for November 11/30, the "11" refers to December 11 new style (not to November 11), so this one entry did occur, according to Sakulin, during the crucial period of rewriting and rethinking (ibid., 244). However, the entry provides no substantial clues to the formation of the novel; it is primarily a rehash of old material in which the Umetsky family plays the dominant role.

30. Dalton, *Unconscious Structure in "The Idiot,"* 173.

31. Sakulin and Bel'chikov, *Iz arkhiva*, 198.

32. The 1974 editors also stress the importance of the phrase "Prince Christ." They find this idea to be an old one of Dostoevsky's. In April 1864 just after the death of his first wife Dostoevsky revealed his understanding of the commandment to love your fellow man as yourself. "He wrote, 'the highest usage which a man can make out of his own personality, out of the completeness of his own *I* is to destroy that *I*, to give it back as a whole to all men and to each man separately and wholeheartedly.' In these words the

writer formulated his highest moral ideal, the fullest incarnation of which was attained, from his point of view, only by Christ" (9:365).

33. On May 16, 1868, Dostoevsky's firstborn daughter, Sonya, died. The second entry after Sonya's death, on May 24, reflects Dostoevsky's desire to be done with the novel. Here he has outlined an ending in which a rehabilitated Nastasya has married the Prince, whose house is turned into a school. Everything generally comes out well. But this outline reflects a poignant desire to be finished with the tormenting work rather than a possible solution to the problems raised in the novel. Dostoevsky quickly rejected the entire plan (9:268–70).

34. The 1974 editors, in a comparison of *The Idiot* with *Crime and Punishment,* draw a similar conclusion and find that "all these features of the poetic style of *The Idiot* receive further development in *The Possessed, A Raw Youth,* and *The Brothers Karamazov*" (9:410).

# Flights from *The Idiot*'s Womanhood

NINA PELIKAN STRAUS

*The Idiot* exhibits an experiment in terms of "the feminine" that distinguishes it from Dostoevsky's other novels. In *Notes from the Underground*, *The Gambler*, and *Crime and Punishment*, traces of the turbulent 1860s transform relationships between male characters and female characters who embody "new woman" heroinisms. If Sonya and Dunya do not immediately redeem Raskolnikov, and if Liza cannot entirely change the underground man's dedication to spite, their feminine powers are nevertheless acknowledged. If Polina does not bring Alexei toward love and self-knowledge, she at least exercises the wit to escape from his sadistic ambivalence. Up until *The Idiot*, several of Dostoevsky's principal women characters embody a polyphonic and quasi-feminist consciousness that his heroes in part assimilate.

With his apparently favorite hero, "Prince Christ" Myshkin, Dostoevsky breaks this narrative pattern. In the denouement (for which the whole novel was written, as Dostoevsky informed his niece),[1] Myshkin is represented as having assimilated and imitated everything but having understood nothing. Despite Nastasya Filippovna's extraordinary capacity for self-dramatizations of women's sufferings and Aglaya's talk of women's emancipation, Myshkin remains at the end of the novel as he was at the beginning. Caryl Emerson argues that Myshkin is the most "monologic" of Dostoevsky's characters,[2] and one who monologizes others. In this chapter I suggest that this monologism is related to Dostoevsky's displacement of "the woman question" to an "answer" in anachronistic Christianity. Myshkin is offered as a solution for the second sex's problems in Russian society, as an alternative model for masculinity, as an antitype to male violence toward women personified by Rogozhin, and as an antidote to

Western patriarchal rationality and secularism. Myshkin is a salve for women's psychological self-degradation, a Christ without a sword who is ready to take on more than one woman as his Magdalene. Dostoevsky's "idiot" fascinates us because he embodies tremendous confusion about gender and sexuality linked to ideas about faith and religion.

As his biographers note, Dostoevsky's period of unrest came to an end shortly after he married Anna Snitkina, and this fact (as well as his desperate need for money) influenced his writing of *The Idiot.* His letters indicate that he soon came to love his wife and to anticipate children with her. *The Idiot* registers the "split consciousness" regarding women that Dostoevsky explored in his heroes earlier, but the split is not internalized as it was in Raskolnikov. Rather, it is externalized through the "good" Myshkin and "bad" Rogozhin. Dostoevsky's need to imagine and present to his reading public an "altogether good man" was perhaps prompted by the future he faced as Snitkina's husband and the father of their children. His decision to become a better sort of man himself, felt so deeply as he stood by the bier of his first wife,[3] perhaps motivated his wish to create a hero intent on saving women, rather than one whom women attempt to save. But the novel also expresses large literary-nationalistic ambitions beyond these biographically motivated impulses, and these ambitions account for the novel's chaotically narrated, structurally alogical elements.

What is possible or impossible in terms of future relations between men and women is the central problem of *The Idiot*, at least in its most coherent section, part 1. Yet Dostoevsky does not describe the novel in these terms, even though his first notes for the novel record anecdotes about girls and women, nor does part 2 develop the focus initiated in part 1. In *The Idiot*, the tale, the teller, and what is told have unusually labile narrative relations to one another. Discourse that appears initially as polyphony later verges on cacophony, with Myshkin's character remaining oddly monologic throughout. In part 1, for example, the reader may experience a pleasurable sense of collaboration with the author's irony, sharing with him a secret hidden from other characters or even readers: that Myshkin only appears to be an idiot but has come into the world to save women like the beleaguered and proud Nastasya. But this impression does not hold its focus. By part 2 the centrality of Myshkin's relation to Nastasya is dispersed by various subplots. The narration becomes increasingly allusive and paradoxical, intimating that readers are about to witness the modernized crucifixion of a Russian Christ figure but must simultaneously participate voyeuristically in the murder of a beautiful woman. The connections between sex and religion are part of the novel's often discussed "mystery."

Mystery and obscurity are part of the total effect, as is the rivalry/brotherhood between "Prince Christ" and Rogozhin. Perhaps, as Harriet Murav puts it, Dostoevsky cannot imagine an ultimate goodness that does not involve beholding "the spectacle of our own folly."[4] Folly and intelligence, Christian and phallic metaphors are so compounded in *The Idiot*, however, that a feminist reader may suspect she is confronting a series of particularly masculinist confusions. Among them is the author's representation of his hallucinated wish to save women "through Christ," subverted by a perhaps unconsciously dramatized apprehension of the ways Christianity makes that wish impossible to fulfill.

The novel remains the site of contested and perhaps inevitable misreadings that center around the notion of *idiocy*, the holy and sometimes not-so-holy foolishness Myshkin continually exhibits. Contemporary traditionalists like David Bethea who find "danger in reading Dostoevsky through Western eyes" emphasize Dostoevsky's apocalyptic vision and interpret Nastasya's death as a "tragic composite of the two temporalities."[5] Bethea does not imagine how apocalypse could be a danger to Dostoevsky himself. What might the novelist *not* have created if *The Idiot* had met with success? Fortunately for late twentieth-century readers, the book appears in much criticism as the most puzzling and least popular of Dostoevsky's "great" works. Even Russians at the time of the novel's publication in 1868 greeted Dostoevsky's religious intentions with skepticism. There were nineteenth-century Russians who asked how one could "value" Dostoevsky's version of "this truth" and wondered "who is interested in these pathological sensations, besides epileptics?"[6]

Interpretations of the "mystery" of Prince Myshkin reveal opposing kinds of responses, one of which moves toward Slavophilism and the other toward the at present un-Russian deconstructions of psychoanalytic and feminist theory. Recently some readers have described the "feminization" of Myshkin's character, although they have not pursued "the woman question" as the heart of Myshkin's trouble.[7] Why Dostoevsky reserves a whole chapter for the expression of Evgeny Pavlovich's idea that Myshkin is obsessed with democracy and the woman question is the piece of the puzzle analyzed later in this chapter.

The puzzle involves the way the novel connects a universalist, supposedly timeless subject, the advent of a "Prince Christ" into decaying Russia, with the timely theme of bringing Myshkin into contact with adventurous young women and changing sexual mores. Modernist negotiations between men and women are framed so that Myshkin's intended innocence and "holy" sickness (epilepsy) subordinate issues of sexuality and women's liberation to transcendent and final liberations "in Christ." Two ideals of liberation seduce the novel's women, and part of their quest is to decide how opposed they are: that is, whether, as Aglaya first supposes, Myshkin could be a good husband for an emancipated woman; or, as Nastasya at first imagines, Myshkin could be her savior. "Myshkin" develops as a symbol of fantastic investments through which women like Nastasya are seduced into hoping that the dangers their sexuality provokes in men will evaporate. The attempted erasure of sexual desire as part of the "love" Myshkin incarnates for both Nastasya and Aglaya is a symptom of Dostoevsky's experiment with eliminating *eros* and substituting *caritas* as the force that binds men and women together. But Myshkin's nonparticipation in sexual reality also functions as the obscurity around which all problems in the novel circulate. Moving in and out between the sacralized, desexualized heaven that is Myshkin's idea of love – which turns out to be a hell of its own – the women characters of *The Idiot* experience a suspension of the traditional orders of male-female relations.

Nastasya's attraction to Myshkin represents a feminist delusion that she could escape into the nonpatriarchal, nonviolent shelter of presexual innocence. He appears to embody her potential emancipation. Her delusion signals Dostoevsky's attempt to imagine a third sex that is not quite a man, a human being who loves women but not the way men in Russian society generally do. As a dream figure whose attitude to women contrasts significantly with Dostoevsky's other male figures, excepting Alyosha Karamazov, Myshkin appears as a man whom an emancipated woman might love. Yet, when Nastasya Filippovna accepts his marriage offer, the result is her death by Rogozhin's knife.

Commentaries on the novel are drawn to the murder scene that ends the novel, and I also approach its woman question by discussing its ending first. I note that Dostoevsky positions Myshkin and Rogozhin near Nastasya's dead body as if the two male characters were meant to interpret the meaning of the scene they are in. This peculiar writing-reading situation, where readers and characters meet together in a final scene that is also a stalemate, indicates how the problem of interpreting the meaning of the dead woman only begins when the novel ends. *The Idiot* conflates what is first and last, backward and forward, what is external and internal, what is idiotic and wise, salvational and destructive, feminine and masculine, even dead and alive. Myshkin is still breathing in the novel's last scene, but he has reverted to a stupefaction that is not exactly "life." It should surprise no reader that at Nastasya's deathbed neither Myshkin nor Rogozhin can interpret what they have done; without Aglaya's or Nastasya's voices, they have no quasi-feminist discourse and thus no explanation available to them. The last picture in the novel is of the dead Nastasya and the half-dead Myshkin caught in the vise of Russian culture's absolutist polarities – Christianity and sexual liberation – and resurrected by neither.

French feminism's insight that language veers toward incomprehensibility and away from the logic of (arguably male-dominated) "reason" when longings for some New Order are attempted may account for impasses in *The Idiot.* The novel appears utopian and unreasonable; it exhibits a flight from masculinity; it dramatizes the exaltation in depression that Suslova marked in Dostoevsky's personal temperament; it subverts its own raison d'être by compromising the patriarchal-Christian salvational structure in which Dostoevsky believes. Overtly, "Prince Christ" is the savior whom nobody recognizes and who dies to this world because he is too good for it. Covertly, Myshkin is a cultural sponge whose capacity for absorbing pain and evil sacralizes passivity. The novel thus appears to appropriate the "feminine" myth of the *mater dolorosa* so that the last scene is a pietà with the genders reversed. This fantasy not only disturbs canonical renderings of Golgotha, but insists upon a surrealist version that is arguably "feminist" in its semiotics because it undermines Jesus Christ's gender role and puts the woman, Nastasya, on the cross.

Provoked by Dostoevsky's comments about the novel's meaning, a feminist reader might be tempted to read this last scene in terms offered by the French feminist Julia Kristeva. Kristeva builds upon Jacques Lacan's theory of the "phallocentric symbolic order" that represents the sense of "the feminine" or "woman" and thus lays claim to "transcendental subjectivity." Kristeva argues

> that there are feminine forms of signification which cannot be contained by the rational thetic structure of the symbolic order and which therefore threaten its sovereignty and have been relegated to the margins of discourse. . . . [Yet for Kristeva] the feminine is a mode of language, open to male and female writers.[8]

Clare Cavanagh's claim that Kristeva's theory articulates an immature, and in Russian-Soviet terms, an ahistorical poetics is persuasive.[9] But if Dostoevsky cannot be consigned to a "feminine mode of language," as he invents the sublime passivity of desexualized Myshkin whose mission is to save women, what description of language suits the discourses of *The Idiot*? The novel's failure to deliver a savior plus the regressively "feminine" dimensions of Myshkin's character are an open target for psychoanalytically minded interpreters. But suggestions that the novel exhibits a pathological structure go only part of the way: the structure reflects a pathology in Russian society that links femininity, even sacralized femininity, with degradation. Myshkin embodies holiness because he is foolish and he is exalted because he is degraded. But while the figure of the holy fool runs through Russian literature as a whole, Dostoevsky's male and female versions of it have very different functions. Female holy fools, such as Sonya of *Crime and Punishment* and Maria Lebyadkina of *The Possessed*, expose men to what men most deeply deny. Dostoevsky associates Myshkin with "the lower body of Russian culture"[10] that may embody ideas about women, birth, and sexuality, but unlike Dostoevsky's female holy fools, Myshkin can do nothing for the women he encounters. Instead, through "Prince Christ," Dostoevsky marks the place where Christianity and sexual relations destroy each other.

Some psychoanalytic commentators have focused on the relation of Myshkin's "pathology" to the author's, reducing the fiction to autobiography in a way both insightful and incomplete. With reference to the fact that Dostoevsky's mother died when he was seventeen, Elizabeth Dalton argues that "Nastasya represents for Myshkin the abused mother, and his identification with her in her masochism is so strong that he can do nothing to prevent her from being destroyed."[11] What also matters as we reread the sadomasochistic, guilt-laden sign language of the novel's last frame, with Myshkin and Rogozhin embracing as they lie near Nastasya's dead body, is that images of nineteenth-century Christian suffering have shifted for Dostoevsky from the masculine to the feminine spheres: from Christ and his Father to the Mother and Son, with the son left paralyzed by the shift.

Dostoevsky's intensely religious impulse, represented by Myshkin's wish to transform his mother country and reconcile "all things," finds its expression through a carnal hermeneutics, a staging of bodies intended to speak more, or differently, than words. This staging is configured throughout the text by many moments of speechless gesture and "marginalized" or even incoherent phrases that make Kristeva's remarks about a "feminine mode of language" less implausible. Dostoevsky first foreshadows the final death-stupefaction scene in part 1, when Nastasya is struck dumb (the characters say she has become insane) by Myshkin's marriage proposal. The foreshadowing continues each time Myshkin is stricken after his epileptic seizures, and on the several occasions when he is able to do nothing but repeat the words of others like a stuck record. Freud remarks in *Beyond the Pleasure Principle* that repetitions occur when the patient cannot remember what is repressed, and that what he cannot remember is most essential to his cure.[12] Dostoevsky's repetitive discourse throughout *The Idiot* is the condition of the novel's theme, a condition that parallels Myshkin's psychic structure expressed most obviously in the least readable sections of part 2. Repetition, like ritual, produces the novel's trance-like effect, but it also symbolizes Dostoevsky's attempt to work through anxiety about men's and women's relations in a transitional and quickly changing society.

Readers invariably note the part played in the novel by the print of Holbein's Dead Christ, with its extremely realistic portrayal of a body from a morgue. Myshkin and Rogozhin are bound by this deadly Christ image as they are bound by their "love" for Nastasya, and perhaps as Dostoevsky was bound imaginatively by composite fantasies of dead wife, dead mother, and the symbolically dead "new" woman (perhaps Suslova) he once loved. "I've seen this [Holbein Christ] painting abroad and I can't forget it," says Myshkin to Rogozhin, noting that it's a painting "that might make some people lose their faith" (*I* 238). The resemblance between the positioning of the Holbein Christ (with feet pointed toward the viewer's face) and the description of Nastasya's dead body with its "tip of a bare foot" protruding from the sheet reinforces the effect, suggesting exactly how faith is lost. Lying upon the bed murdered, it is Nastasya and not Myshkin who now resembles Christ, a figure de-feminized, de-eroticized, and neutered. "All that could be seen was that a human figure lay stretched out at full length" (*I* 623).

The reduction of her once desirable body to this *kto-to,* literally a "something" deprived of gender, may strike readers cognizant of the history of death and eros in many nineteenth-century novels as an aberration. Instead of the sexual arousal that haunts Thomas Hardy's description of the beautiful hanged body of Tess Durbeyfield, in contrast to the sexual innuendos of Flaubert's Emma Bovary's death (with dark blood like menstrual fluid coming from her mouth), and in particular contrast to Tolstoy's description of Anna Karenina's feminine gestures as she, "with a light movement," plunges under the train to her death[13] – Dostoevsky's female corpse is depicted as altogether sexless. The Nastasya whose "beauty" has acted so demoniacally upon men throughout the novel, providing them with the opportunities for rivalry, madness, and murder, now appears to be de-fetishized. Her transfiguration in death is the opportunity for Myshkin's and Rogozhin's final male bonding, revealing how she has served as "traffic" between them.[14] Her absent femininity suggests a point where the concepts of "good" and "bad" men, the sacred and profane, the personal and the (sexual) political, cancel each other out.

In contrast to this moment of revelation, the living, desirable, fetishized body of Nastasya has appeared as the primum mobile of the novel's beginning and middle text. Nastasya has been the main reason for Prince Christ's being *in time,* the main opportunity for his experiment with redeeming the world. Fantasies about "the feminine" thus frame Dostoevsky's notion of the exact time of Christ's symbolic second coming. Descriptions of physically expressed apocalyptic human emotions also parody symptoms of female hysteria connected to certain ideas about how woman's organs influence their emotions. Simone de Beauvoir's theory of genderized binary oppositions – the way femininity is mythologized as *immanence* and masculinity as *transcendence* – throws light on the disturbing compound Dostoevsky invents in *The Idiot.* In this most strained of his novels, to understand Christ is to become immersed in something like feminine hysteria, feminine "weakness," and feminine lack of control. It is to imitate a passive succumbing to a violating, entering God-force, a Spirit that penetrates, possesses, and *epilepsizes*. The passage in *The Idiot* that articulates this fantasy is often quoted:

> Thinking about the [epileptic] moment afterward . . . he often told himself that all these gleams and flashes of superior self-awareness and, hence, of a "higher state of being" were nothing other than sickness. . . . And yet he came finally to an extremely paradoxical conclusion. . . . "What does it matter if it is abnormal intensity, if the result . . . turns out to be the height of harmony and beauty . . . of reconciliation, an ecstatic and prayerlike union in the highest synthesis of life?"

Myshkin concludes that "one might give one's whole life for such a moment!" (*I* 245–46). The fusion of orgiastic madness with religious ecstasy, of entry into the "demoniacal beauty" of Nastasya as into the frenzy of the "epileptic" moment, is completely symbolized only in the still life of the denouement. Here Christ's body and Nastasya's become one, echoing the gender fusion Nastasya experiences when she enters psychologically into Myshkin's idiocy also coded as a "higher" level of consciousness. Nastasya's quest is for a terminal experience – like epilepsy and like dying – that would cancel her former degraded identity as Totsky's whore: "I always imagined someone like you," Nastasya tells Myshkin just before she throws Rogozhin's hundred thousand rubles into the fire, "kind, honest, and good, and so stupid he would suddenly appear and say, 'You are not to blame, Nastasya Filippovna, and I adore you!'" (*I* 192).

What Myshkin is for Nastasya, epilepsy is for Myshkin: a flight into completion and ultimate suspension of the all-too-human and ambivalent self. In both cases these flights involve extraordinary states: the one a brain seizure, racking the whole body; the other a penetration into disembodied *other* consciousness. When Myshkin declares himself willing to marry her, Nastasya appears to lose her mind:

> She continued to sit there and for some time gazed at everyone with a strange, wondering expression, as if she could not under-

> stand what had happened and was trying to make sense of it. Then she suddenly turned to the prince and glared at him with a menacing frown, but for only a moment. . . .

Nastasya's temptation, to identify herself as somebody worthy of "pure" love, is dramatized as a loss of reason that links her consciousness to Myshkin's. If initially, in her role as a "fallen woman," she is capable of irony, a realistic assessment of men's motivations concerning her and even a dangerous playfulness with them, her "pure" self is expressed as a lapse into silence. If Myshkin's epilepsy is a surrogate for Nastasya's erotic passion, her madness is a displaced form of the Idiot's eventual insensibility. Her "insane" physical movements carry the text's style, constricting or enlarging its coherence. Only when she inspires love in Myshkin does his emotional life begin. Only her death certifies that the meaning of *The Idiot* has concluded. Her bodily responses are clues to be intensely watched and interpreted, signaled by the most important scene in part 1 in which men are assembled to watch her every move and to interpret her choices. As the text's visual fetish, she performs its eruptions, gaps, and closures:

> perhaps she had imagined for an instant that it was all a joke, a deception; but the sight of the prince's face told her at once that it was not. She reflected a moment, then smiled again, as if she herself did not really know what she was smiling at. (*I* 187)

Nastasya's body does things and she says things that "she herself did not really know." Writing to Aglaya, Nastasya coaxes her to marry Myshkin, but also declares that she is in love with Aglaya, that "every day she looks for an occasion to see [her], even from a distance" (*I* 454). As Myshkin's Heraclitean flux, Nastasya embodies a ceaseless movement. She is his reminder that he cannot escape from a "fallen" world symbolized by a woman's sex-exploited, "fallen" history that he has come to redeem. This is a rather large prospect for an epileptic who has no theory as to why women are so often subjected and degraded in the first place. In this sense Dostoevsky comes close to writing a tragic comedy, but as I suggested earlier, no consistent tone or choice of literary genre sustains his discourse.

While Myshkin's identity as a redeemer is associated with his ability to remain statically monologic, to merely observe and witness, Nastasya's identity is marked by her compulsion to keep moving. She takes flight toward and away from Myshkin, toward and away from Rogozhin's "knife," toward and away from her "good" and "bad woman" identities, and toward and away from hatred and love of Aglaya. As such, the text imitates a kind of tragic carnival of the feminine body, a movement both toward and away from archetypal images of women that duplicate Dostoevsky's construction of Myshkin as an archetypal saint moving upward and a diseased idiot moving downward in desacralized history. Part of the tragicomedy of Myshkin's failed (sexual) masculinity is that he imitates the various stereotypically coded feminine rhythms – hysteria, indecision, marginality, undecidability, and self-degradation – that are Nastasya's forte. Through Nastasya's fainting, running back and forth, flashing of eyes, through the "two spots of color . . . on [her] cheeks" (*I* 163), and her suffering eyes, Myshkin is "pierced" into a resemblance of life. What binds him to women is the physical experience of being pierced or stabbed by excess of feeling. Confronted with Nastasya, he "speaks in a trembling voice" (*I* 182); in front of Aglaya even his "lips tremble" (*I* 454). He laughs hysterically and inappropriately when he hears how a man burns his finger in a candle at Aglaya's provocation, then "bursts into tears" (*I* 593). After the furious scene between Aglaya and Nastasya, he is found "stroking" Nastasya's head and face "with both hands as if she were a little child . . . laugh[ing] when she laughed and ready to cry when she cried" (*I* 589).

The relation of Myshkin's holy foolishness to socially constructed femininity is dramatized by his inability to make up his mind (or as his not having a mind to make up). What Michael Holquist calls the novel's "failure to express the holy"[15] is linked to Myshkin's disintegrative bodily and speech rhythms, to a holy foolishness that saves no one, and to the way feminine hysteria and the Prince's epilepsy move along the same discursive continuum in the novel. This brings us to the question of why, at this point in Dostoevsky's artistic career, he was compelled to imagine such a continuum: to create a text whose rhetoric seems to imitate a male's imagining of the movements of a woman's body, perhaps a Suslovian body desired and betrayed. Myshkin's epilepsy appears as a pathological equivalent of, if not exactly orgasm, as Elizabeth Dalton suggests, then the climactic emotional frenzies to which "fallen," "passionate," or "new" women are supposedly driven. Like mythologies of femininity that embrace the idea of "woman" as "the body" or "nature," a "tempest" or a "swamp of feeling,"[16] *The Idiot* deploys its repertoire of gestures to suggest that "Prince Christ" can embody the transfiguring "Beyond" only by figuring himself as female.

Is Dostoevsky hinting that the true Christ is anima, a female soul? Are we to understand Myshkin as suffused not with his Father's spirit but with Sophia (divine wisdom)? Dostoevsky insists on epilepsy as the transcendental marker, but that marker is also associated with Nastasya's being driven into epileptic-like frenzies and stupors as she is objectified by Rogozhin as a female commodity. Epilepsy may be the symbol of the Son's connection to his eternal Father, but it is also the sign of Myshkin's hysterical identity with degraded femininity. No attachment to the Father can ensure his efficacy in *this* world; yet his feminized soul does not ensure his transcendence into the other world either.

Nastasya's and Myshkin's identities are further analogized by violent physical experiences and through the trope of penetration. Dostoevsky brings together strange ideas about woman's biological vulnerability and fantasies about Christ's experience of embodiment so that Christian and feminine subjectivities are allied through the trope of knives and piercing. While Nastasya's madness is linked to her fear of being penetrated by Rogozhin's knife, the movement of the image of the knife structures the text itself. The image of a knife floats within Rogozhin's, Nastasya's, and the Idiot's consciousness. The knife floats "outside" too, in the shopwindow Myshkin sees, and throughout the surrealist atmosphere of the novel that penetrates the reader's consciousness. The Russian verb *pronzat'* (to pierce) is repeated throughout the text in various ways, forming a leitmotif that connects the piercing of Christ by soldiers to the "piercing" eyes following Myshkin in his hallucination, to the way Nastasya's face "had pierced [Myshkin's] heart forever" (*I* 588), and to Rogozhin's knife piercing Nastasya's body. The "piercing" the characters experience is part of *The Idiot*'s narrative coding of sex and violence as the crucifixion of the Spirit, closely allied to fantasies about the phallus and its destructive potentials.

Christ the male warrior, whose emblem is the sword and not the plowshare, is completely absent from Dostoevsky's conceptualization, as is Christ the church organizer absent from Ivan Karamazov's conception of Jesus in *The Legend of the Grand Inquisitor. The Idiot* foreshadows *The Legend*'s analysis of the problem of Christian (feminine) gentleness as politically impotent, in contrast to tyrannical (male) aggressiveness as ecclesiastical power incarnated in the patriarchal Inquisitor himself. If Rogozhin plays the part of inquisitor-prosecutor in *The Idiot*, Myshkin plays the part of Jesus, with the "new woman" Nastasya caught between them, her tragically ambivalent position foreshadowing "the new man" Ivan's intellectual struggles.

In other ways too *The Idiot* reads like a rehearsal for themes more successfully realized in Dostoevsky's later work. But the novel remains particularly interesting in terms of the woman question because it displays in its own narrative structure a confusion about one part's relation to another, about orders and hierarchies, and about subordinations and dominations that have gendered connotations. It is significant that part 4, in which Myshkin becomes the erotic-spiritual fetish literally "fought over" by Nastasya and Aglaya, is a narrative inversion of part 1, in which Nastasya is surrounded by men and is offered the choice between Myshkin and Rogozhin. In the scandalous scene of part 4, women who were pursued by men become a man's pursuer, and the man who once pursued women becomes the object of female rivalry. In this world of shifting gender roles that leads toward the wedding day and Nastasya's death, Myshkin plays out with Nastasya and Aglaya the role that Nastasya played out earlier with Rogozhin and Myshkin. Instead of men's rubles thrown into the fire, we have letters between the female rivals (that Myshkin hopes will disappear). Instead of Rogozhin exultantly running off with Nastasya, we have a scene in which Aglaya runs out after watching Myshkin run after Nastasya. The gender reversals inscribed in these scenes, the fact that Nastasya chooses the "wrong" man (Rogozhin) in the first scene and Myshkin chooses the "wrong" woman (Nastasya) in the last, suggests that *choice*, sexual and otherwise, is completely de-centered in this novel.

While part 1 (chapters 13–16) dramatizes a fantasy in which all the men desire and literally "play for" Nastasya with money and promises, part 4 (chapter 8) expresses a man's desire to be fought over by two beautiful women and to win reconciliation with his "world" through love of both of them. What Myshkin discovers, however, is that women cannot be pulled into his synthesis, nor can they accept traditional ideals of Christian reconciliation. Neither Aglaya nor Nastasya serves the patriarchal religious fantasy, even if they are the objects of it and the test cases for Dostoevsky's version of it. Nastasya and Aglaya together, like Grushenka and Katerina Ivanovna in *The Brothers Karamazov*, appear to incarnate forces for dispersal and negation of much that is sanctioned by masculine versions of religious goodness. In *The Idiot* neither woman allows herself to be a vehicle for Myshkin's choice between the two different ideas he believes they represent.

What Mochulsky describes as Myshkin's struggle with an "idea of beauty . . . embodied in the two images of his heroines, Nastasya and Aglaya,"[17] involves a choice between a "new" woman and a "fallen" woman. That both images of women are "beautiful," that both draw Myshkin toward the split that paralyzes him, has been persuasively described by Louis Breger.[18] While Aglaya offers Myshkin the sort of risk that would bring him into a new world of emancipated men and women, Nastasya bonds him to the Christian allegory of forgiveness for sexual sins that throws him back to the past. But Myshkin cannot and does not choose between these versions of the world, between past and future. Nor is he, ultimately, the only object of their quarrel. The scene between Nastasya and Aglaya suggests a quarrel that is also about the identity of "woman," for which "Myshkin" is an excuse. It is a quarrel between feminism and traditionalism that Katerina Ivanovna and Grushenka will also experience in the chapter called "Lacerations in the Drawing Room" in *The Brothers Karamazov.*

Like Katerina Ivanovna, Aglaya symbolizes ideas about feminine freedom and modernity and naive self-expansion. Olga Matich argues that "Nastasya's incipient and inclusive revolt against the female role . . . characterizes the behavior of her rival Aglaya, whose portrayal is clearly influenced by political considerations." Aglaya reads banned books, wants to become a teacher, and desires a relationship with a man that will defy social conventions. She chooses the "idiot" Myshkin, whom Matich describes as "a man with female attributes" as she describes Aglaya and Nastasya as "nascently masculinized women."[19] While Nastasya's fallen identity is reinforced by the way she succumbs to both Myshkin and Rogozhin, Aglaya acts upon feminist impulses and flies from men's intimidations. Her hope, like Nastasya's initial but undermined fantasy, is that Prince Christ will understand her desire for freedom.

> "I've been thinking about it over a long time [she tells Myshkin], and I've finally chosen you. . . . I don't want them to laugh at me at home. I don't want to be taken for a little fool, I don't want to be teased. I realized all this at once and I refused Evgeny Pavlovich point-blank because I don't want them always marrying me off! . . . I want to run away from home, and I've chosen you to help me!" (*I* 448)

Myshkin's ambivalent repudiation of Aglaya, dramatized as a symptom of his infinite "pity" for Nastasya, is the sign that he cannot go forward with the woman question. He reaches an impasse like the Gambler's forgetting of Polina, and like Raskolnikov's fall into "oblivion" after he kills the female pawnbroker. Myshkin's way out is to vow that he wants to love both women. But as Evgeny Pavlovich rightly observes, this may be an excuse for his loving neither, an intuition that drives both women to enact their disgust with Myshkin's passivity by attacking each other:

> Finally Aglaya looked firmly straight into Nastasya Filippovna's eyes and at once read clearly all the malice gathering in her rival's look. Woman understood woman. . . . "Ah! So then you have come to 'fight' me? Just imagine, I thought you were – cleverer."
>
> They looked at each other no longer concealing their malice. One was the woman who had been writing such incredible letters to the other. And here all that had vanished into thin air at their first encounter and their first words. . . . However extravagant the other was with her disturbed mind and her sick soul no predetermined intention of hers could, it seemed, stand against the venomous, purely feminine contempt of her rival. The prince felt certain that Nastasya Filippovna would not mention the letters herself . . . – and he would have given half his life if Aglaya would not mention them either. (*I* 582–83)

Positioned precisely between the two women in a way that mirrors the way Nastasya is positioned between her "rivals" Myshkin and Rogozhin, Myshkin's "goodness" appears as a failure of self-recognition and a failure to recognize the larger subject of the women's quarrel. The narrator speaks of "purely feminine contempt" much as Losnitsky in Suslova's *The Stranger and Her Lover* speaks of "perfectly feminine traits." But the narrator cannot control the feminist theme Dostoevsky has set in motion or the reader's reaction to Myshkin's inability to respond to it.

Dostoevsky's strong impulse to create a thoroughly "good" man who will appeal to women's love, as if in penance for his narcissistic rebel figures, operates at last to reveal certain delusions that his other novels have obscured. While Raskolnikov can at least control Sonya to the extent that she is addicted to bringing him to God, Myshkin has no control over either Nastasya or Aglaya as the novel draws to its close. The wish for a termination of the deepest conflicts about women leads to the most intense rendition of confused masculine consciousness that Dostoevsky has yet imagined. While his "kind" and "good" Prince Christ appears initially as a penitential fantasy, by the end "a pattern of sadistic feeling shapes all the principle erotic relationships in *The Idiot*."[20] The act of writing *through* the idea of a "pure" male holiness to discover the sadistic component in patriarchal constructions of "the holy" is a purgation for Dostoevsky: it released him toward the critiques of patriarchy and *Übermensch* culture to be inscribed in his last and greatest works *The Possessed* and *The Brothers Karamazov*. In *The Idiot* Dostoevsky dissolves the sublimity he first constructs, leaving in its wake questions about the "purely feminine" and about masculine motivations for Evgeny Pavlovich to decipher.

Evgeny Pavlovich's voice interrupts the narrative precisely the way Porfiry's intercedes in Raskolnikov's rationalizing thought processes in *Crime and Punishment*. Piercing an increasingly muddy metaphysics, Evgeny's voice articulates a skeptical modern perspective. As various convincing interpretations for Myshkin's behavior are being offered in the narration, Evgeny ushers the woman question to the forefront of the conversation. The question of why and how Myshkin became involved with Nastasya is at last addressed.

> "You must admit, Prince" [says Evgeny] "that in your relations with Nastasya Filippovna there was from the very start something *conventionally democratic* (I put it this way for the sake of brevity), the fascination, so to speak, of the 'woman question' (to put it still more briefly)."

In part 4, chapter 10, Evgeny Pavlovich is described as "sensibly and clearly, and we repeat, with extraordinary psychological insight," drawing for Myshkin "a vivid picture of all the prince's past relations with Nastasya Filippovna." This man "rose to positive eloquence," the narrator tells us, when he asserts that "there were lies between [the man and the woman] and whatever begins with lies must end with lies, for that is a law of nature." Arguing that "the fundamental cause of all that has happened is . . . [Myshkin's] innate experience," Evgeny argues that Myshkin's relations with women were grounded in nothing but "intellectual convictions."

> "For you see I knew all about the curious and scandalous scene that took place at Nastasya Filippovna's when Rogozhin brought his money. If you like I shall give you a systematic analysis of yourself, I shall show you yourself in a mirror."

Evgeny's mirror shows Myshkin a naive but benignly ambitious young man who has read too many books, who has "longed for Russia as for a land which is unknown but full of promise," but who is finally "seized" in the "heat of enthusiasm" with the idea of saving some women. Evgeny's rational enlightenment discourse, with its denigration of enthusiasm and seizures, glances ironically toward Myshkin's own valuation of his epilepsy as a sign of spiritual depths. Evgeny's conviction that "everything is perfectly clear" is a bit suspect, however, considering that his own motivation to analyze Myshkin comes from his disappointment at Aglaya's refusing him. He is nevertheless persuasive in describing how, after meeting the "fantastic, demonical beauty," Nastasya, Myshkin

> seized the opportunity to declare publicly the magnanimous notion that [he], a prince and a man whose life is pure, does not consider a woman dishonored who has been put to shame not through her own fault but through the fault of a revolting aristocratic libertine.

Shifting the blame to the revolting Totsky is the smallest part of Evgeny's analysis. The point he wishes to emphasize, and with which Myshkin agrees, is that Myshkin's own feeling may not be "genuine." Evgeny reveals to Myshkin that the Prince himself cannot tell the difference between "intellectual" and "genuine" feelings, between a "fascination (so to speak)" with "the woman question" and a genuine commitment actually to improve the concrete life of a particular woman.

> "The point is, was this the truth, was your feeling genuine, was it a natural feeling or merely intellectual enthusiasm? In the temple a woman was forgiven, but do you think she was told that she had done well, that she was deserving of all honor and respect?"

Evgeny moves swiftly through difficult questions about the motives of the woman "chosen," the idea of a man like Myshkin choosing a woman to save, and the problem of men's relations with women in general. He may need to degrade Myshkin to console himself, but Myshkin has no response to Evgeny's interpretation except to repeat, "Yes, yes, you are right. Oh, I do feel I am to blame!" Unable to resist or answer Evgeny's skepticism, he can work up no self-transformative *dialogical* energy that would enable him, as it enables Raskolnikov, to break through to more authentic relations with women. Myshkin ratifies, in effect, Evgeny's diagnosis that his trouble has been some sort of "bad faith" regarding them: what Dalton calls the Prince's passive-aggressive psychology and lack of "genuine" or "natural" feeling.

Myshkin's identity as a failed savior devoted to the beautiful *image* but not to the efficacy or dialogic potential of Christ suggests that Dostoevsky might be moving at this late point in his novel toward the redemptive laughter of carnival described by Bakhtin. There is much in *The Idiot* to suggest "the reversal of the hierarchic levels," the toppling of official authority, even some parody of official religion and the figure of Christ himself. But this potentially modernist element is aborted by certain blockings of the "as yet unpredetermined *new word*." What Bakhtin claims Dostoevsky to be incapable of, a "monosemantic seriousness,"[21] shows up in *The Idiot* as a defense against the revelation that there is nothing funny about Christianity's inability to save women. If any sort of liberation is expressed in the novel, it is achieved at the expense of the author's monologic Christian ideology. The "articulate" Evgeny Pavlovich voices a dangerously modern clearance in his novel: a moment when the text's official myth of Myshkin's identity collapses and no laughter emerges.

Evgeny suggests that Myshkin has exploited the role of savior for his own regressive and delusive purposes. He has "seized the opportunity to declare publicly" his "magnanimous notion" that fallen women should be forgiven and exalted. Myshkin's acts of "love" have been a public spectacle, Evgeny intimates, and Myshkin has misunderstood his relation to the woman question. Playing an inquisitorial role that is markedly like Porfiry's, Evgeny elicits a response from Myshkin ("you are right") that echoes Raskolnikov's admission that he is "no Napoleon." What binds the profane hero of *Crime and Punishment* to the sacred hero of *The Idiot* is the "fall" from a superman status.

Bound by conflict, burdened by a traditionalist Christian mythology that strangles men rather than channels them toward new possibilities with women, Myshkin allows Evgeny to destroy his illusions just as surely as he allows Rogozhin to destroy Nastasya. Shadowing the last chapters that lead to Myshkin's ultimate stupor is a covert idea that connects feminist to religious utopian thinking: If the true Christ came to Russia, his mission would be to allow women to save themselves from the masculinist erotic culture that confuses love either with the phallic knife or the castrated phallus.

---

In *The Idiot*, the narrator's flights, loops, plunges into intertextual interpretation, obscurity, and paradox suggest what Bakhtin calls an "internally dialogic dissociation." Dostoevsky is in love with the freedoms released by the rhetoric of idiocy and the poetics of epilepsy. But this same discourse involves him in regressive Christian delusions of grandeur that the figure of Myshkin cannot realize. Myshkin's relation to "the feminine" serves mainly to defend him against his unresolved feelings about masculine power. Explaining himself to Evgeny Pavlovich, Myshkin says: "If only Aglaya knew, if she knew everything – I mean absolutely everything. For in this matter, you have to know *everything* about another person, when we have to, when that other person is at fault." This incoherent statement, which the Prince knows is incoherent, ends in further mystification. "There's something here I can't explain to you," he insists, even when Evgeny insists that "most likely, you never loved either one of them" (*I* 599–600). Between the Prince's idea that there is "something here" that cannot be explained and Evgeny's notion that women are the clue to Myshkin's whole identity, the suppressed "feminine" emerges as the "mystery" of the novel. This mysterious "something" may be related to what Mochulsky and Robert Hingley have described as the germ from which *The Idiot* grew:

> An entirely different figure [from Myshkin] had obsessed Dostoevsky from the beginning: a tempestuous woman with a huge sense of grievance, the eventual Nastasya Filippovna. Somehow this image arose out of a real-life court case involving a teen-age Moscow girl, Olga Umetskaya, who had four times set fire to her family home after being savagely misused by her neglectful and sadistic parents.

Hingley concludes that finally "there is far more of Miss Suslova in the finished Nastasya Filippovna" than Umetskaya; and he suggests Anna Korvin-Krukovskaya as the model for Aglaya.[22] But the connection Hingley makes between feminine imagery and the early notes for *The Idiot* is more interesting than finding the exact biographical sources for Dostoevsky's women characters. More suggestive is the link between images of abused femininity and the idea of a feminized male savior figure. The close identification of Myshkin with women points the late-twentieth-century reader to the transformations in the novel that are now becoming more obvious to us,[23] for "it is impossible to dissociate the questions of art, style and truth from the question of women": "One can no longer seek her, no more than one could search for woman's femininity or female sexuality. And she is certainly not to be found in any of the familiar modes of concept or knowledge. Yet it is impossible to resist looking for her."[24]

In *The Idiot* two of Dostoevsky's favorite personas, the idiot-saint and the sexist criminal, cannot help looking for Nastasya. Bakhtin notes that Nastasya is "reduced to a search for herself and for her own undivided voice beneath the two voices that have made their home in her."[25] But two male voices may not be enough to create even one woman's identity. Dostoevsky's male characters continue this quest in *The Eternal Husband*, a short novel that replicates as it revises those scenes of male rivalry and knife/razor play that haunt *The Idiot*. *The Eternal Husband* returns to the psychological realism of

*Notes from the Underground* and *The Gambler* in which modernist uncertainty, men's impulses to tyrannize women, and questions about otherness predominate. As a corrective to *The Idiot*'s finally exploded fantasy that an asexual Prince Christ could save the world, *The Eternal Husband* offers mocking youthful feminist voices convinced that only *authentic* respect for women's sexuality can transform the future.

## NOTES

Quotations are from *The Idiot*, trans. Henry and Olga Carlisle (New York, NAL, 1962). Cited in text as *I*.

1. "Almost the whole novel," Dostoevsky informed his niece in a letter, "was thought and written for the sake of the denouement." See 28.2:318; October 26/November 7, 1868.

2. Caryl Emerson, "Problems with Baxtin's Poetics," *Slavic and East European Journal* 32 (1988): 503–25.

3. See Dostoevsky's letters and his various biographers' descriptions of this event.

4. Harriet Murav, *Holy Foolishness: Dostoevsky's Novels and the Poetics of Cultural Critique* (Stanford: Stanford University Press, 1992), 174.

5. David M. Bethea, *The Shape of Apocalypse in Modern Russian Fiction* (Princeton: Princeton University Press, 1989), 101.

6. See Murav's description of Dostoevsky's dissatisfactions with the novel and her analysis of the "two tendencies" – including Burenin's as cited above (*Holy Foolishness*, pp. 73–74).

7. See, for example, the commentaries of Konstantin Mochulsky (*Dostoevsky: His Life and Work*, trans. and introd. Michael A. Minihan [Princeton, N.J.: Princeton University Press, 1967]), and Tamira Pachmuss (*F. M. Dostoevsky: Dualism and Synthesis of the Human Soul* [Carbondale: Southern Illinois University Press, 1963]) supporting the religious interpretation in contrast to the more skeptical commentaries of Richard Peace (*Dostoevsky: An Examination of the Major Novels* [Cambridge: Cambridge University Press, 1971]) and Michael Holquist (*Dostoevsky and the Novel* [reprint; Evanston: Northwestern University Press, 1986]).

8. Chris Weedon, *Feminist Practice and Poststructuralist Theory* (Oxford: Basil Blackwell, 1987), 69.

9. Clare Cavanagh argues in "Pseudo-Revolution in Poetic Language: Julia Kristeva and the Russian Avant-Garde," *Slavic Review* 52 (1993): 283–97, that in Julia Kristeva's work the "'Symbolic Order,' the 'Father' or the 'Law'. . . all seem to mean simply society as such with no regard as to whether the particular 'society' is democratic or tyrannical" (29).

10. Murav, *Holy Foolishness*, 6.

11. Elizabeth Dalton, *Unconscious Structure in "The Idiot": A Study in Literature and Psychoanalysis* (Princeton: Princeton University Press, 1979), 173.

12. Sigmud Freud, *Beyond the Pleasure Principle*, vol. 18 of *The Standard Edition of the Complete Psychological Works of Sigmund Freud*, trans. James Strachey, in collaboration with Anna Freud, assisted by Alix Strachey and Alan Tyson (London: Hogarth Press and the Institute of Psycho-Analysis, 1955), part 3.

13. The description of Anna's last moment conforms to a stereotyped vision of femininity, including the accoutrement of the "red hand-bag" that is flung aside before she jumps. See Leo Tolstoy, *Anna Karenina*, trans. Joel Carmichael (New York: Bantam, 1960, 1988), 816.

14. Again, I refer the reader to Eve Kosofsky Sedgwick's discussion, in *Between Men: English Literature and Male Homosocial Desire* (New York: Columbia University Press, 1985), of women as intermediate objects or "traffic" between men who cannot otherwise establish their (homosexual or homosocial) bonds.

15. Holquist, *Dostoevsky and the Novel*, 196ff.

16. See the chapter "Myths," in Simone de Beauvoir, *The Second Sex*, trans. H. M. Parshley (New York: Knopf, 1952).

17. Mochulsky, *Dostoevsky*, 380.

18. See Louis Breger's chapter on *The Idiot* in *Dostoevsky: The Author as Psychoanalyst* (New York: New York University Press, 1989).

19. Olga Matich, "The Idiot: A Feminist Reading," in *Dostoevsky and the Human Condition After a Century*, ed. Alexej Ugrinsky, Frank S. Lambasa, and Valija K. Ozolins (New York: Greenwood, 1986), 55–56.

20. Dalton, *Unconscious Structure*, 97.

21. Mikhail Bakhtin, *Problems of Dostoevsky's Poetics*, ed. and trans. Caryl Emerson, introd. Wayne C. Booth (Minneapolis: University of Minnesota Press, 1984), 165–66. Also see Bakhtin's discussion of the carnivalesque in *Rabelais and His World*, trans. Hélène Iswolsky (Bloomington: Indiana University Press, 1984), 303.

22. Ronald Hingley, *Dostoevsky: His Life and Work* (New York: Scribner, 1978), 414ff.

23. In the early 1990s, two male-authored feminist novels received much attention: Norman Rush's *Mating* (New York: Random House, 1991) and Peter Haug's *Smilla's Sense of Snow* (New York: Farrar, Straus & Giroux, 1993). Both novels, though authored by men, explore feminist questions and are narrated by women's voices.

24. Jacques Derrida, "Becoming Woman," *Semiotexte* 3 (1978): 130.

25. Bakhtin, *Problems*, 235.

# *The Idiot:* Historicism Arrives at the Station

DAVID M. BETHEA

*That devilish Iron Horse, whose ear-rending neigh is heard throughout the town, has muddied the Boiling Spring with his foot, and he it is that has browsed off all the woods on Walden shore, that Trojan Horse, with a thousand men in his belly, introduced by mercenary Greeks! Where is the country's champion, the Moore of Moore Hall, to meet him at the Deep Cut and thrust an avenging lance between the ribs of the bloated pest?*
—*Henry David Thoreau, Walden*

*What is this that man has done?*
*He has set off on the iron road,*
*And I feel the threat of our iron century.*
—*Fyodor Glinka, "Two Roads"*

For good or for ill, Russian literature has long been known for its so-called messianism, and there is no writer who struggled more than Dostoevsky to give legitimacy to the "Russian idea," to the belief that Russian history is uniquely inscribed with a biblical End. Yet Dostoevsky was no mystic, at least in the sense of one who tries to peer *beyond* the End and tell about it (see, e.g., Rozenblium, "Tvorcheskie dnevniki," 13–15). If he had occasion to resort to the figures and codes of Revelation,[1] he did so allusively; as a novelist he was keenly aware that his texts must first be grounded firmly in nineteenth-century history and that whatever lies on the other side of personal death is not to be captured *in words*, is not the stuff of a story told over time. As his epoch's most eloquent voice in the dialogue between logic (*rassudok*) and belief (*vera*), he apparently had similar thoughts about the promised interregnum of the Antichrist and the Second Coming of Christ as prophesied by John of Patmos.

Modern criticism often speaks of novels as being "end-determined"[2] or somehow written in reverse, with the shadow of a foreordained conclusion cast backward over the various elements of narrative structure. Such an approach, one suspects, could certainly be applied to much of Dostoevsky's writing, and to *The Idiot* especially, of whose haunting final scene the author wrote his niece S. A. Ivanova, "almost the whole novel was thought out and written for the sake of the denouement" (28.2:318; October 26/November 7, 1868).[3] But it would be a mistake to do so too hastily, if only because the neat and self-regarding "structure" touted by modern criticism is such a vexed issue in the context of Dostoevsky the great vitalist. The implicit danger in reading Dostoevsky through Western eyes is to impose cultural paradigms and critical orthodoxies that have limited meaning when projected back to the Russia of the 1860s and 1870s. In this regard, *The Idiot* has been a powerful magnet for some spectacular misreadings.[4] René Girard's fascinating but remarkably uninformed account of what he calls the "Dostoevskian apocalypse" in *Deceit, Desire, and the Novel* is a prime example of this (see 256–91). Indeed, if we are to judge by what Dostoevsky had to say about the logically closed ideologies swarming in the air of his time, he would have harsh words for the way that language has evolved from a medium of ethical choice to a system of systems. In the end one would have to agree with Edward Wasiolek who, as the Western scholar most familiar with Dostoevsky's notebooks, points out that *The Idiot* is, of Dostoevsky's major fiction, the work most resistant to "elegant" structural analysis: "We cannot go to *The Idiot* with theories of the organic fitness of every part, of the necessity of every positioning, every image, every sound. . . . Structure, I hazard, is never as exquisite as our current theories would have it, at least not in this novel" ("Introduction" in *Notebooks*, 9).

One issue is not in doubt: as the threat of revolution entered the public consciousness, Dostoevsky and the tradition his work grew out of became increasingly obsessed by the notion of apocalypse. Whether or not history, in Herzen's metaphor, followed a "libretto," the threat of a communist-inspired "violent tempest – dreadful, bloody, unjust, and swift" – was something that people anticipated, depending on their political orientation and the part they saw themselves playing in the unfolding drama, with either fear or joy (*Sobranie sochinenii*, 6:104). Moreover, this apocalypticism could not but leave some trace on how Dostoevsky's fiction is composed and narrated.[5] Here *The Idiot* is particularly noteworthy: it is Dostoevsky's first major work in which the Apocalypse, as metaphor for "anti-life" (death), "anti-history" (timelessness), and indeed "anti-narrative" (end, silence) is ironically the prime mover of plot. There is good reason why the novel has been called Dostoevsky's most "untidy masterpiece" (Wasiolek, "Introduction" in *Notebooks*, 19) and why efforts to invest it with a structure it apparently lacks have so often gone awry. This central paradox – namely, that *The Idiot* is about an end it cannot tell but only foretell – is the subject of this chapter. To pose the question in terms of the novel's life in our own times: this end, foretold, held in linguistic limbo by the "différance" (in the sense of both differentiation and deferral) of Dostoevsky's telling – is it a true End, a transcendental presence whose "time has come"? Or is it simply an end like any other, a provisional presence that resolves nothing and leaves everyone, characters, reader, and author, stuck on the tracks of an ongoing historicism? I shall briefly establish a context for Dostoevsky's apocalypticism within his epoch and his own oeuvre, then look more closely at how the novel gathers narrative momentum and proceeds toward its end. Our focus will be on the image of the train, which as metaphor for mechanical force, "iron logic," and unregenerate *chronos*, is both the chief semantic and compositional source of this momentum and one possible key to Dostoevsky's conceptualization of the role of apocalypse in history.

---

The most authoritative statement ever made by Dostoevsky on the idea of the End came in a notebook entry of April 16, 1864, as he stood vigil at the bier of his first wife. The occasion provided ample opportunity to contemplate the nature of death, the possibility of resurrection, and the meaning of history. The entry itself is especially interesting both because of its unguarded frankness and because of its timing on the eve of Dostoevsky's major period: the first part of *Notes from the Underground* had just appeared that March and *Crime and Punishment* and the other novels were soon to follow. It is also striking that the questions raised by Dostoevsky as he reasoned passionately with himself are directly implicated in the themes and storyline of *The Idiot*, the novel written after *Crime and Punishment*, in the first years of Dostoevsky's self-imposed exile in western Europe (September 1867–January 1869).

> Masha is lying on the table. Will Masha and I ever see each other again?
>
> It is impossible to love one another *as oneself* according to Christ's commandment. . . . Only Christ could do this, but Christ was eternal [*vekovechnyi*], an eternal ideal [*ot veka ideal*], toward which man strives and must, by the laws of nature, strive. At the same time, after the appearance of Christ as *the ideal of man in the flesh* it became clear as day that . . . the highest use to which man can put his personality is . . . to destroy, as it were, that *I*, to give it back in full to each and every one selflessly and wholeheartedly. And this is the greatest happiness. Thus the law of *I* merges with the law of humanity and in this merging both [the *I* and the *all*] . . . attain the highest goal of their individual development.
>
> It is precisely this that is the paradise of Christ. All history – both that of mankind and of each man separately – is only the development of, struggle with, urge for, and attainment of this goal.
>
> But if this is the ultimate goal of mankind (at whose attainment there will no longer be a need to develop . . . [and], therefore, to live), then it follows that man, having once attained [his goal], also ends his earthly existence. Hence man on earth is a being that is only developing, and therefore not completed, but transitional.

But to attain such an exalted goal is, to my mind, totally senseless, if in the attainment of the goal all is snuffed out and disappears, that is, if there is no more life for man upon the attainment of the goal. It follows then that there is [i.e., there must be] a future life in paradise. . . .

NB. The Antichrists are mistaken when they attempt to refute Christianity with the following main point of refutation: (1) "Why doesn't Christianity reign on earth if it is [the] true [religion], why does man suffer to this day and not become a brother to others?"

Well, it's not easily understandable why – because this is the ideal of the future, completed life of man, while earthly man is in a transitional state. This ideal will come, but it will come after the attainment of [life's] goal, when man will have been completely reborn by the laws of nature into another form that neither marries nor is given in marriage;[6] and, second, Christ Himself taught this lesson only as an ideal, prophesying that until the end of the world there would be struggle and development (His teaching about the sword) for such are the laws of nature, because on earth life is developing, while there [i.e. the other world] is an existence that is complete in its synthesis, eternally joyous and full, for which, it would seem, "time" shall be no more. . . .[7]

Hence man strives on earth for an ideal that *opposes* his nature. When man doesn't fulfill the ideal of striving for the ideal, that is, doesn't *in an act of love* make a sacrifice of his *I* to other people or another being (Masha and I), he experiences suffering and calls that suffering sin. Hence man must constantly experience a suffering that is counterbalanced by the heavenly [*raiskii*] delight in fulfilling the law, that is, by sacrifice. Herein lies our [sense of] balance on earth. Otherwise the Earth would be without meaning (*Neizdannyi Dostoevskii*, 173–75).

I have quoted this extraordinary passage at length because in it we see the mind of a great storyteller trying, step by step, to compose a plot for life that *encompasses* death. As in the finale of *The Idiot*,[8] where Myshkin and Rogozhin contemplate the corpse of Nastasya Filippovna, Dostoevsky strikes repeatedly at the mystery of this ultimate threshold. The fascination with spatiotemporal brinks and border crossings that is his hallmark[9] and that so marks the writing of *The Idiot*[10] is here distilled to a radical essence of logic and belief. Dostoevsky works back from the fact of his wife's death to the story of every human life. Death frames life, gives it a conclusion so that what has come before can have a beginning, middle, and end (see Kermode, *Sense*, 58–59). Yet only if the conclusion can be set, as it were, in a larger story does this structure have a meaning, and the forward movement ("struggle and development") a goal (the synthesis of "Masha" and "I"). Dostoevsky's Christian logic is trying to posit the ultimate story whose authorial viewpoint cannot be known. To resort to the language of narratology, without some larger employment of faith, humanity's attempts to serialize the tale of its strivings *beyond* life's conclusion are deprived of any absolute or meaningful placement in time. There is no divine "draft," no "Finis" in paradise, only endless embellishment and retardation.

In short, although Dostoevsky's internal monologue does not express the argument so explicitly, the future author of *The Idiot* is feeling his way toward the head-on collision between Christianity and historicism, between an atemporal ideal and the relentless march of *chronos*, that lies at the center of his most elusive plot. Indeed, many of the motifs that reappear, artistically shaped, in *The Idiot* are set forth here in unmediated fashion: the silent corpse and what it means; Christ as an ideal that entered history and became flesh; the final tableau and tragic ensemble of competing loves; the sense of harmony and synthesis – Dostoevsky's metaphor for God – that, like a freely rotating eyeball, sees the present (life "in the middest") from the vantage of eternity (life "at the end"). All of these are vital to the plot of *The Idiot*, and we shall return to them in due course. For the moment suffice it to say that Dostoevsky was sensitive to the dangers of positivistic thinking that lie in wait for the vacillating believer.[11] His unkind words for the "Antichrists," "atheists," and "materialists" of the 1860s are evidence of this.[12] And, as will be seen shortly,

Dostoevsky felt that the logic of such thinking condemned the (hi)story of a human life and a people to be told in terms of a tragic and unavoidable end.

---

As an artist, Dostoevsky had to find a way to invest these tensions ("here"/"there," "now"/"then") in story form. He needed some verbal picture of interlocking time-space relations to embody the notions of personal and national history that occurred to him in *his* time. This picture, which Bakhtin has termed the chronotope, is the novelist's (or narrative poet's) way of translating notions of time (open/closed, public/private, changing/static) into ready-made images of narrative space (the public square, the road).[13] One of the most celebrated and visually arresting means of proceeding down the road of life and history is the steed, which entered Russian literature and culture – both reflecting the shape of contemporary history and, indeed, contributing to that shape – as a powerful symbol for contemporary readers. In the Russian context, the horse was employed both as local color (a mode of conveyance, a domestic animal) and as mythical image (a symbol of imperial might or manifest destiny), so that in certain works it actually became a focal point where opposing concepts of time (everyday-epic) could intersect and collide. Here the horse's role in folkloric and chivalric tradition elided with its role in the emerging realistic tradition; the site of this collision – the "cliff" over the "abyss" in Saint Petersburg in Pushkin's *The Bronze Horseman*, the "steppe" in Gogol's *Dead Souls* – functioned as an all-important visual field for organizing the reader's response to contemporary history.

Thus, Senate Square served as the "betwixt-and-between" site where different classes of people (Peter–Evgeny) and the different times they represented could have their "duel." And the steppe, with its sprawling expanse and seemingly endless horizon line, became a metaphor for the openness and infinite possibility of Russian historical time, a time whose direction and meaning were as yet unknown: "Whither art thou soaring away to, then, Russia? Give me thy answer! But Russia gives none" (Gogol, *Dead Souls,* 304). As he entered on the period of his major fiction, Dostoevsky turned with increasing fervor to the central questions of Russia's history, to the "whither" and "why" raised by his forebears. His later works constantly take into account the time and space that has been traveled *since* these earlier historical poses first captured the attention of contemporary audiences.

Although the horse's role in the chronotope of Pushkin and Gogol was not, properly speaking, "apocalyptic" (that is, no *explicit* connection was made between its movement and the End prophesied in the Book of Revelation) one thing is certain: over time, this role began to acquire an increasingly dark coloration. What was once implicit was now, under the pressure of contemporary history, "revealed" to subsequent generations. If in the first half of the nineteenth century certain thinkers, notably Chaadaev and Herzen, had seen Russia's lack of a significant past as an opportunity to avoid the pitfalls of Western bourgeois civilization (Herzen visualized this as the pristine "openness" of Siberia), then in the second half of the century others such as Leontiev and Solovyov saw their country's historical mission more pessimistically, in terms of closure, not openness. Leontiev, for example, so feared the process of democratization promoted by the left that he claimed that "Russian society . . . is racing faster than any other along the path of universal mixing [*vsesmeshenie*], and, who knows . . . suddenly we may . . . give birth to the Antichrist" ("Nad mogiloi Pazukhina," *Sobranie sochinenii,* 7:425). In addition, the myth surrounding Saint Petersburg in Pushkin's poem was gradually being re-finished by other "catastrophists": rather than the floodwaters that were often seen in early nineteenth-century poetry (V. Odoevsky, Lermontov, M. Dmitriev, V. Pecherin) as a *natural* form of retribution, by the turn of the century it was the notion of a flaming end (*ekpyrosis*), to be fueled by terrorist bombs and the *man-made* fires of social revolution, that came to dominate the descriptions of this doomed city.[14]

Dostoevsky's later fiction marks a distinct turning point in this tradition: in it the connection between the end of the biblical plot and the direction of Russian history is made explicit. Dostoevsky was the first Russian prose writer[15] to visualize the movement of an individual life and a national history in terms of the apocalyptic horse and rider. That which was left unsaid in the duel between Evgeny and the Bronze Horseman is now fully articulated in the love triangle of Myshkin, Rogozhin, and Nastasya Filippovna as it is employed in the Petersburg world of the 1860s. Dostoevsky's allusions to a coming apocalypse can be traced to a visit to the 1862 London Exhibition, which he subsequently described in *Winter Notes on Summer Impressions* (1863). Here he voices his disgust at the Western "worship of Baal" for the first time, but the reference seems, in context, closer to a metaphor for corruption than to a literal prophecy.[16] By the 1860s, however, and particularly in *The Diary of a Writer*, Dostoevsky had apparently begun to insist on an actual and imminent coming of the Antichrist: "The Antichrist is coming to us! He is coming! The end of the world is near – nearer than they think" (Timofeeva, "God raboty," 170).[17] Sometime during the intervening years between the publication of *Winter Notes* and the serialization of *Diary* Dostoevsky had shifted his focus from individual to national salvation, from death as a personal apocalypse to revolution as a political one. And, indeed, a closer look reveals evidence of this shift in the three long novels written during this period: *Crime and Punishment* (1866), *The Idiot* (1868–69), and *The Devils* (1871–72).

In *Crime and Punishment*, Raskolnikov's dream of the mare draws heavily on a similar description in Nekrasov's long poem *About the Weather* (written 1863–65) (*Pss* 2:169–70). Nekrasov and Dostoevsky replace the powerful male steed (*kon'*) of folklore with a bedraggled female nag (*kliacha*), implying that this horse symbolizes the silent (nonverbal), long-suffering Russia of the *narod* (common folk).[18] The potential murderer raises his hand against a world of "Christian" time, the world of Lizaveta, Sonya, and Raskolnikov's own child-self. This horse is a far cry from the proud steed of Peter, raised on its haunches and poised, like Russia, to leap into the future,[19] or the spirited troika of Gogol, emerging, like Russia again, from the multiform countryside onto the highroad of history. Here the death of the horse is still not "apocalyptic," since the narrator stops short of linking its end with the larger shape of Russian history. It can be inferred, however, that human beings are capable of bringing on their own end and the end of those around them as soon as they replace *higher* reason (guided by moral "intuition") by *lower* reason (simple verbal logic), thus enabling the conclusion that murder can be an act of the mind alone. That Dostoevsky was now coming closer to an apocalyptic view of Russian history, with Raskolnikov's dilemma expanding into the larger issue of Russia "at the crossroads," is seen in the hero's last dream in Siberia. Raskolnikov is finally made to understand, by the sprung logic of a dream, what his mind has managed to avoid throughout the long and circuitous telling of his story up to this moment: when used to measure morality, reason is a plague (see the locusts that have "human faces" and are arrayed like "horses for battle" of Rev. 9:1–11), presumably emanating from the West,[20] that will bring on the wholesale destruction of humanity. Immediately following this revelation Raskolnikov has his silent conversion ("They [Sonya and Raskolnikov] wanted to speak, but couldn't find the words") and his story crosses a narrative threshold that words cannot describe ("But here begins another story . . . ") (6:421–22).

In *The Idiot*, which will be examined more closely in a moment, Dostoevsky makes broad use of the Johannine Apocalypse, including pointed reference to the third and fourth horses of Revelation 6:1–8. By this time the nagging premonition that *mundi termino appropinquante* was entering the author's consciousness through a variety of channels: (1) the patriotic feelings he felt moved to express in frank correspondence with his friend the poet Apollon Maikov, who during this same period (February–July 1868) was working on a new verse translation of the Apocalypse (28.2:298; May 18/30, 1868); (2) his growing anxiety as he followed the latest news from Russia, including details of the Zhemarin murders (to be reproduced in *The Idiot*) in the March 10 issue of *The Voice;* (3) his close-hand view of Mikhail Bakunin and the Russian revolutionary movement in exile at a conference in Geneva the previous fall (September 1867); and (4) his gathering animus against Europe (especially Switzerland), which was beginning to reach a fever pitch.[21] Dostoevsky embodies these concerns in his art not only thematically but structurally; he visualizes the shape of contemporary history, including what he felt to be the critical 1860s, by reincarnating the flesh-and-blood horse of biblical and folkloric tradition in the horse of modern times: the train (see Bazanov, *Esenin*, 153–58). Similarly, the open road that once lured Chichikov and his vegetative Russia into a future of epic proportions becomes the rails of historicist logic that lead to a radically different terminus, one in which Russia's sleeping beauty can never be awakened.

By the writing of *The Devils*, the apocalyptic movement that began in *Crime and Punishment* and gathered momentum in *The Idiot* reaches national and international proportions. The narrative opens with a description of Stepan Trofimovich Verkhovensky, the "free thinker" of the 1860s, who is modeled on the famous Professor Timofei Granovsky and represented as "father" to the coming minions of the Antichrist, as progenitor of the "Time of Troubles" that begins two decades later. As a way into the mentality of those early years, when Dostoevsky himself fell under the sway of the liberal Belinsky and then the more radical Petrashevsky Circle (see Frank, *Seeds*, 159–291), the narrator hilariously recounts a poem written by Stepan Trofimovich in his youth, a parody of the minor poet and one-time liberal V. S. Pecherin.[22] But the humorous veil of parody is torn by a thrust of high seriousness when the reader suddenly realizes that the silly decorative image of a "youth of indescribable beauty [entering] on a black horse" (10:10)[23] is in fact the Stavrogin of the 1860s. Like Stepan Trofimovich, the handsome and daring Stavrogin was modeled on a real-life figure of the 1860s, Nikolai Speshnev, a revolutionary of almost mesmerizing charm.[24] Significantly, the youth "depicts death, which all peoples are thirsting for" (10:10).[25] In the characterization and field of action accorded to Stavrogin then, whose name, suggestive of the Antichrist, is a combination of *stavros* (cross) and *rog* (horn), Dostoevsky takes the final step begun in the earlier works: he joins the image of the apocalyptic horseman with that of the coming revolution, and thereby makes explicit what had hitherto been largely implied. When later in the novel Pyotr Verkhovensky ecstatically identifies Stavrogin with "the leader of the flagellants, Ivan Filippovich, [who] had been seen ascending into heaven on a chariot before a multitude of people" (10:326), we are confronted not only with a cherished folk image – the prophet Elijah (Ilya) – but, more important, with a Gogolian vision of horse-drawn deliverance, of movement up and out of this world and time. Dostoevsky's irony of course is that what for the benighted people appears to be a savior is in fact a parody, a mask, a straw man, and that what seems like an ascent into a better place and time is on the contrary a descent into revolution, chaos, death.

Dostoevsky's last significant use of the horse-and-rider motif comes in *The Adolescent* (1873), his penultimate novel. Arkady Dolgoruky, the title character, has a vision of Saint Petersburg, the new Babylon, as it disappears into an abyss. All that remains of the city's original splendor is the striking outline of the bronze statue on the "hotly breathing, *driven* [*zagnannyi*] steed" (13:113):[26] Pushkin's steed, once a prime mover of Russia's imperial ambitions and a symbol of its national will, is being driven from the stage of Russian history (see Dolgopolov, "Roman A. Belogo," 219). To Dostoevsky at least, its time has come and gone. In the years to follow, as the "realistic" novel yields its position of privilege to shorter forms with their fin-de-siècle aesthetic and metaphysical concerns, the Symbolists will be responsible for an explosive proliferation of this same equine motif. But, closer to the coming revolution and consumed by an ever greater and more self-destructive urgency, they will reverse the formula and equate the soon-to-be-unleashed fury of the *narod* with the force of an avenging Bronze Horseman. Still employing the mythological imagery of Dostoevsky and his predecessors, they will stand his essentially conservative political worldview on its head. In Bely's *Petersburg* in particular, the ambiguous historical role of Peter – Is he an authoritarian father figure or a rebellious son? – will be seen as a chief source of apocalyptic tension, and the Bronze Horseman and the new Evgeny (Dudkin), as paternal and filial extensions of the same chaos, will join hands in a pact with universal death.[27]

---

*The Idiot* is the first of Dostoevsky's novels, and indeed one of the first Russian novels,[28] in which the railroad assumes a significant role. The first railroad in Russia, a short line, had been opened between Saint Petersburg and Tsarskoe Selo as early as 1837,[29] and Moscow was joined to Saint Petersburg by rail in 1851 (while Dostoevsky was still doing hard labor in Siberia). But it was only under Alexander II (ruled 1855–81) that Russian railroading developed in earnest. In 1856 construction was undertaken to extend rail lines from Saint Petersburg both westward (to Europe) and eastward (to Siberia). In James Billington's words, "For Russia, the new railroads brought the first massive intrusion of mechanical force into the timeless, vegetative world of rural Russia, and a great increase in social and thus class mobility throughout the empire. . . . Railroads . . . became a symbol of progress to the new materialistic and egalitarian students of the sixties" (*Icon*, 384). We get some sense of the liberal intelligentsia's early naive faith in the machine (*mashina* meaning both "machine" in general and train in particular) and their attachment to it on the semantic level of such notions as "progress" and "usefulness" (*pol'za* was a term of special odium to Dostoevsky) from a lead essay written in 1839 by a certain A. Bashutsky for the journal *Notes of the Fatherland:*

> The application of steampower to movement over water and dry land, [and] the railroads, which are obliged to the steam engine for their miracles . . . these are the great forces stimulating growth in the physical and rational capabilities of man. . . . Movement is a given [*dvizhenie dano*], and the enlightened world cannot stop; it must continue always to move forward; success is essential; its is a status that is compulsory [*vynuzhdennoe*], already unalterable, a basic condition for existence.
>
> It is in vain that we would begin now to judge and pontificate at

> random – this is not the time to heed the cries of fear and indignation, the gloomy predictions of old men, the irrational assumptions of the short-sighted and the ignorant: the shining core [or nucleus: *svetiashchee iadro*] has been set in motion, it flies on, swallowing space and illuminating cities, seas, and deserts beneath itself. And peoples, who have been separated from one another for a long time and perhaps at odds, can [now] be tightly joined together by the bonds of fellow-feeling and mutual interest" ("Parovye mashiny," 6).

This view of the train as a vehicle capable of penetrating not only hitherto unreachable geographical but also social or class boundaries will be taken up from the first pages of *The Idiot*, where a prince, a merchant's son, and a down-and-out government official meet in a third-class coach of the Warsaw–Saint Petersburg express. Here high class meets low, East (Russian native traditions) meets West (Poland, Europe, Dostoevsky's hated Roman Catholicism) in that raucous, melting-pot atmosphere of "polyphony" described by Bakhtin (*Problems*, 5–53).[30] The literal terminus for all this movement, both physical and dialogic, is the station, the place in *The Idiot* that frames or is the site of numerous scandal scenes.

The railroads became then a vital question to the liberals of the 1860s (Belinsky being their chief spokesman) and to the "enlighteners" of the 1860s (Chernyshevsky, Dobrolyubov, Pisarev).[31] In his memoir of Belinsky, Dostoevsky recalled how the famous critic met him once in the late 1860s near the Znamenskaya Church and led him to the construction site of the new Nikolaevsky Station (21:12). The two talked about the future of railroading, about how trains would change the economic face of Russia through their rapid and cost-efficient distribution of commodities such as timber. But the context and setting of this remembered conversation are curious. As the same episode is recounted in the drafts of *The Devils* (10:73), it is Belinsky's atheism, his sarcastic attempts to "convert" the young Dostoevsky, who was still impressionable and deeply attached to his naive ideal of Christ, that triggers the recollection of the talk about railroading that follows immediately.[32] In this respect, Belinsky's (and the young Dostoevsky's) "progress" from church to station may be relevant, suggesting that homage at a traditional temple was being undermined and replaced by homage at a new and more modern place of worship. Whatever the precise meaning of these events, after his years in Siberia and his genuine conversion (in a direction that would have made Belinsky turn in his grave), Dostoevsky did come to associate the railroad with the spread of atheism and the spirit of the Antichrist. This new awareness is demonstrated in *The Idiot* on many occasions.

At the same time that the train as a symbol of progress and mechanical force was being viewed with an optimism bordering on euphoria by Belinsky and his followers, it was being viewed with anxiety and skepticism by those of a more conservative stripe (the "*old* men," with their "*irrational* assumptions," in the passage quoted above).[33] If the horse had ties to an older agrarian or nomadic view of the world, one in which the controlling hand, either at the plow or in the saddle, belonged to an *individual*, then the train had ties not only with the concept of newness and progress but with that of *collective* movement. The reins of fate, as it were, were taken out of the individual's hands and given back to the (mechanical) beast; the lone rider on his steed or the lone peasant urging on his workhorse in the field became the group of passengers, the societal microcosm, being driven by the train. As Prince Vyazemsky, Pushkin's old friend, wrote in 1847, "Railroads have already annihilated, and in time shall completely annihilate, all previous means of transportation. *Other fires, other steams have long ago put out the fire of the winged horse*" (*Pss* 2:353). Dostoevsky himself, in a heavily satiric piece entitled "On the Road" (1874), made the mythic connection between the folkloric steed that was by then all but extinct as a major mode of public conveyance and the iron steed that had come to replace it: "I have in mind the road [traversed by means] of steam, [that of] the train and the steamship. As one peasant recently expressed it, we, the inhabitants of capitals, have begun to forget completely the roads of former times, the roads 'driven by horse'" (21:159).[34]

It is also true that Dostoevsky was never narrowly consistent. His view of the railroad could be either xenophobic and negative or jingoistic and positive, depending on whether he was looking toward Europe, where, as we learn from an important passage in *The Idiot*, the network of railroad lines was poisoning the "waters of life" (Rev. 7:17, 8:10, 21:6), or whether he was looking toward home, where for political reasons the training of "practical" railroad personnel and the construction of more efficient and extensive lines needed to be made a national priority.[35] Still, Dostoevsky's letters and journalism, while often supplying the source material and point of departure for a theme, are not the same as his art, where that theme may be reworked according to a wholly new set of demands. What, on balance, can be said is that the "Slavophile"[36] Dostoevsky of the late 1860s and 1870s was genuinely concerned by the inroads of Western materialism into the "organic" world of the *narod*, and that he "novelized" this abstract fear with the help of a concrete image for time (inroad = railroad). His thoughts would probably have been very close to those of a rector of the Riga Theological Seminary, who when asked in 1872 to bless a new railroad bridge expressed the following doubts: "Will it [the new route] not be in part the expediter of that would-be civilization, which under the guise of false all-humanity and common brotherhood of all . . . destroys . . . true humanity, true brotherhood?" (cited in Billington, *Icon*, 382).[37]

No discussion of railroading in the context of *The Idiot* would be complete without brief mention of that other great novel of the period in which the contest between competing loves (erotic-maternal) launches the heroine on an "iron path" to suicide.[38] *Anna Karenina* (1873–77) was written just a few years after *The Idiot*, and it is noteworthy, if not remarkable, that Tolstoy resorts to precisely the same symbol complex (the train, the horse) to prefigure Anna's ruin. Although the styles, subjects, and worldviews implicit in the "realisms" of Tolstoy and Dostoevsky are versts apart, the great chronicler of Russia's aging patriarchal order and aristocratic *moeurs* was as deeply concerned as Dostoevsky about the erosion of traditional values and as anxious to find a way, in novelistic terms, to express the momentum of this deterioration. Tolstoy's remarks to Turgenev, in a letter of April 1857, show to what extent his feelings toward the railroad anticipate the ideational structure of both his and Dostoevsky's novels: "The railroad has the same relationship to travel as a brothel does to love: just as convenient but just as *inhumanly mechanical* and *murderously monotonous*" (Tolstoi, *Perepiska*, 95; my emphasis). Like Dostoevsky, Tolstoy frames his heroine's story, the beginning and end of her "journey," with pivotal scenes at the train station. Anna first meets Vronsky at the station in Moscow and is frightened ("It is a bad omen" [*Anna Karenina*, 60]) by the death of the watchman that anticipates her own. On her return trip to Saint Petersburg, she falls into a dangerously impressionable state in which the snowstorm raging outside the coach mirrors her inner turmoil and, pursued by Vronsky, gives him the hope he seeks; on this same trip she also has her first dream of the peasant who is associated with a dreadful squeaking and clattering sound and with someone "being torn to pieces" (93) and who reappears at the rails at the moment of her suicide. Even her son, Seryozha, the chief victim of the affair, is figuratively drawn into it when, abandoned by his mother, he is told by his tutor not to play the "dangerous game" of railways (638).

As in the case of Nastasya Filippovna, there is something both noble and pathetic in Anna's dilemma; she too is a victim of her own life force and sexuality, of a "fall" that divides her biography into a once meaningful "before" and a now unanchored, chaotic "after." In some sense she is the embodiment of Russia herself, with her "excess vitality" (36), at a crossroads of history, but this same vitality becomes her undoing when its sole outlet is mediated by the Western values of Saint Petersburg high society. Tolstoy's placing of *French* words, the language of Anna's circle, in the mouth of the terrifying native peasant of her dreams is additional evidence of how confused her value system has become. In the moments leading up to her suicide Anna's eyes are riveted to one image: the large iron wheels

(692, 694, 695) that, moving pitilessly along the rails, are both the instrument of her death and a constant reminder of the vicious circle of her love ("Then, realizing that in her attempts to quiet herself [in Vronsky's absence] she again *completed the circle* she had gone round so often, and had returned to her former cause of irritation [i.e., jealousy], she was horror-struck at herself" [671]).

This confusion as to the past, tradition, "Russianness" itself, is further reinforced in the famous episode at the races. Here, rather than Levin's massive, plodding workhorses, we find high-strung thoroughbreds gathered for society's entertainment. These latter perform no vital function in Russia's agrarian life, but, for the sheer sport of it, are made to endanger themselves and their riders by leaping a series of artificial obstacles along an elliptical track. Vronsky's horse, a mare, is given the French name Frou-Frou (which, in terms of sound repetition, suggests a foreign version of *Anna*)[39] and several other traits (unruly mane, excitability, sparkling eyes, "thoroughbred quality" [166]) obviously reminiscent of the heroine. Vronsky breaks the back of his favorite horse just as his self-centered Western values, his relentless amorous attentions followed by his equally inevitable cooling, will eventually crush Anna. In various ways, he is unable "to keep pace" (Blackmur, "Dialectic," 907). Although he tries to legitimize their relationship as best he can given the fact that he knows only how to run "unalterably and inevitably along . . . [the] customary rails of social and regimental connections and interests" (138), his love affair with Anna is no more than an exhibition, a thrilling contest set in a closed, and ultimately deadly circle with no other goal in sight save an arbitrary finish line. Thus Tolstoy, like Dostoevsky, prefigures his heroine's doom through a series of mechanical and equine images of relentless movement in a novel far more symbolically patterned than earlier works. For manifest aesthetic and philosophical reasons, he does not mention the Apocalypse in this context, nor does his novel in any explicit way suggest a transfiguration of the biblical plot. Nevertheless, the structural parallels between *The Idiot* and *Anna Karenina*, especially the way in which a thematic motif is gradually transformed into a "world picture" of Russian history in crisis, are profound and worthy of closer study.

———

The scene that opens *The Idiot* is sufficiently dramatic to attract the attention of any reader, and one must assume that this was Dostoevsky's primary intention.[40] But the drama here, involving Myshkin, Rogozhin, and Lebedev, also sets up a metaphysical pro and contra that the author, a past master of the use of mystery and tension in narrative form, knew he would have to resolve at some later point. The visual field of the narrative is immediately dominated by Myshkin and Rogozhin, who are seated "opposite one another" (*drug protiv druga*) at the same time that they are bound by a hidden kinship through the anaphoric use of "both" (*oba*):

> Two passengers had found themselves sitting *opposite one another* by the window of one of the third-class compartments since daybreak – *both* of them young men, *both* traveling light, *both* far from fashionably dressed, *both* of rather striking appearance, and, finally, *both* anxious to start a conversation *with one another.* Had they known what was so extraordinary about them at this moment, they would no doubt have been surprised that chance should have strangely placed them *opposite one another* in a third-class compartment of the Warsaw-Petersburg train. (Mag 27; 8:5; my emphases)

Here at the very outset we find an unmistakable shaping of the story to come. The narrator's admission that "had they known what was so extraordinary about them at this moment" and that "chance should have strangely placed them opposite one another" implies that the meeting is pregnant with possibility and that significant happenings are in store. The superficial comparison of these young men, so alike at the first sweep of the narrative eye ("both"), will soon recede before the more important *differences* of character that set the story in motion. The arrangement of Myshkin and Rogozhin in the space of the coach suggests what the narrative will soon bear out: they are, as it were, metaphysical Siamese twins, unable to move without straining the painful integumentary seam of their different loves for Nastasya Filippovna. They want to talk, to enter into discourse "with one another," but a communality of words will always elude them. In this sense, their stance will remain, as Bakhtin would argue, dialogic, "one against the other" (*drug protiv druga*).

Nevertheless, the function and ultimate purpose of this dialogic relationship is *not* to keep conversation (and narration) "open." It is an "opening" and "openness" only *for a time*, since what begins here starts the process toward the closure, the total blackout and eerie silence, of Nastasya Filippovna's death. In this initial meeting of the heroes, as in the final one at her deathbed, the heroine is mentioned in absentia. And indeed, the Nastasya Filippovna for whom Myshkin and Rogozhin compete will never be fully present either as her "ideal" or as her "real" self, but will always be caught somewhere in between. Perhaps most telling, the bustling, volatile movement of this beginning, which the train embodies ("The Warsaw train was approaching Petersburg at full speed" [Mag 27; 8:3]) and by which Nastasya Filippovna comes to be constantly driven,[41] disappears in the end of the novel: the terminus so painfully sought after will at last be reached, and the heroes, this time with desperate gestures revealing the failure of words, will once again sit down "opposite one another" (Mag 652; 8:303) to contemplate the fate of their Sleeping Beauty. All this is not of course to suggest that Dostoevsky had the ending of his novel in mind when he wrote the beginning. Such an argument would be another instance of literally "getting ahead of ourselves" where the history of the text does not warrant it (see Hollander, "Apocalyptic Framework," 123–31). It would be more accurate to say that the relationship between Myshkin and Rogozhin initiated on these rails is bound to lead somewhere, and, as the narrative progresses, a conclusion, not inconsistent with what has come before, gradually emerges.

The role of the train in this opening scene is first of all realistic. It provides a place for these three characters to meet and carries them to Saint Petersburg, one of the novel's two primary settings. Along with other features, it also gives the novel a stamp of "modernity." But its figurative function for the novel's subsequent development is no less important. It brings a Russian who knows nothing of his country's present into contact with a Russian who lives fully in, and is a product of, that present. (Lebedev's role in the opening is significant, as indeed it will be later on, for as go-between and "know-it-all" [*vseznaika*] he is able to supply information of which the innocent Myshkin is unaware and which the sullen Rogozhin would be apt to withhold.) The Prince comes from a romantic Switzerland – not the object of derision found in Dostoevsky's letters, but a land of waterfalls, mountain vistas, and the pathetic "fairy tale" about Marie.[42] Dostoevsky thus creates the narrative effect of dropping a hero onto earth from another planet. An orphan in various senses, Myshkin has no past continuous with the present; his bout with epilepsy and gradual recovery in a foreign country constitute a temporal vacuum that others might fill with memories of youth. He is, we might say, a character of beginnings (he offers Nastasya Filippovna "new life") and ends (he is obsessed by thoughts of execution and death), but never of any continuous middle. He cannot "develop" in any traditional sense because he is Christlike and "positively beautiful" to begin with.[43] Also, because he is the last of an aristocratic line without any means – that is, sexual potency – of extending it, his very genealogy, and the historical future of his kind, must be brought in question. Like Christ, who is sent into time by God, the Prince is sent into the "moment" of the story by his author to explain to the other characters that there are meaningful beginnings and ends beyond the aimless flux of the middle. That is to say, Myshkin, according to our typology for apocalyptic fiction, is that "messenger" figure come, as it were, from another space-time to deliver his "revelation" to those trapped in this world.

Rogozhin, on the other hand, is the essence of the struggling middle that Dostoevsky identified with human nature at the bier of his first wife. His family has links with the Old Believers, those vociferous advocates of religious tradition and opponents of the

Petrine Antichrist.[44] Moreover, the greed of the father is visited on the son in the form of possessive sexual passion. The father's death, retold in the context of Rogozhin's attempts to buy Nastasya Filippovna with diamond earrings, inspires no real change in the status quo but only effects a transfer of money from one generation to the next. Taken together, these legacies serve to mire Rogozhin in the continuous present. Both as actual mode of conveyance with a geographical destination and as chronotopic symbol for movement with no higher goal beyond itself, the train is a logical site for this confrontation. Not only does it join opposing concepts of space (the Prince's idyllic Switzerland versus Rogozhin's capitalistic Saint Petersburg); more significant, it joins opposing concepts of time (the beginning and end beyond history versus the middle that is synonymous with it).

Throughout part 1 the train continues to be used as a framing device with thematic import. As we learn from Myshkin himself when he retells his experiences in Switzerland to the Epanchin sisters, the period of his "new life" began the moment he left the waterfall, the children, and the memories of Marie behind and boarded the train for Russia: "As I sat in the train [*vagon*], I thought: 'Now I'm going among people; I may not know anything, but a new life has begun for me.' . . . When I had taken my seat in the carriage and the train started, they [the children] all shouted 'Hurrah!' and stayed on the platform until the train was out of sight" (Mag 102–3; 8:64–63). And as he goes on to exclaim in almost the same breath, "Listen, when I came in here a short while ago and looked at your dear faces . . . and heard your first words, I couldn't help thinking that perhaps I am lucky, for, you see, I know you don't often meet people to whom you take a liking at once, but I met you as soon as I left the train" (Mag 103; 8:65). In this rapid file of impressions, the train functions as a kind of time machine, moving the hero from an idyllic[45] and now separate past of happy endings (the children shouting "Hurrah!") to an uncertain, but still hope-filled present (the "new life" associated with the Epanchin daughters and the childlike Lizaveta Prokofievna). It is also noteworthy that the story of Marie, with its disturbed and guilt-ridden heroine finally finding forgiveness through Myshkin, is an obvious template for the story of Nastasya Filippovna to come.[46] Here difference seems to outweigh similarity, however: the setting (time-place) of the new heroine's tragic story will be contemporary Saint Petersburg. When later in part 1 the Prince meets Nastasya Filippovna face to face, he is drawn to recount, in the manner of a preface, how her story first came to his attention *on a train:* " 'Early this morning, in the train, before I arrived in Petersburg, Parfyon Rogozhin told me a lot about you' " (Mag 134; 8:89).The end of one love story and the beginning of another are therefore fused in the motif of the train.

The image of the apocalyptic steed also makes its first elliptical appearance in part 1. The heroine's full name is Nastasya (from Anastasya, "woman returned to life") Filippovna (daughter of Filip, "lover of horses") Barashkova (from *barashek,* "lamb"). She is, furthermore, the only major character whose story remained essentially intact from Dostoevsky's various plans to the final version, a fact indicative of the author's sharply focused and unwavering conception of her from beginning to end (Wasiolek, "Introduction" in *Notebooks,* 10–12). As it turns out, her given name involves a bitter irony: like the Mary Magdalene on which she and Marie are modeled, she wants desperately to be returned to (prelapsarian) life, to that innocent condition existing at Otradnoe before the "fall" at the hands of Totsky;[47] her patronymic, however, binds her to an inherited passion for horses, that is, to an urge to incorporate into her life story the speedy and inevitable means to its apocalyptic end.[48] Unlike Marie, Myshkin's other heroine cannot separate the guilt of her past from the continuous present. And so, like the lamb of her surname, she remains forever a sacrificial victim awaiting Rogozhin's knife.[49] When, at the conclusion of part 1, she refuses the Prince's proposal (the "new life" she desires), leaves her birthday party (an occasion signifying a return to origins and lost innocence), and flees with Rogozhin in a flurry of troikas to a "terrible orgy at the Ekaterinhof Station" (Mag 208, 210; 8:148, 150), her future assumes a definite shape for the first time. The repeated references to her as a "lost" or "doomed" woman (*pogibshaia zhenshchina*)[50] make the connection clear. Thus while the favorite animal of the "Prince Christ" is the ass (*osel*), the alter ego in the animal world for the frantically driven and ultimately suicidal Nastasya Filippovna is the horse.[51]

---

The first half of part 2 (chapters 1–3) takes place in Saint Petersburg; the second half (chapters 6–12) takes place in Pavlovsk, a "green world" of dachas and country living outside the city. In each of the first three parts of the final version of the novel Dostoevsky begins with prominent mention of the train, but it is in the early chapters of part 2 that the image and its surrounding context take on marked apocalyptic overtones (Hollander, "Apocalyptic Framework," 131). Now, prepared by the wild conclusion to part 1, the reader witnesses a tangible *foreshortening* of those options only recently open to Myshkin and the other characters. If the effect of his Christian goodness and unwillingness to judge was heretofore an "open book," from this point on we can sense a definite and ominous narrowing in his story. In addition, the ending, with explicit reference to Rogozhin's knife, is alluded to for the first time.

This new narrowing of possibilities is most keenly felt when the hero, having visited, in a six-month interval, other parts of Russia and mixed with the *narod*, begins to act in a manner qualitatively different from what we have come to expect. Suddenly he is given an all-too-human trait: he is able to judge. In his mind he imputes evil intentions to Rogozhin that then – quite in accordance with the law of the Dostoevskian world which stipulates that the reality of thought is prior to that of action – materialize. The fact that Myshkin does not *want* to judge his "brother" and indeed tries every means to repress his fear is of no matter, since the thought *exists*. It is as if the two temporalities associated with Myshkin and Rogozhin, which in part 1 were perceived as separate and counterbalancing, have been conflated within one consciousness, brought together and applied as a dual optic through which to interpret the meaning, the *causality*, of events. The result is a combined sense of prescience and modal disorientation (a "revelation") as to which point of view should be determining our response. This disorientation begins at the train station and thereafter continually reasserts itself there. Hence, rather than the distinct messenger of biblical revelation who delivers knowledge of a higher design to a member of the elect, Myshkin becomes both messenger from beyond *and* victim (and *victimizer*) within history. This is an extraordinary gambit on Dostoevsky's part: his "positively good" hero, without any particular motivation, is now seen as not only incapable of healing those sick at heart but as actually contributing to their affliction with his benignly discontinuous spatiotemporal model. In fact, he himself seems strangely prone to ambient infection. (The Prince's sudden vulnerability to the wages of a continuous, postlapsarian temporality is most obvious, as shall be seen, in the first appearance of his special affliction, the "falling sickness.") To be sure, Myshkin is not now, nor will he ever be, fully dimensionalized as a fallible human character; it is simply that an important, if incremental, first step has been taken in that direction. In any event, while the question of causality remains moot, one could argue that the hero's flawed perception, his "judgment" of his friend, is brought on by the excitability preceding an epileptic attack. As Dostoevsky explained to his niece in an oft-quoted letter written on the eve of his work on part 2, "The main idea of the novel is the depiction of a positively good man. There is nothing on earth more difficult than that, and especially *nowadays*" (28.2:251; January 1/13, 1868; my emphasis). It is at this juncture in the novel that the "nowadays," the forceful and combative voice of the 1860s, begins to take the upper hand in its dialogue with the positively good Myshkin and his ecstatic temporality.

The change in the Prince's character generates an attendant shift in narrative momentum, and this shift is in turn announced through a constellation of interrelated motifs. These motifs are not merely atmospheric; they attach themselves to specific temporal categories (past, present, future) and to their narrative counterparts (beginning, middle, end). They can be summarized as follows: the garden (*sad*) signifies past/beginning; the railroad (*zheleznaia doroga*) and the machine (*mashina*) signify present/middle; and the station (*vokzal*) and the knife (*nozh*) signify future/end. As the temporalities represented by Myshkin and Rogozhin meet once more and clash, there is, not unexpectedly, a certain semantic overlap. The machine, for example, can suggest both the engine/train motif *and* the guillotine/knife motif. That is to say, it can serve to introduce the meaning of future/end into the context of present/middle. Or the knife can be of the "garden" variety, thereby fusing in one semantic unit notions of past/beginning and future/end. This obviously makes for a difficult and in some ways confused narrative, but one entirely adequate to the larger task of "revealing" the hero's dilemma in terms of temporal disjunction: both we and the hero must ask, In *which* time is my story unfolding? Dostoevsky often returns to these motifs to create a sense of mounting tension; they will culminate in Rogozhin's attempt on Myshkin's life at the conclusion of chapter 5. With regard to narrative structure, the attempt to end Myshkin's life is also coterminous with a temporary end to the Saint Petersburg chapters; immediately thereafter the story resumes in a strikingly different setting, at Pavlovsk.

Part 2 begins with a brief recapitulation of the happenings at Ekaterinhof Station that framed the climax of part 1 (8:151).[52] In this prefatory first chapter we also learn of the existence of a suitor for Adelaida Epanchin, a certain Prince Shch., who pursues what is "useful" – *poleznyi*, always a suspect word in Dostoevsky's vocabulary – and who has been engaged in the "planning of one of the most important of the newly projected railroad lines" (Mag 216; 8:154, 155). Just a few pages later the generation of the 1860s is caricatured in the person of Lebedev's nephew: this peevish young man turns out to be an outspoken atheist who supports himself by working on the railroad (8:162). The third such occurrence takes place two chapters later when Myshkin explains to Rogozhin how an atheist he met on a train managed to miss the point in his condemnation of religion: "He didn't seem to be talking about that [i.e., God]" (Mag 231; 8:182). Thematically interrelated, these three episodes establish a kind of genetic bond in the reader's mind between the religious (that is, atheistic) and political (that is, rationally self-serving) ideas of the 1860s, on the one hand, and the spatiotemporal metaphor for their dissemination, on the other.

As soon as the Prince returns to Saint Petersburg at the beginning of chapter 2, he feels a strange, piercing glance coming from somewhere in the crowd at the station:

> Two or three days after the Epanchins had left for Pavlovsk, Prince Lev Nikolaevich Myshkin arrived from Moscow by the morning train. No one met him at the station, but as he left the train, the prince suddenly became aware of two strange, burning eyes staring at him. . . . When he looked more attentively, he could no longer see anything. Of course he had only imagined that he had seen those eyes, but it left a disagreeable impression. Besides, the prince, as it was, was pensive and sad and seemed to be worried about something (Mag 220–21; 8:158).

What is curious about this passage is that the eyes, which seem to burn into Myshkin's soul and read his thoughts, are present *before* he actually judges Rogozhin (compare 8:171). They are evidence both of his coming guilt and impressionable pre-epileptic state (the two, to repeat, are not mutually exclusive, but may be seen as different, contemporaneous aspects of the same phenomenon: Myshkin's imminent "fall"). Equally noteworthy is the setting of this inchoate guilt and physical affliction. Unlike the motif that brought Myshkin and Rogozhin together at the outset of part 1, the station is now the location where *alienation* between friends, brought about by the Prince's rival love for Nastasya Filippovna and Rogozhin's jealousy, is underscored. It is no longer the place for a *first* entrance from afar, but is the frame for an arrival with an existing "prehistory"; the hero's notion of time, with its a priori rejection of judgment and of a present continuous with the past (the eyes are "of course . . . only imagined"), has become implicated in the time of his foil, with its rejection of forgiveness and of a present without prior, ulterior motives (the actual awareness of the "strange, burning eyes"). Depending on *whose* eyes are viewing this return, Myshkin's appearance at the station is either innocent or cynical, disarming or threatening. From the station Myshkin proceeds to Lebedev's house. There he meets the entire Lebedev household, including the buffoonish widower himself. Lebedev's role appears to have expanded since part 1. Now, despite his constant lying and pulling of faces, he makes statements that must, in this context, be taken seriously. He claims that the nephew's insistence on personal rights rather than on mercy is tantamount to committing the Zhemarin murders, for that is where such logic leads. Then he speaks, in another access of seriocomic hyperbole, of the death of Countess Du Barry on the guillotine. These comments are particularly telling: they recall Myshkin's story of the condemned man in part 1, when the Epanchin sisters were told how it would feel to experience time at the moment of death and to hear overhead "the iron come slithering down." At this moment, Myshkin had mused, one's brain operates like "an engine [literally *mashina*, 'machine'] going at full speed" (Mag 228; 8:56). Lebedev's reading of this experience is remarkably similar to that of the Prince: "Seeing that he [the executioner] was bending her neck down under the knife and kicking her from behind . . . she began screaming: *'Encore un moment, monsieur le bourreau, encore un moment!'* . . . And for that little moment the Lord will perhaps pardon her, for a greater *misère* than that it is impossible to imagine for the human soul" (Mag 228; 8:164).

It is directly after this outburst that Lebedev accompanies the Prince into the garden[53] and tells him of the present condition of Nastasya Filippovna:

> "Tell me, how did you leave her?" "She was after something" [*I-iskatel'na*]. "After something?"
>
> "I mean, she seemed to be looking for something, just as if she had lost something. . . . She's restless, sarcastic, double-faced, short-tempered . . . ."
>
> "Double-faced and short-tempered?"
>
> "Short-tempered, for she nearly seized me by the hair last time because of something I said. I was quoting the Apocalypse to her."

> "What do you mean?" the prince asked, thinking that he had misheard him.
>
> "I was reading the Apocalypse. . . . She agreed with me that we've arrived at the time of the third horse, the black one, and of the rider who has a pair of balances in his hand, for everything in our present age is weighed in the scales and everything is settled by agreement, and all people are merely seeking their rights: 'A measure of wheat for a penny, and three measures of barley for a penny.' And, on top of it, they still want to preserve a free spirit and a pure heart and a sound body and all the gifts of the Lord. But they won't preserve them by seeking their rights alone, and there will therefore follow the pale horse and he whose name was Death, and after whom Hell followed" (Mag 231–32; 8:167–68).

This heavy-handed passage indicates to what extent the author has, as it were, laid his tarot cards on the table. Clearly Dostoevsky knew that only a character such as Lebedev, performing in the tradition of the Shakespearean "wise fool," could manage such a balancing act between high seriousness and comic bathos. Suddenly the little narratives (Lebedev's argument with his nephew, the anecdote about Countess Du Barry) within the larger narrative (the story of Myshkin, Rogozhin, and Nastasya Filippovna) make sense. The references to death (the Zhemarin murders), the guillotine (a knifelike engine of death), and fear of the end (the "un moment" of Du Barry) can be decoded in terms of Nastasya Filippovna's frantic search "for something" and Lebedev's unorthodox exegesis of the Book of Revelation.[54] According to Dostoevsky's *porte-parole* (spokesman), the plot being worked out in contemporary Russian history and in the fate of Nastasya Filippovna, a victim of that history, is equivalent to *the distance traveled between the third and fourth horses of Apocalypse*, between a society increasingly atomized by its insistence on "rights" and the actualized impulse to self-destruction implied in such a human-centered system of justice (see Girard, *Desire*, 256–89).

Myshkin's next visit is to Rogozhin's. He proceeds to the crossroads (*perekrestok*)[55] of Gorokhovaya and Sadovaya Streets where, full of agitation, he looks over the facade of his friend's house (Mag 235; 8:170).[56] The Prince pauses for a moment as if to take in not only the meaning of the building but the spatiotemporal choice, the "fall" into history, involved by crossing its threshold. He is entering into this "temple" of tradespeople and money changers, as Christ once did, to make his case for a higher currency of exchange among human souls. Once across the threshold, Myshkin is met by Rogozhin, who recalls the time before their rivalry in terms of the *first* train ride: "Remember how we traveled in the same coach from Pskov last autumn – me coming here and you – you wearing that cloak and gaiters – remember?" (Mag 237; 8:171–72). But Myshkin can only think of the burning eyes of the present that betoken his coming fall: "When I got off the train this morning, I saw a pair of eyes that looked at me just as you did a moment ago from behind. . . . I think I must have imagined it all. . . . I'm afraid, brother Parfyon, that I feel almost as I did five years ago when I still used to have my fits [*pripadok* – literally 'a falling down']" (Mag 235; 8:171).

What is implied at this point is that the *horizontal* train ride stands in for the *vertical* motion of the guillotine (the *mashina*) mentioned earlier. *Nozh* (knife), *mashina*, and *zheleznaia doroga* (iron road) are kindred symbols for a time that, if not already fallen, is in the process of falling, a time that cannot be turned back. Myshkin fully understands the force and trajectory of what has been set in motion when he exclaims, "If she marries you [Rogozhin], she will certainly perish" (*za toboiu ei nepremennaia gibel'*) (Mag 239; 8:173). As a possible ending to the love story, the version feared by the Prince is still, for the moment, only an uncut page; hence the image of the *garden* (*sadovyi*) knife in the volume of Solovyov's history that is presented to Rogozhin as a gift by Nastasya Filippovna.[57] But as the strained exchange between Myshkin and Rogozhin continues, the motif of the knife is invoked so frequently and pointedly as to seem hypnotic in its gathering momentum. Rogozhin tells Myshkin that Nastasya Filippovna wanted at one point, in a fit of anger, to kill him with a knife; Myshkin speaks agitatedly of his premonition that Rogozhin will slit Nastasya Filippovna's throat; in her thoughts of marriage,

Nastasya Filippovna is described by Rogozhin as going, like a sacrificial victim, "under the knife"; Myshkin recounts an anecdote (directly after that of the atheist on the train) of a man who "butchered his friend like a ram" over a gold watch. By now there can be little doubt that someone, probably the heroine, will eventually be driven to fill that uncut page of history not with a comic epithalamium but with a tragic bloodletting. Any other ending would frustrate expectations and make this momentum and its shaping ironic in a way inconsistent with what has come before. Dostoevsky is here bound to follow the logic of his fictional method, to see what must happen as he transposes the idea of (wo)man as "transitional being" in history to narrative form.

The final episode in this drama takes place between the time the Prince leaves Rogozhin's and the time Rogozhin tries to kill him on the hotel landing. When Myshkin goes to "The Scales" to find Kolya Ivolgin, he begins to move mechanically, "like a machine" (*mashinal'no*) (8:186).[58] He senses that he may be to blame for something and, as he loses himself in thought, he notices that he has turned up on the platform of the Tsarskoe Selo railroad. After deciding to buy a ticket for Pavlovsk – and thus *not* to go to Nastasya Filippovna's and to arouse Rogozhin's jealousy – he prepares to board the train, but then suddenly, for no apparent reason, he tosses away the ticket and leaves the station. From there he walks on in a daze, driven forward by an "unconscious impulse" (*bessoznatel'noe dvizhenie*) (8:187), until he feels the urge to verify an item that recently attracted his attention in a shopwindow. This urge also provokes more anxiety and confusion about time, since now Myshkin realizes that he has definitely entered his "pre-epileptic stage" (*pripadochnoe vremia*), a time when the categories of past, present, and future interpenetrate and lose their distinct boundaries. The idée fixe is of course a knife, and in the Prince's disoriented mind the potential murder weapon is associated with the train station and Rogozhin's accusing eyes:

> That object, consequently, had impressed him so much that it had attracted his attention at a time when he was in a state of utter

> confusion just after he left the train station. He walked back, looking in anguish to the right, and his heart beat with uneasy impatience. But there was the shop – he had found it at last! . . . He now clearly remembered that it was just then, while standing in front of that shop window, that he suddenly turned around, as he had done only a short time before when he caught Rogozhin's eyes fixed upon him. . . . He felt that he must think it all over very carefully; it was now clear that he had not imagined it at the railway station, that something had really happened to him that was most certainly connected with all his former uneasiness (Mag 257–58; 8:187).

It is of no little significance that only now, shortly before the murder attempt by Rogozhin, does Myshkin have his dramatic monologue about the positive and negative effects of his (and his author's) falling sickness. The sense of higher life, of harmony, joy, and otherworldly synthesis, that the hero experiences during a moment of the aura before the onset of the actual seizure is, he surmises, worth an entire lifetime. The price of this gift, this escape from the chains of history, is the stigma(ta) of "idiocy." At this point Dostoevsky offers one of his most vexing paradoxes, for the reader's praise or censure of the Prince now depends entirely on whether the "idea" he embodies is in any way "tellable." After all, is it possible to tell the story of a character willing to trade his role in a continuously developing plot for an ulterior, extranarratorial vantage that undermines the temporal reality of that plot? How can a fictional hero in the middle of a life, or a reader in the middle of a text, pose questions that can be answered only from *beyond the end?*[59] The author seems to be saying that to look at Myshkin *within* time (narrative, biographical, historical) is to judge him a sick man and a failure: "Reflecting about the moment afterwards, he often said to himself that all those gleams and flashes of the highest awareness . . . were nothing but a disease" (Mag 238; 8:188). But to look at him *outside of* time, when all the struggle that comes between life's beginnings and endings collapses into an instant, is to see only his spiritual beauty: "a great calm . . .

full of understanding and the knowledge of the final cause" (Mag 238; 8:188).

Yet because such spiritual beauty exists, as Myshkin himself says, quoting Revelation 10:6, when "there shall be no more time" (8:189), this paradoxical knowledge is also, as it were, his cross, his "rood of time." It is the burden that must be shouldered because he has been blessed (cursed?) with *both* viewpoints – life before and after the fall – and is unable to superimpose the one on the other. The central contradiction of Myshkin's character brought into focus is that the moment of his salvation and the moment of his fall are simultaneous. Any attempt to join them in a temporal causality (the euphoria is posterior to, and hence derives from, the sickness, and so forth) is to fall back into the "error" of the novel form, with its *différance*, its story of the relation over time between contiguous moments. Here as elsewhere, Dostoevsky shows a remarkable sensitivity to the competing, and, as it were, self-canceling narrative modalities associated with developing or retarding a story, on the one hand, and ending it, on the other. And yet, while his "dialogic" imagination never ignores the opposing elements of an argument, there should be little doubt on which side of the pro and contra his sympathies lie.[60]

The Prince awakens from his reverie to find himself sitting, not fortuitously, on a bench in the Summer Garden. In the hot and heavy air that bodes a thunderstorm, he quickly returns to his former "train of thought." He leaves the garden where he had his vision of harmony and, overcome by the temptation to see Nastasya Filippovna, proceeds along "almost without noticing his way" (*pochti ne zamechaia svoei dorogi*) (Mag 260; 8:189). Once more the topoi converge, but now with even greater intensity, like musical motifs intertwining in a final crescendo:[61]

> "Isn't it criminal, isn't it base of me to assume such a thing [i.e., that Rogozhin would murder] with such cynical frankness?" he exclaimed, his face flushing all over with shame. He was amazed, he stood still in the roadway, as though rooted to the spot. He

> remembered all at once the Pavlovsk station that afternoon and the Nikolaevsky station in the morning, and the question he had asked to his [Rogozhin's] face about those *eyes*. . . . The prince wanted to turn back to his hotel at once; he did, indeed, turn back and go the other way, but a minute later he stopped, thought it over, and went back again in the first direction [*po prezhnei doroge* – literally, "along his former way"] (Mag 261–62; 8:190–91)[62]

Clearly the hero is being drawn toward Nastasya Filippovna (who is not at home) and toward the lapse in faith and brotherly love that a visit to her represents *as if along rails.* Having fallen victim to the strange temporality of what he will later call "double thoughts," he has no strength to turn back. He believes he is going to save Nastasya Filippovna from history *at the same time* that his judgment of Rogozhin causes him to fall back into history. This is presumably what Myshkin means when he acknowledges that a demon of doubt "whispered to him in the Summer Garden" and that this doubt led by its own logic to the picture of Rogozhin standing in the station "like an accuser and judge" (Mag 263; 8:193). The distance between the garden and the station, between the aura and the convulsions, between life "in" and "out" of history is equal, in the collapsed and hopelessly ambiguous time-space of Myshkin's present state, to the path of tragic contradiction covered en route to Nastasya Filippovna's. It is her residence (as it will be Rogozhin's at the end of the novel) that is the psychological "terminus" for this section of the narrative.

Finally, this duel of temporalities is brought to a momentary climax when the Prince, having failed to locate Nastasya Filippovna, arrives at his hotel. He spots Rogozhin in a niche on the landing, and, as the latter emerges from the shadows with a knife in his hand, shouts, "Parfyon, I don't believe it!" (Mag 267; 8:195). The pun is more obvious in the original, where Myshkin's exclamation is rendered literally as "I don't believe" (*ne veriu*). The verb phrase suggests both that the speaker does not believe his friend is capable of murder *and* that the speaker simply does not believe. In the paradoxical temporality of this confrontation, Myshkin has at once kept and lost his faith. Although the first (sanguine) meaning is more in keeping with the character of the hero, both are possible. And as might be expected, it is immediately after his outcry, *in the same instant,* that Myshkin has his *fit* (*pripadok*) of *falling sickness* (*paduchaia*) which, ironically saves him "from the inevitable blow, already *falling* [*padavshego*] at him, of the knife" (Mag 268; 8:195). Dostoevsky manages to spare his favorite hero and continue his story about the end by a kind of optical illusion. By eliding the notions of salvation and judgment, and by describing with the contiguity of words what has just happened simultaneously, he arrests the narrative in midstep and shifts the setting to the green world of Pavlovsk.

---

The shift in setting from Saint Petersburg to Pavlovsk is of considerable importance. Here the story will remain until the very end, when the three lovers return to the city for the novel's climax. As numerous commentators have noted, the structural waywardness of *The Idiot* derives in large part from these very Pavlovsk chapters, since it is in them that the author seems to lose his way. The Myshkin–Aglaya–Radomsky triangle and the impending fate of Ippolit gradually come to the fore just as the original story retreats backstage, creating the impression that the entire artistic enterprise has been bereft of a center. One possible motivation for this sudden atomization of the plot is its hitherto rapid forward movement and eschatological impulse: from this point forth Nastasya Filippovna must remain mostly in the background because her story has progressed *too far;* as was remarked earlier, its ending is in sight and would be difficult to retard convincingly if she were constantly under scrutiny. On the other hand, the Pavlovsk chapters manage to sustain, however circuitously, the relentless momentum begun in the Saint Petersburg chapters. They do so by a sort of narrative detour, a switch to different, but parallel tracks. The obsession with endings characterized earlier by Nastasya Filippovna's constant flight between lovers will be transferred to other characters, most notably to Ippolit. In spite of our expectations, the rustic surroundings of Pavlovsk[63] will not function to disarm the tension between competing egos, to offer a brief "whistle-stop" in the middle of history's ride. Once the human being has entered history there is no way back to Otradnoe. Hence Dostoevsky is able to write his large novel about the End only by *postponing* the climax and inserting in the middle a series of subplots that, while interrelated thematically, have little direct impact on the main plot. The greatest "structural flaw" in *The Idiot,* if it is helpful to pose the problem in such terms, is that the narrative, being concerned with ends, points too soon to its own without being ready to fulfill it. Without diversions, "a story about the End" can become a contradiction in terms.

If Nastasya Filippovna is fated to disappear for much of the last half of the novel, then the author needs an additional cynosure in order to keep his apocalyptic design in plain view.[64] This new focus falls on Ippolit, whose strange and poignant confession constitutes the emotional climax of part 3, Ippolit has much in common with Nastasya Filippovna (see Skaftymov, "Tematicheskaia kompozitsiia," 149–54). In fact, one might go so far as to say that in the story of the consumptive boy Dostoevsky has, mutatis mutandis, reincarnated the story of Nastasya Filippovna. Both characters are "condemned persons" who lash out – the one physically, the other verbally – at an intolerable status quo; both are morbidly consumed by thoughts of impending death; both are volatile mixtures of kindness and cruelty, self-abnegation and self-absorption; and, most revealing, both are forced to choose between the temporalities and attendant moralities embodied by the Christlike Myshkin and the Antichrist-like Rogozhin. Dostoevsky then had ample reason for calling Ippolit "the main axis of the entire novel" (9:277). In this "unleasher of horses"[65] he had found a way to start over and continue an apocalyptic story that had "gone too far." Correspondingly, in neither the notebooks nor the final version is there a character (except for Nastasya Filippovna) more closely associated with apocalyptic motifs, and, indeed, one whose narrated life is more apocalyptically shaped than that of this embittered adolescent.

Like Nastasya Filippovna's outburst at her own birthday party, Ippolit's rambling cri de coeur is set at a similar occasion, this time Myshkin's. The chief difference, one reflective of how far we have progressed from part 1, is that the heroine's hope for a new beginning is now countered by Ippolit's urge to make an appropriate end. The only activity of any significance left open to him by the advanced state of his illness is suicide. His confession is preceded by Lebedev's longest and most pointed seriocomic digression. Once more Dostoevsky's fool returns to his favorite topic, the Apocalypse, and to the lines about the polluted waters of life that, when read through the prism of modern life, yield up an image of the railroad.

> "Our question is whether the 'waters of life' have grown weaker or not with the increase of . . . "
>
> "Railways?" cried Kolya.
>
> "Not of railway communications . . . but of the whole tendency, of which the railways may serve, as it were, as an illustration, as an artistic expression. They hustle, they roar, they rend the air with their noise, they hurry, they say, for the happiness of mankind. 'People are getting too noisy and commercial,' some recluse of a thinker complains, 'there is little spiritual peace.' 'That may be so,' triumphantly answers him another thinker, who is always on the move, 'but the rumble of the carts bringing bread to starving humanity is perhaps better than spiritual peace,' and he walks away conceitedly. But, vile man that I am, I do not believe in the carts that bring bread to humanity! For carts bringing bread to all humanity without a moral basis for that action, may quite deliberately exclude a considerable part of humanity from the enjoyment of what they bring." (Mag 412–13; 8:311–12)

This is as close as the reader will come to a full disclosure of the railroad motif. Lebedev (and his author) question the moral and psychological motivation for material progress. His remarks become more obvious when viewed in the context of a polemical exchange that took place between V. S. Pecherin and Alexander Herzen in

1853 (see 9:393). Pecherin wrote Herzen of his fear that the rising tide of commercialism would engulf the spiritual calm and harmony within the *narod,* but Herzen, a representative of the liberal generation of the 1840s for whom the later Dostoevsky felt only scorn, retorted, "What are you afraid of? Can it be the noise of wheels bringing daily bread to the starved and half-clad masses?" (*Sobranie sochinenii,* 11:402.) By parodying this argument in the pages leading up to Ippolit's confession and by closing the tirade with a lament over the loss of a "binding idea" ("Show me anything resembling that force [i.e., of the 'binding idea'] in our age of vice and railroads" [Mag 417; 8:315]), Dostoevsky lays the tracks, as it were, for the response of the young nihilist who must face the injustice of his own end.

With the possible exception of Kirillov in *The Devils,* there is no other character in all of Dostoevsky's fiction more obsessed with the *now* of his end than Ippolit. This sense of urgency is generated in the very patterns of his language. Over and over again he resorts to some form of *chas* – the Russian word for "moment," "hour," and (in the plural) "watch/clock" – until the time has arrived, by his calculations, to shoot himself.[66] He begins his last will and testament with a series of precise temporal phrases, at least one of which is a familiar allusion to the Apocalypse:

> "What time is it? [*Kotoryi chas*] Don't bother; I know what time it is. The hour is at hand [*Prishel chas*]. Now is the time [*Teper' samoe vremia*]. . . . Tomorrow 'there shall be no more time.' . . . But don't worry. It won't take me more than forty minutes to read – oh, an hour [*chas*] at most." (Mag 420–21; 8:318)

Between the biblical "hour at hand" that gets Ippolit's story under way, the sixty minutes that it takes him to narrate it, and the "now" (*seichas;* literally, "this moment") that serves as the mnemonic prod to pull the trigger (8:348), we witness the full range of how he, and by implication his generation, experience life by the biological clock. All the apocalyptic motifs with which he invests his narrative, including the melodramatic breaking of the seal, the prophecy of universal catastrophe in the pathetic "Après moi le déluge," and the image of the scorpion (see Hollander, "Apocalyptic Framework," 134) suggest that Ippolit wants his passing to be a genuine threshold, something memorable and full of high drama, not, as his nihilism would dictate, "in the nature of things." It is his passionate wish that the time he has chosen – the sunrise following Myshkin's party – be "final" or "ultimate" (*poslednii*). During the hour allotted he vows to speak "only the truth, ultimate and triumphant" (8:322) and to demonstrate how he came to his "ultimate conviction" (8:337).

What Ippolit rebels against is the *injustice* of his early dying, the traducing of his *right* to a longer life. But in Dostoevsky's world it is never justice that bestows grace.[67] Hence the use of an apocalyptic framework for Ippolit's story is primarily ironic. That is to say, this story avails itself of familiar topoi from the Book of Revelation, but not with the aim of telling about the vindication of the righteous. Like the underground man, whose tone may be alternately sincere and sarcastic or indeed both at the same time, the youth does not fully believe in what he is saying. Rather, he uses the occasion to create good theater. On the other hand, as Dostoevsky's ingenious method of narration ensures, it is not for us – just as it is not for the other characters – to judge (see R. Miller, *Dostoevsky and "The Idiot,"* 90–222). The Apocalypse is, first and foremost, about judgment, and Ippolit's story, ostensibly following yet at a more basic level subverting the logic of the biblical text, is about the judgment of one who wants to die having *earned*, through his torments, the good judgment of others. That, however, according to his author's version of theodicy, is impossible without a prior desire for Christian forgiveness and mercy. Ippolit wants to forgive the others their good fortune, but the others deny responsibility for this turn of events. The others (rather haughtily, to be sure) want to forgive Ippolit his embarrassing display of emotion and pathetic suicide attempt, but he refuses "to be judged." For this story to have a "happy ending" the forgiveness would have to come *before* the right to judge, which again implies a totally different and "ahistorical" temporality, not after, as a result of, or reward for, one's tribulations. In the end what emerges from the

"Necessary Explanation" is a second version, or cynical parody, of the Book of Revelation. Its "ghost writer" would not be Christ, but Antichrist, and its sense of overwhelming bitterness and futility accords perfectly with the "just punishment" of its participants, especially Ippolit, who are judged by the implied reader in inverse proportion to their ability to forego judgment (see R. Miller, *Dostoevsky and "The Idiot,"* 203–19).

Ippolit has two visions that open and close his narrative. The first is the dream about his dog Norma and the second is the imagined visit of Rogozhin set within a delirious recollection of Holbein's painting *Christ in the Tomb* (1521). As becomes clear, these episodes are not only powerful indices of psychic health (or disease) and subconscious motivation; more important, they offer a precise reckoning of the changes wrought in Ippolit over time by his rebellion and loss of faith. In the dream about the now dead Newfoundland, a younger Ippolit is trapped in his room with a "terrible creature, a sort of monster" that "looked like a scorpion, but was . . . more hideous" (Mag 427; 8:323). Because of its tridentlike shape and resemblance to a scorpion, this monster has been identified with the Antichrist (Hollander, "Apocalyptic Framework," 135).[68] Yet Norma, though fully aware of the danger ("There was something . . . almost supernatural in Norma's terror" [Mag 428; 8:324]), saves the child from the sting of death he so fears. What is significant about the scene is that she too is afraid and that, in saving the child, she is destroyed. At the end of this passage, as if to link the waking and dreaming worlds and to reinforce the analogy with Christlike self-sacrifice and a human (here the child's) triumph over death, Ippolit declares, "Then I awoke, and the prince came in" (Mag 429; 8:324). Subconscious feelings have intuitively chosen the logic of a wisdom tale/parable and a nonverbal image from the animal world to express what would be inadmissible to the logic of positivism or materialism.

The second vision is a mirror opposite of the first. Describing Holbein's painting of a mutilated and all too human Christ, it is totally dominated by the spirit of death:

> Here [i.e., in front of the painting] one cannot help being struck with the idea that if death is so horrible and if the laws of nature are so powerful, then how can they be overcome? . . . Looking at that picture, you get the impression of nature as some enormous, implacable, and dumb beast,[69] or to put it more correctly, as some *huge engine* [lit., "machine" (*mashina*)] of the latest design, which had senselessly seized, crushed, and swallowed up – a great and priceless being, a being worth the whole of nature and its laws, worth the entire earth, which was perhaps created solely for the coming of that being! (Mag 447; 8:339)

Now the laws of nature, which dictate that all must die, even he who was "most beautiful," are in control. Instead of Norma catching and crushing the beast in her mouth, it is the beast that seizes, crushes, and swallows the "priceless being." And the *mashina* – which Magarshack translates nicely as "engine" (in various senses) – is the root image for this cruel, inhuman force. Furthermore, as if to complete the mirror symmetry, Ippolit associates the end of the vision with the entry of Rogozhin, the incarnation of the all-powerful spirit of death. The moment of truth is made more forceful by the knowledge that the latter's house, with its links to commercial Saint Petersburg, is the setting for the Holbein copy that earlier had captured Myshkin's attention. Thus the "progress" narrated by Ippolit's story is from a meaningful end (Norma/Myshkin) to an end without meaning (machine/Rogozhin). After the boy's suicide attempt, little more can be done to squeeze additional drama from his story; like Nastasya Filippovna, its overplayed hero must dwell in the shadows for much of the remainder of the novel.

By the last chapters of part 4, the narrowing of options once open to the Prince has reached its outer limit. There is no longer any doubt that his good intentions weigh cruelly on those around him. The Prince loses control of himself in a rambling monologue made during a party in his honor and then, in the initial stages of a fit, breaks a Chinese vase, an Epanchin family heirloom that perhaps symbolizes the artistic sense of proportion and grace that he lacks. When the party is disrupted on

Myshkin's account, the formidable patroness Princess Belokonskaya (*belyj kon'*, "white horse") judges him a "sick man" and a social misfit (Mag 396; 9:459). He is further isolated from "proper society" when pity forces him to choose the fallen Nastasya Filippovna over the virginal Aglaya in the dramatic confrontation between heroines. The implied irony is that Myshkin, in following his best Christian instincts, can do nothing to avert the coming tragedy. Quite the contrary, his efforts to move upstream against the powerful current of historical time seem now only to redouble the forces converging rapidly on the climax. The end of the novel becomes not only inevitable, as indeed it has been for several hundred pages, but at last imminent when the author breaks off the Myshkin-Aglaya-Radomsky subplot and returns the major characters and their triangle to center stage.

The novel's final scandal scene takes place on Myshkin's and Nastasya Filippovna's wedding day. Like the birthday parties that earlier played a strategic role in the apocalyptic subtext, this festive occasion might be seen as a fresh start, another new page in the story of life. But Nastasya Filippovna, in her last change of heart, refuses to make such a start. Once again, her story has progressed too far to be rewritten with a happy ending. As she leaves for the church, she catches sight of Rogozhin in the crowd of admirers and screams, "Save me! Take me away! Anywhere you like – now!" (Mag 638; 8:493). Rogozhin responds by seizing her in his arms, passing a hundred ruble note to the nearest coachman, and urging on the latter with, "To the station [*na zheleznuiu dorogu*], and if you catch the train [*a pospeesh' k mashine*] there's another hundred for you!" (Mag 638; 8:493). With this final convergence of money, speed, and iron force, the apocalyptic race, as it were, enters its last leg.[70] The couple returns to the city by train, and Myshkin follows the next day. Perhaps most intriguing, the neutral word for train – *poezd* – that Dostoevsky had employed from the first sentence of the novel is now nowhere to be found.[71] Instead these two return trips are repeatedly described in terms of the *mashina*, a word rich in nineteenth-century folklore and the popular belief/fear that the train is the ultimate "machine" (8:493, 495, 504). This reading is further corroborated by the notebooks, which show a marked role for the word in a scene following the wedding fiasco: originally there was to be, *in the presence of Ippolit*, a "lecture on *machine production* [*mashinnoe proizvodstvo*]" and its ability to "swallow everything"; and the Prince himself was supposed to speak (deliriously?) "about machines" (9:284). The implication is that Dostoevsky, recalling the implacable machine of Ippolit's second vision and intent on working the motif into the narrative, transformed these planned conversations into the actual images of locomotion that accompany the three principals back to Saint Petersburg and the novel's denouement.

The final scene is the most powerful in the novel. It is so not only because that which has been dramatically retarded for hundreds of pages is at last accomplished, but also because the poetics of space and time employed earlier to suggest precipitous forward movement is now used to depict its utter absence. The reader experiences a macabre sense of déjà vu precisely because all this has happened before, but in altered circumstances. Again Myshkin and Rogozhin sit down "opposite one another" (*drug protiv druga*) (8:503); again we realize that the pro and contra of their respective temporalities have been the source of all tension, conflict, movement. Only now there is no tension, as there is nothing for these temporalities to compete for. Neither the "ideal" nor the "real" Nastasya Filippovna is present. The Saint Petersburg station, their initial destination, has been replaced by the morgue-like house at the crossroads of Gorokhovaya and Sadovaya Streets.[72] The heroine has merged into a tragic composite of the two temporalities: the dead bride. Her death epitomizes the curse of judgment, of past lapses forbidding present change, while her wedding dress shows how much she longed for a new beginning. At last she has fully traversed the distance between the black horse and the pale horse. From her hysterical movement *na mashine* (on the train) (8:504) she has, on this *white night* in Saint Petersburg, come to rest against the pale immobility of the setting:

> The prince's heart beat so violently that it seemed it could be heard in the room, in *the dead silence* of the room. But his eyes had

> already got used to the dark, and he could make out the whole bed; someone lay asleep on it in an *absolutely motionless* sleep; not the faintest rustle could be heard, not the faintest breath. The sleeper was covered, from head to foot, with a *white* sheet. . . . All around . . . clothes were scattered – a rich *white* silk dress, flowers, ribbons. On the little table at the head of the bed diamonds, which had been taken off and thrown down, lay glittering. At the foot of the bed some sort of lace lay in a crumpled heap, and on the *white* lace, protruding from under the sheet, the tip of a bare foot could be made out; it seemed as though it were carved out of marble, and it was *dreadfully still.* The prince looked, and he felt that the longer he looked the more *silent* and death-like the room became. Suddenly a fly, awakened from its sleep, started buzzing, and after flying over the bed, settled at the head of it. The prince gave a start. (Mag 631–52; 8:503; my emphases)

All these images of whiteness and stillness surrounding Nastasya Filippovna's nuptial bier reveal to what extent she has realized her personal mythology. The whiteness of virginity is now at one with the paleness of death. Her ride on history's train is over. Whatever motion is left in this *nature morte* is provided ironically by the hovering fly, one of those insects that in Dostoevsky's world are sooner associated with death and physical corruption than with buzzing biological life (see Tate, "Hovering Fly," 17–23). And if Dostoevsky's roots in nineteenth-century realism would not permit such a naked analogy, this heroine, as Vyacheslav Ivanov first noted, also in some sense symbolizes Russia the bride, who must choose *in time* between Christ and Antichrist as suitors. Dostoevsky often expressed exaggerated hopes for his homeland in his correspondence,[73] yet in the honesty of his art, where time must have its own reality, those hopes were transmuted into tragic insight.

---

In a celebrated recent study of Dostoevsky's fiction, Michael Holquist has argued that the central idea of *The Idiot* is "an inspired moment that subsequently fails to change anything" (*Dostoevsky*, 104). This perhaps most difficult of Dostoevsky's major works is primarily, as Holquist continues, about the inability "of *kairos* to affect *chronos*" (122). Such a line of reasoning has its cogency, for it posits a certain tension and dialogic openness characteristic of the *middles* of Dostoevsky's novels. Moreover, Holquist is correct to identify *chronos*, time in history, as the force capable of undoing whatever kairotic ends the Prince might insert in the story of his and the others' lives. It is true that Dostoevsky's view of human life in time is tragic ("der Christ muss scheitern" [the Christian must run aground, be wrecked], as the Swiss theologian Walter Nigg once said).[74] Therefore, to state that in this story of clashing temporalities the idea of time as inevitable continuity comes to dominate the idea of time as radical change is logical, even self-evident, inasmuch as it allows that story in the first place.

But Holquist's reading does not adequately account for the final scene at the bedside of the heroine. Here one finds it difficult to argue that "discourse is open." The dark forces of history without God may have defeated this Ivan Tsarevich and his sleeping princess, but it would be almost perverse to claim that the chief implication of the silence and immobility is ongoing dialogue, continued movement, never-ending struggle. What one can say is that the end of this novel is appropriate to its beginning and middle. It is the end that we knew would come and that now has. To imply that it is another failed epiphany is to see it *within history*, that is, to judge it through the eyes of the characters (and narrator) who ostracize Myshkin. But this death, after all, comes at the *end*, at that privileged moment when the reader leaves the temporality of the narrative to enter the temporality of his or her world. As we know from the notebook entry written on the occasion of his first wife's death, Dostoevsky was painfully aware of the difference between life "in the middle" and life "at the end." In this sense, the viewpoint of his implied reader, who judges the novel's meaning *from the end*, from a temporal vantage above or beyond that which generated the plot, may be taken a step further. A study of the interrelation between aesthetics and metaphysics in Dostoevsky would begin with the assumption that any reader's life is in turn part of a larger plot whose meaning is evaluated by its reader only at the appropriate "Finis." Perhaps then it is not reading too much into this ending to reverse Holquist's conclusion and suggest that Nastasya Filippovna's death *does* represent qualitative change and *is* meaningful in its silence. It is a meaning that is implied rather than stated. It symbolizes the end of the ride, the pale horse whose name is death, the Apocalypse that has come for these people personally and, by an associative logic of which Dostoevsky was certainly aware, *will* come for their country. If it is not a sanguine meaning, it is a meaning nonetheless.

Bakhtinian theory can, like any body of thought, impose its own orthodoxy. What is *only* open can also be closed. To Bakhtin and his followers Dostoevsky's works are best characterized by the sound of competing voices.[75] And in terms of narrative time, this means that the Dostoevskian plot "is set up to do nothing else so relentlessly as to dramatize the absence of essence in chronology, the separation of moment and sequence" (Holquist, *Dostoevsky*, 110). Yet such a viewpoint, apt for a plot in progress, cannot adequately respond to the sense of an ending, where silence and the discontinuation of dialogue obtain – be it Raskolnikov's conversion or Stavrogin's suicide. For Dostoevsky death and rebirth are not merely convenient ploys with which to end a story. They become meaningful when placed in the larger context of God's plot. Apocalypse, lest we forget, means an "uncovering" or "disclosing," and, depending on how one views human history and one's place in it, its revelation can be positive or negative, justificatory or retributive. An end, therefore, may involve a tragic and just punishment, as it does for Stavrogin, or it may involve a new beginning, as it does for Raskolnikov, but both possibilities have their place in the higher design. The forces of history would be victorious and the dialogue would remain open in the event that such characters as Stavrogin and Svidrigailov went "unpunished." Then we might indeed say that an ending is nothing more than a convention, a literary whistle-stop. Yet that is not the case. So it seems only fair, in the ongoing pro and contra generated by Dostoevsky's art, to balance the scales by proposing that he was at least as concerned with giving appropriate artistic form to what he felt was the end of discourse as he was with keeping that discourse open. What lies beyond that end, whether it be of a novel, a life, or a history, was not, as we noted at the outset, within his purview as an artist or an orthodox believer.

## NOTES

1. Parenthetical references to Dostoevsky are to the *Polnoe sobranie sochinenii* (*Pss*). The English translation of *The Idiot* used in this study is that of Magarshack and is abbreviated in the text as "Mag." Liberal changes have been made in the Magarshack translation for the sake of semantic clarity and precision.

A perceptive discussion of the effect of Dostoevsky's apocalypticism on the narrative structure of his "threshold" works – particularly *Diary of a Writer* – is found in Morson, *Boundaries*, 24–26, 33–38. For possible apocalyptic motifs in *The Idiot*, see Cox, *Between Earth and Heaven*, 164–91; Leatherbarrow, "Apocalyptic Imagery"; and esp. Hollander, "Apocalyptic Framework." See as well Mochulsky, *Dostoevsky*, 353–62; Peace, *Dostoyevsky*, 109–24; and Dostoevskii, *Pss* 9:393, 439, 442, 445–48.

2. The phrase is Frank Kermode's. See his influential *The Sense of an Ending* as well as Friedman, *Turn;* D. A. Miller, *Narrative and Its Discontents;* Richter, *Fable's End;* and Torgovnik, *Closure.*

3. For the sake of consistency I shall be using the Russian calendar in all references to Dostoevsky's correspondence. During the period under discussion (1860s) the Russian calendar lagged behind the Western calendar by twelve days.

4. Such misreadings would include, in my opinion, Krieger's making the smug and ultimately judgmental Radomsky into the author's mouthpiece ("Dostoevsky's 'Idiot,'" 49–51); Lord's conclusion that Myshkin is a "princely humbug" and "an open sore, a paranoiac introvert" (*Dostoevsky*, 84, 88); and Dalton's interpretation of Rogozhin's attempt on Myshkin's life in terms of the hero's sexual fantasies and Freudian "primal scene" logic (*Unconscious Structure*, 107–16).

5. The studies by Cox, Leatherbarrow, and Hollander mention numerous possible apocalyptic motifs, but they stop short of showing how an

apocalyptic framework might affect the actual narrative structure of *The Idiot.* For the understanding of apocalyptic time (the difference between *chronos* and *kairos*) as it applies to *The Idiot,* see Holquist, *Dostoevsky,* 102–23; and Terras, "Dissonans," 64.

6. The phrase "neither marries nor is given in marriage" is an allusion to Matthew 22:30.

7. The allusion to Revelation 10:6 ("there shall be no more time"; in RVS, "there should be no more delay") will be taken up at significant moments by Myshkin and Ippolit in *The Idiot.* See below.

8. Cf. the similar situation in "The Meek One" ("Krotkaia"). There too the silence of a dead woman is juxtaposed with the arguments raised by her conscience-stricken husband.

9. "Everywhere and in everything I go to extremes; all my life I have always overstepped the mark" (28.2:207; August 16/28, 1867, to A. Maikov). On the threshold in Dostoevsky see Arban, "Porog"; and Bakhtin, *Problems,* 71–74, 85, 170–74, 204–6.

10. Dostoevsky's obsessive preoccupation with debts, deadlines, and gambling up to and during the writing of *The Idiot* suggests that at some level he *needed* to feel the danger of a crisis situation in order to bring out untapped resources within himself, to perform at the threshold of nervous (and often epileptic) collapse. He even came to look at *The Idiot* in gambling terms as his last possible wager: "In a word, I am throwing myself into the novel as though into an attack [*na ura!*] – headfirst, everything on one card, what will be, will be!" (28.2:227; October 9/21, 1867, to A. Maikov).

11. As Dostoevsky said of himself in a now famous letter of late February 1854 to N. D. Fonvizina, "I am a child of the century, a child of faithlessness and doubt until now and (I know this) until the grave" (28.1:176).

12. In a letter of August 16, 1867, to A. Maikov, Dostoevsky called the 1860s a period that "in terms of its crisis and reforms is nearly as important as that of Peter" (28.2:206).

13. See the discussion of the chronotope in the Introduction to *The Shape of Apocalypse in Modern Russian Fiction.*

*14. Examples are provided by Odoevsky's Russian Nights,* Lermontov's (?) "The Flood" ("Navodnenie"), M. Dmitriev's "The Submerged City," Pecherin's *The Triumph of Death,* and others. See Antsyferov, *Dusha;* and Weidlé, *Zadacha,* 203–27. Numerous examples of the apocalyptically tinged fire motif in turn-of-the-century literature are found in the novels of Valery

Bryusov (*The Fiery Angel*), Remizov (*The Pond, Sisters in the Cross*), and Bely (*Petersburg*). In *Sisters* (1910), for example, the Bronze Horseman is portrayed as a fireman – an allusion that Bely seems to have known, since his character Sophia Petrovna ("Holy Wisdom, daughter of Peter") has a vision of the Bronze Horseman that turns into a fire truck speeding to a fire. See as well *Fiery Russia*, Remizov's book about the revolution.

15. To be sure, there had been a number of Russian "eschatologists" before Dostoevsky. These might include such eighteenth- and nineteenth-century figures (mainly poets) as A. M. Kutuzov, Semyon Bobrov, S. A. Shirinsky-Shikhmatov, M. A. Dmitriev-Mamonov, and V. S. Pecherin. The use of apocalyptic motifs by most of these figures traces to their ties with Freemasonry rather than to medieval Russian tradition. In any event, Dostoevsky is the first major Russian prose writer of whom it can be said that both the form and substance of his work bears the influence of the text of Revelation. For more on the early Russian eschatologists, see Lotman and Uspenskii, "Spory o iazyke."

16. "Something final has taken place here, taken place, and come to an end. It is like a biblical picture, something out of Babylon, a prophecy from the Apocalypse coming to pass before your eyes" (5:70).

17. Cf.: "As a matter of fact, what awaits the world not only in the remaining quarter of this century but even (who knows?) perhaps in this very year? There is unrest in Europe – of this there can be no doubt. . . . It is obvious that the time has come for something eternal, millenarian, for that which has been preparing itself in the world since the very beginning of its civilization" (January 1877; 25:6); "Everyone senses that something final has begun, that an end is coming to former things . . . [and] a step is being taken toward something already completely new . . . and this step is being taken by Russia" (April 1877; 25:94). See the illuminating discussion in Morson, *Boundaries*, 33–38.

18. This dream has important links to an episode in Dostoevsky's youth when he witnessed the beating of a peasant by a government courier. See Frank, *Seeds*, 70–73.

19. Cf. the famous "purple passage" (chapter 2) in Bely's *Petersburg* where Russia is compared to Peter's apocalyptic steed standing poised on its haunches.

20. In the actual text from the "depths of Asia."

21. See, e.g., letters of August 16, 1867–March 21–22, 1868, to A. Maikov (28.2:203–83).

22. Pecherin is the same "eschatologist" mentioned above (note 14). His polemic with the liberal Herzen over the significance of trains figures prominently in Lebedev's long digression on the Apocalypse in *The Idiot* (8:303–16). See discussion below.

23. In Pecherin's original the rider is, significantly, on a *white horse.* See his *Torzhestvo smerti,* in Ginzburg and Kiseleva-Sergenina, *Poety 1820–1830-kh godov,* 2:483.

24. A number of commentators have also mentioned the name of the notorious anarchist Mikhail Bakunin in connection with Stavrogin.

25. Dostoevsky seems to be playing off both Pecherin and the apocalyptic equine motif when he has Pyotr Verkhovensky link his idol Stavrogin with "the leader of the flagellants, Ivan Filippovich, [who] had been seen ascending into heaven on a chariot before a multitude of people" (10:326). Pecherin also has waves of doom appear in "triumphant chariots" (*Torzhestvo,* 2:483). Here the assumed patronymic "Filippovich" (son of Filip [lover of horses]) may be noteworthy when seen against the names of the two characters in *The Idiot* most influenced by the apocalyptic subtext: Nastasya *Filippovna* and *Ippolit* ("unleasher of horses"). To what extent Dostoevsky and his readers were aware of such Greek etymologies is, however, open to doubt. See below.

26. On Dostoevsky's changing attitudes toward the mythical character of Petersburg, see Weidlé, *Zadacha,* 203–27.

27. On this tradition of a split role for the tsar, see Lotman and Uspenskii, "Spory o iazyke," 268–79.

28. The only immediate impact of the first (Saint Petersburg–Pavlovsk and Tsarskoe Selo) railway line on Russian "literature" was in the area of vaudeville: P. S. Fyodorov's "A Trip to Tsarskoe Selo by Railway" (performed seventeen times in Petersburg between 1838 and 1841). By the early 1860s, the theme of the railroad begins to appear elsewhere: e.g., V. A. Sologub's "Adventures on the Railroad," a piece published in *The Dawn* (*Utrenniaia zaria*) for 1842. See Baehr, "The Troika and the Train." The train also plays a role in other works by Dostoevsky: see, e.g., its function in the pseudo-travelogue framework of *Winter Notes.* It of course begins to appear most prominently in works with a travel theme, such as Turgenev's *Smoke* (1867). For more on the railroad as a symbol of revolutionary change, see Al'tman, "Zheleznaia doroga."

29. As one contemporary expressed it, this first railway was a "toy of the

idle" going from "the capital to the pub [i.e., the 'Vauxhall' adjacent to the station in Pavlovsk]" (letter from N. N. Muravyov to Nicholas I of December 3, 1838, in M. Krutikov, ed., "Pervye zheleznye dorogi v Rossii," *Krasnyi arkhiv* 74 [1936]: 87, 127; cited in Baehr, "The Troika and the Train"). This *voksal* (later spelled *vokzal*) in Pavlovsk becomes an important part of the setting in *The Idiot.* Some of the nineteenth- and twentieth-century literary subtexts for the *vokzal* (leading up to Mandelshtam's poem "At the Station") are discussed in Ronen, *An Approach*, xvii–xx, 290.

30. A good example of the social and linguistic melting pot associated with first-, second-, and third-class railroad travel is found in a "physiological sketch" published by an anonymous author ("S") in vol. 54 of the journal *The Contemporary* (*Sovremennik*) for 1855: "The Railroad between Petersburg and Moscow," 43–71. Here the train is repeatedly referred to as a new and potentially perilous *mashina;* there is a sense of bustle and rapid mindless movement as the passengers board the train at the station and say farewell to friends and relatives; and within the different class coaches social boundaries are continually threatened and traduced. Confusion reigns above all in the second-class coach because the passengers don't know how to deal with competing views of difference/equality: one woman, for instance, is angry because she is forced to occupy space that is shared by charwomen, whereas a man nearby complains that, though "we are all equal here" (31), a young dandy has taken the liberty to smoke.

31. As Nikolai Kibalchich, one of the technophiles of the 1860s who would eventually become a revolutionary and plot the 1881 attempt on Alexander II's life, exclaimed: "For Russia railroads are everything. This is the most necessary, most vital problem of our time. *Covering Russia by sections with an interconnected network of railroads* such as exists for example in England, we shall prosper and blossom forth [with] unheard-of progress" (cited in Billington, *Icon* 383; my emphasis). Cf. this passage with the digression by Lebedev (8:303–16).

32. For Dostoevsky's very ambivalent feelings toward Belinsky, see Frank, *Seeds*, 172–98. "If Belinsky had not really introduced Dostoevsky to socialism, he had introduced him to *atheistic* socialism – and this was the only kind that the Dostoevsky of the 1860s believed to be spiritually honest and intellectually self-consistent. . . . The mechanical 'scientific' materialism that Belinsky admired in Littré did succeed in becoming the philosophical dogma of the Russian left for much of Dostoevsky's life. And moral

values were derived from a utilitarian egoism which, if it stemmed more directly from Bentham than from Max Stirner, fully shared the latter's supreme contempt for all sentimental humanitarianism. . . . Dostoevsky thus had good reason to regard his disputes with Belinsky as having foreshadowed the major issues posed by the later development of Russian sociopolitical and cultural life; and his encounter with Belinsky certainly colored his own reaction to such changes" (196–97).

33. In order to calm the fears of those who felt that this mechanical intrusion would destroy faith, Russian railway officials were compelled to hang icons in terminals, to build railroad lines to or near monasteries, and, in the case of the Trans-Siberian Railway, to include a church car with bells and a cross on top (Baehr, "Troika and Train"; see also Massie, *Land of the Firebird,* 174, 376).

34. Cf. Gleb Uspensky's article on the "Suburban Peasant": "Yes, doesn't the same fate sooner or later await the most remote Russian backwater [*medvezhii ugol*] that has already happened in these parts [i.e., the Novgorod province]? Sooner or later a stone and, perhaps, an iron road will proceed through these quiet parts where recently a witch was burned" (*Pss* 6:469–70).

35. Although Dostoevsky could not be called a Slavophile in a narrow chronological sense, he did derive a number of his most cherished ideas from their movement and came to see himself, as letters to Maikov indicate, squarely within their tradition. His hatred of Roman Catholic authority ("unity without freedom") in the West and of the Roman juridical tradition that had developed there into "legalistic" niggling over rights ("individual over community") as well as his advocacy of the "Russian idea" of *sobornost'* (free unity) and of Russia's privileged position in history owe much to the writings of Ivan Kireevsky, Khomyakov, and others. On the difference between Dostoevsky and the traditional Slavophiles, see Kirpotin, *Dostoevskii,* 73–90.

36. See letter of March 21–22, 1868, to A. Maikov in 28.2:277–83. Cf. beginning of part 3 of final version of *The Idiot* (8:268–70), where the narrator bewails the lack of "practical" railroad men and extends the analogy to families (e.g., the Epanchins) who have "slipped off the rails."

37. Apparently the Metropolitan of Moscow had a similar reaction to the proposed railroad line from Moscow to the Trinity-Sergius Monastery: "Pilgrims would come to the monastery in railroad cars, on which all sorts of tales can be heard and often dirty stories, whereas now they come on foot,

and each step is a feat pleasing to God" (Del'vig, *Vospominaniia*, 3: 29; trans. in Westwood, *History of Russian Railways*, 45). Cf. the conservative Leontiev's fear of corrupt Western values as expressed in a train metaphor: "And may the raging and thundering train of the West hurtle past us into the abyss of social anarchy" (cited in Levitskii, *Ocherki*, 126).

38. Both the train ride and steeplechase scenes in *Anna Karenina* have been discussed often. See, e.g., Al'tman, *Chitaia Tolstogo*, 111, and "Zheleznaia doroga"; Browning, "Death of Anna Karenina"; Christian, *Tolstoy*, 204–7; Jahn, "Image of the Railroad"; Muchnic, *Russian Writers*, 134; and Wasiolek, *Tolstoy's Major Fiction*, 134ff.

39. As Eikhenbaum (*Lev Tolstoi*, 190) has shown, the name Frou-Frou appears to have originated from a popular French play of the same name by Henri Meilhac and Ludovic Halévy. Published in 1869, it dramatizes the plight of a heroine who abandons her husband and son for a lover.

40. See R. Miller's perceptive comments on Dostoevsky's various narrative strategies in *Dostoevsky and "The Idiot,"* 11–45, 223–31.

41. When outlining in his notebooks scenes involving Nastasya Filippovna, Dostoevsky returns repeatedly to the word *beg* (flight) and its variants.

42. On a possible Rousseau connection in *The Idiot*, see Kovacs, "Genezis."

43. It is one of the fascinating vagaries associated with this novel, which went through eight drafts, that the "Idiot" of the early versions had a cruel and vindictive streak not inconsistent with the character of a typical Dostoevskian anti-hero. These traits were later dispersed among other characters, including Ganya lvolgin, Rogozhin, and Ippolit, while the idea of a troubled but at heart magnanimous youth would have to wait for the character of Arkady Dolgoruky in *The Adolescent*. For a full and informed treatment of the notebooks, see R. Miller, *Dostoevsky and "The Idiot."*

44. The name "Rogozhin" suggests "burlap" or "burlap sack" (*rogozha*), perhaps an allusion to the character's working-class origins. See Peace's interesting observations on the link between Rogozhin's name and the sect of schismatics (*Dostoyevsky*, 86). I disagree with Peace that the clues to a Castrate-inspired fanaticism within the Rogozhin family imply sexual sterility. There is the implication of sterility to be sure; however, what is sterile is not the passion per se, but rather its possessiveness, its underlying spiritual greed, and its ultimate self-destructiveness.

45. This is not to say that nothing "evil" happens in the story of Marie. She is ostracized by the moralists of the village and taunted (at first) by the children. But, against the background of the Swiss countryside, this story comes to have a happy ending: Marie's fallen state is redeemed by her prince's kiss; both are united with the children; and she dies in a state of bliss.

46. For more on the similarities and differences in the *telling* of the Marie and Nastasya Filippovna stories, and the implication this has for the dialogic structure of the novel, see Kovacs, "The Poetics of *The Idiot.*"

47. The estate has definite associations with an Edenic paradise. See Holquist, *Dostoevsky*, 115.

48. See Peace, *Dostoyevsky*, 84, on the connection between the Flagellants and her patronymic. She is referred to always by her given name *and* patronymic, whereas Aglaya is referred to simply by her given name. It may seem at first glance far-fetched to interpret the *Greek* etymology of the heroine's patronymic (see note 25 above). What meaning could that have for Dostoevsky and his reader? On the other hand, Nastasya Filippovna is repeatedly associated with a carriage drawn by white horses (8:250, 233–54, 262), Ippolit in his doomed life appears to be living up to the activities of his namesake (see note 65, below), and Ivan Filippovich, the leader of the Flagellants mentioned in *The Devils*, is reported to have been seen ascending into the sky in a chariot: all this suggests that Dostoevsky may well have been aware of the etymology. A decoding of Stavrogin's name (Greek, *stavros*, "cross," + Russian, *rog*, "horn") also involves a Greek etymology.

49. As early as part 1 Nastasya Filippovna says that Ganya would "slit her throat like a ram" (8:137); in part 2 Rogozhin speaks of Nastasya Filippovna's marriage as "going under the knife" and laughs convulsively when he hears Myshkin's anecdote about the peasant who "butchered his friend like a ram" over a gold watch (8:179, 183). See below.

50. See 8:148–49. It is intriguing that Myshkin is also alluded to in this context as "a man [who is] cultured, but doomed" (Mag 201; 8:142).

51. Also offering additional grounds for assuming a proto-apocalyptic framework for the novel *before* part 2 is the presence of the secondary character Princess Belokonskaya (White Horse). First referred to in the notebooks innocuously as "the aunt" (9:334), and remaining offstage in the final version until near the end of the novel, where she passes judgment on the Prince (8:459), she is seen as the chief patroness of the Epanchin family and guiding spirit of the *beau monde.* It seems more than chance that the author, who was

sensitive to the nomenclatural level of his art, would choose a character with this name to be society's keeper. It is Belokonskaya's daughter whom General Ivolgin, a notoriously unreliable narrator, claims to have insulted while traveling on a train, and it is this same little anecdote, told by the General, that provokes his cry of *svetoprestavlenie* (literally, "doomsday" [8:94]) and that initiates the scandal scene culminating in Ganya Ivolgin's slapping Myshkin in the face.

52. Dostoevsky enjoined himself repeatedly in his notebooks to resume the narrative "at the station." See 9:220, 224, 228, 230, 234, 356, 360. It seems significant that his first mention of the Apocalypse in the notebooks takes place on the next page of the same March 11, 1868, entry in which the "scene at the station" is outlined (9:221).

53. The motifs of garden (*sad*) and bench (*skam'ia, skameika*) will be taken up later in the summer garden and in Pavlovsk. See 8:166, 189, 301, 351.

54. The black horse has traditionally symbolized famine.

55. Information about the reputed location of Rogozhin's house in nineteenth-century Saint Petersburg is provided in 9:440. According to G. A. Fyodorov, the house originally serving as the source for Dostoevsky's description was no. 33.

56. For Dostoevsky and other Romantic realists the physical appearance of a dwelling often offers clues to the psychology of the dweller. See Fanger, *Dostoevsky*, 195–98.

57. It seems likely that Dostoevsky was consciously singling out Solovyov. More than any other historian in the 1870s, he advocated *linear* history, the glories of material *progress*, the indispensability of Peter the Great (see, for example, his public lectures on Peter given in 1872 for the bicentenary celebrations at Moscow University), and the statist worldview. In other words, what Solovyov stood for was the very opposite of Dostoevsky's apocalypticism.

58. Rogozhin, who is caught in the same ineluctable forward movement, but from "the other side," is also described as shaking Myshkin's hand *mashinal'no* (8:182).

59. Cox implies something like this with his notion of "completeness within flux" (*Between Earth and Heaven*, 172). This in turn sounds close to the condition of transcendent breakthrough à la Shelley, of "the loss of the individual self in oneness," described recently by Jay Clayton in *Romantic Vision and the Novel*, 19–26, 160–74. The core texts treated by Clayton are

*Clarissa, Mansfield Park, Wuthering Heights, Little Dorrit, Adam Bede,* and *Women in Love.*

60. As Strakhov once related Dostoevsky's words on the nature of the aura: "For several moments I experience a happiness that is impossible in a normal condition and that other people can have no understanding of. I feel complete harmony in myself and in all the world, and this feeling is so strong and sweet that for several seconds of such bliss one could give ten years of one's life, perhaps one's entire life" (cited in *Pss* 9:441–42).

61. Cf. "For some obscure reason he kept remembering Lebedev's nephew . . . just as sometimes one cannot help remembering some persistent *and* stupidly tiresome musical motif" (Mag 260; 8:190).

62. Cf. the same motifs in Mag 264; 8:193.

63. The potentially regenerative powers of Pavlovsk are mentioned several times in the text. Ippolit, for example, is attempting to rely on them when, at the Prince's prompting, he trades the urban anguish of "Meyer's wall" (8:321–22) for Pavlovsk's trees. Yet as it turns out, Ippolit comes to the country not to restore his hopes but to parade the bitter irony of his imminent death in these surroundings.

64. For Dostoevsky's mention of the Apocalypse in his notebooks, see 9:221, 233, 262, 269, 277.

65. Ippolit's name is a russified version of Hippolytus, the bastard son of Theseus and the Amazon Hippolyta. Hippolytus was thrown from his chariot and dragged to death when a monster sent by Poseidon (one of whose names was Hippios) frightened the horses. Dostoevsky could also have in mind Hippolyte, the innocent victim in Racine's *Phèdre.* See note 25.

66. See, e.g., 8:318, 321, 322, 333, 337.

67. Cf. the very different deaths of Marmeladov and Katerina lvanova in *Crime and Punishment.*

68. Cf. this scorpion and the tarantula of the second vision with the apocalyptic *piccolo bestia* of *Diary* (September 1876): "Everyone is waiting, everyone is alarmed, over everyone there hangs a nightmare, everyone has bad dreams. Who or what this *piccolo bestia* is that produces such turmoil it is impossible to determine because a sort of wholesale insanity has set in. . . . And yet, it is as if everyone had already been stung" (26:107).

69. Cf. this beast and the fourth and most terrible beast from Daniel 7:7 (one of the major Old Testament Apocalyptic texts): "And behold, a fourth beast, terrible and dreadful and exceedingly strong; and it had *great iron*

teeth [*bol'shie zheleznye zuby*]; it *devoured and broke in pieces* [*pozhiraet i sokrushaet*], and stamped the residue with its feet. It was different from all the beasts that were before it; and it had ten horns [a motif also associated with the beast/Antichrist of Revelation]" (my emphases; *Oxford Annotated Bible*, 1078/*Bibliia*, 1033).

70. The scene is presented in terms that imply flight and hot pursuit: Rogozhin's command *na zheleznuiu dorogu* means literally "onto [i.e., get going to] the iron road"; the coachman whips his horses on to the station; Keller and Burdovsky want "to give chase" (*brosilis' bylo v pogoniu*), but realize they have fallen too far behind; the fleeing couple "gallop to the station on time"; and so on.

71. Up to this point in the novel, Dostoevsky has used the term *poezd* five times (8:3, 158, 186, 210, 268) and the term *chugunka* once (8:303). His only use of *mashina* with the precise meaning of train comes at the end (8:493, 495, 504), where it appears five times.

72. As might be predicted, Myshkin and Rogozhin meet each other for the last time *at a crossroads* before proceeding on to Rogozhin's house (8:500).

73. E.g., "All the world is being prepared for a great regeneration through the Russian idea (which, as you rightly say, is inextricably bound with Orthodoxy) and this will take place in some century – that is my fervent belief" (28.2:260; February 18/March 1, 1868, to A. Maikov).

74. See Nigg's fine essay on *The Idiot* in *Der christliche Narr*.

75. "In the Dostoevskian novel there is no causality, no genesis, no explanations based on the past, on the influence of environment, upbringing, etc. Each action of the hero is entirely in the present, and in this regard is not predetermined; it is conceived and depicted by the author as though it were free"; "The polyphonic novel is throughout dialogic"; "All in life is a dialogue, that is, dialogic opposition"; and so forth (*Problems* 35, 49, 51).

## WORKS CITED

Al'tman, M. S. *Chitaia Tolstogo*. Tula: Priokskoe knizhnoe izd., 1966.

———. "Zheleznaia doroga v tvorchestve L. N. Tolstogo." *Slavia* 34 (1965): 251–59.

Antsyferov, N. *Dusha Peterburga*. Saint Petersburg: Brokgauz-Efron, 1922.

Arban, D. "'Porog' u Dostoevskogo (Tema, motiv i poniatie)." *Dostoevskii: Materialy i issledovaniia* 2 (1976): 19–29.

Baehr, Stephen. "The Troika and the Train: Dialogues between Tradition and Technology in Nineteenth-Century Russian Literature." In *Issues in Russian Literature before 1917: Proceedings from the III International Congress on Soviet and East European Studies*, edited by Douglas Clayton and R. C. Elwood, 85–106. Columbus, Ohio: Slavica, 1989.

Bakhtin, Mikhail. *Problems of Dostoevsky's Poetics.* Translated by R. W. Rotsel. Ann Arbor, Mich.: Ardis, 1973.

Bashutskii, A. "Parovye mashiny, zheleznye dorogi i oborotnye banki," *Otechestvennye zapiski* 1 (1839): 1–17.

Bazanov, Vasilii. *Sergei Esenin i krest'ianskaia Rossiia.* Leningrad: Sovetskii pisatel', 1982.

Billington, James. *The Icon and the Axe. An Interpretive History of Russia.* New York: Random House, 1970.

Blackmur, R. P. "*Anna Karenina:* The Dialectic of Incarnation." In *Anna Karenina: Backgrounds and Sources Criticism*, 2d ed., the Maude translation revised and edited by George Gibian, 899–917. New York: Norton, 1995.

Browning, Gary L. "The Death of Anna Karenina." *Slavic and East European Journal* 30 (1986): 327–39.

Christian, R. F. *Tolstoy: A Critical Introduction.* Cambridge: Cambridge University Press, 1969.

Clayton, Jay. *Romantic Vision and the Novel.* Cambridge: Cambridge University Press, 1987.

Cox, Roger. *Between Earth and Heaven: Shakespeare, Dostoevsky and the Meaning of Christian Tragedy.* New York: Holt, Rinehart and Winston, 1969.

Dalton, Elizabeth. *Unconscious Structure in "The Idiot": A Study in Literature and Psychoanalysis.* Princeton: Princeton University Press, 1979.

Dolgopolov, L. K. "Roman A. Belogo 'Peterburg' i filosofsko-istoricheskie idei Dostoevskogo." In *Dostoevskii: Materialy i issledovaniia*, edited by G. M. Fridlender, 2:217–24. Leningrad: Nauka, 1976.

Dostoevskii, F. M. *Polnoe sobranie sochinenii v tridtsati tomakh.* 30 vols. Edited by V. G. Bazanov et al. Leningrad: Nauka, 1972–90.

Dostoevsky, Fyodor. *The Notebooks for "The Idiot" [by] Fyodor Dostoevsky.* Edited and with an Introduction by Edward Wasiolek. Translated by Katharine Strelsky. Chicago: University of Chicago Press, 1967.

Eikhenbaum, B. *Lev Tolstoi. Semidesiatye gody.* Leningrad: Khudozhestvennaia literatura, 1924.

Fanger, Donald. *Dostoevsky and Romantic Realism.* Chicago: University of Chicago Press, 1967.

Frank, Joseph. *Dostoevsky: The Seeds of Revolt, 1821–1849.* Princeton: Princeton University Press, 1976.

Friedman, Alan. *The Turn of a Novel.* New York: Oxford University Press, 1966.

Ginzburg, L. Ia., and V. S. Kiseleva-Sergenina, eds. *Poety 1820–1830-kh godov.* 2 vols. Leningrad: Sovetskii pisatel', 1976.

Girard, René. *Desire, Deceit, and the Novel: Self and Other in Literary Structure.* Translated by Yvonne Freccero. Baltimore: John Hopkins University Press, 1965.

Gogol, N. W. *Dead Souls.* Translated by Bernard Guilbert Guerney. New York: Holt, Rinehart and Winston, 1966.

Herzen, A. I. *Sobranie sochinenii v tridsati tomakh.* 30 vols. Moscow: AN SSSR, 1954–65.

Hollander, Robert. "The Apocalyptic Framework of Dostoevsky's *The Idiot.*" *Mosaic* 6 (1974): 123–39.

Holquist, Michael. *Dostoevsky and the Novel.* Princeton: Princeton University Press, 1977.

Jahn, Gary. "The Image of the Railroad in *Anna Karenina.*" *Slavic and East European Journal* 25 (1981): 1–10.

Kermode, Frank. *The Sense of an Ending: Studies in the Theory of Fiction.* New York: Oxford University Press, 1967.

Kirpotin, V. Ia. *Dostoevskii v shestidesiatye gody.* Moscow: Khudozhestvennaia literatura, 1978.

Kovacs, Arpad. "Genezis idei 'prekrasnogo cheloveka' i dvizhenie zamysla romana 'Idiota.'" *Studia Slavica* 21 (1975): 309–31.

———. "The Poetics of *The Idiot:* On the Problem of Dostoevsky's Thinking about Genre." In *Critical Essays on Dostoevsky,* edited by Robin Feuer Miller, 116–26. Boston: G. K. Hall, 1986.

Krieger, Murray. "Dostoevsky's *The Idiot:* The Curse of Saintliness." In *Dostoevsky: A Collection of Essays,* edited by René Wellek, 39–52. Englewood Cliffs, N.J.: Prentice-Hall, 1962.

Leatherbarrow, W. J. "Apocalyptic Imagery in Dostoevsky's *The Idiot* and *The Devils.*" *Dostoevsky Studies* 3 (1982): 43–51.

Leont'ev, Konstantin. *Sobranie sochinenii.* 9 vols. Moscow: V. M. Sablin, 1912–13.

Levitskii, S. *Ocherki po istorii russkoi filosofii i obshchestvennoi mysli.* Frankfurt am Main: Possev, 1968.

Lord, Robert. *Dostoevsky: Essays and Perspectives.* Berkeley and Los Angeles: University of California Press, 1970.

Lotman, Ju. M., and B. A. Uspenskii. "Spory o iazyke v nachale XIX v. kak fakt russkoi kul'tury." *Trudy po russkoi i slavianskoi filologii* 24 (1975): 168–254.

Massie, Suzanne. *Land of the Firebird.* New York: Simon and Schuster, 1980.

Miller, D. A. *Narrative and Its Discontents: Problems of Closure in the Traditional Novel.* Princeton: Princeton University Press, 1981.

Miller, Robin Feuer. *Dostoevsky and "The Idiot": Author, Narrator, and Reader.* Cambridge: Harvard University Press, 1981.

Mochulsky, Konstantin. *Dostoevsky: His Life and Work.* Translated and with an Introduction by Michael A. Minihan. Princeton: Princeton University Press, 1967.

Morson, Gary Saul. *The Boundaries of Genre: Dostoevsky's "Diary of a Writer" and the Traditions of Literary Utopia.* University of Texas Slavic Series 4. Austin: University of Texas Press, 1981.

Muchnic, Helen. *Russian Writers: Notes and Essays.* New York: Random House, 1971.

Nigg, Walter. *Der christliche Narr.* Zurich: Artemis, 1956.

Peace, Richard Arthur. *Dostoevsky: An Examination of the Major Novels.* Cambridge: Cambridge University Press, 1971.

Richter, David H. *Fable's End: Completeness and Closure in Rhetorical Fiction.* Chicago: University of Chicago Press, 1974.

Ronen, Omry. *An Approach to Mandel'shtam.* Jerusalem: Magnes, 1983.

Rozenblium, L. M. "Tvorcheskie dnevniki Dostoevskogo." In *Neizdannyi Dostoevskii. Zapisnye knizhki i tetradi 1860–1881 gg. Literaturnoe nasledstvo,* 83:9–92. Moscow: Nauka, 1971.

Skaftymov, A. P. "Tematicheskaia kompozitsiia romana 'Idiot.'" In *Tvorcheskii put' Dostoevskogo,* edited by N. I. Brodskii, 131–84. Leningrad: Seiatel', 1924.

Tate, Allen. "The Hovering Fly." In his *The Hovering Fly and Other Essays,* 17–23. Freeport, N.Y.: New York: Books for Libraries, 1968.

Terras, Victor. "Dissonans v romane F. M. Dostoevskogo *Idiot.*" *Transactions of the Association of Russian-American Scholars in the U.S.A.* 14 (1981): 60–68.

Timofeeva [Pochinkovskaia], V. V. "God raboty s znamenitym

pisatelem." In *F. M. Dostoevskii v vospominaniiakh sovremennikov*, edited by V. V. Grigorenko et al., 2: 122–50. Moscow: Khudozhestvennaia literatura, 1964.

Tolstoi, L. N. *Perepiska s russkimi pisateliami.* Moscow: Khudozhestvennaia literatura, 1962.

Tolstoy, Leo. *Anna Karenina.* Edited by George Gibian. Translated by Aylmer and Louise Maude. New York: Norton, 1970.

Torgovnik, Marianna. *Closure in the Novel.* Princeton: Princeton University Press, 1981.

Wasiolek, Edward. "Introduction." In Fyodor Dostoevsky, *The Notebooks for "The Idiot" [by] Fyodor Dostoevsky.* Edited and with an introduction by Edward Wasiolek. Translated by Katharine Strelsky. Chicago: University of Chicago Press, 1967.

———. *Tolstoy's Major Fiction.* Chicago: University of Chicago Press, 1978.

Weidlé, Wladimir. *Zadacha Rossii.* New York: Chekhov, 1956.

Westwood, J. N. *A History of Russian Railways.* London: Allen and Unwin, 1964.

# Myshkin Through a Murky Glass, Guessingly

LIZA KNAPP

In the wake of the death and destruction at the end of *The Idiot*, readers familiar with Dostoevsky's statements that he wanted, in Myshkin, to portray a "positively beautiful" and Christlike man may well wonder whether something has gone wrong with this novel. Critics have condemned Myshkin (as an ineffectual hero), Dostoevsky (as an ineffectual novelist), and, for that matter, Jesus himself (as an ineffectual savior or simply as a bad role model).[1] And the fact that Dostoevsky expressed some dissatisfaction of his own with the novel (without ever actually denying Myshkin) has only added grist to the critical mill. Others have defended Myshkin, Dostoevsky, and Jesus. Still others have come up with apologetic interpretations of the novel that rationalize the novel's contradictions.

In order to understand the role played by Christ in the novel and Dostoevsky's conception of that role, it is important to remember that Dostoevsky envisioned this "positively beautiful man" to be *like* Christ, even if in the privacy of his notebooks he at times seemed to equate Myshkin with Christ (9:246, 249). *The Idiot* does not ask what would happen if Jesus arrived in Saint Petersburg by train on November 27, 1867. Rather, Dostoevsky set out to give us an imitation of Christ and to portray Christ by indirection. *The Idiot* thus formally imitates the New Testament; as Robin Feuer Miller has pointed out: "The figure of Christ and the style of the Gospels, which portray Him through parables and stories rather than through authorial explanations, provide Dostoevsky with models for characterization and narration."[2] Dostoevsky, in presenting a Christlike Myshkin, makes use of a process something like that practiced by Jesus when he spoke in parables, not defining the Kingdom of God but hinting at what it is like. The process is analogous to simile and metaphor as described by Aristotle: Dostoevsky challenges his reader to contemplate and intuit similarities between Myshkin and Christ so that the reader can, in the process, "learn" (for Aristotle argues that there is a "learning process" involved) something that was not previously known or obvious; it is often intended to be shocking.[3]

When it comes to the "fantastic," which Dostoevsky understood as matters bridging life and death, full knowledge and, for that matter, direct expression of partial knowledge are impossible, at least on earth. To use Paul's metaphor, we see "through a murky glass, guessingly" rather than "face to face."[4] And given the fact that *The Idiot* is a novel, with a Christ*like* hero, we are beholding Christ through many layers of murky glass.

As Hugh McLean has shown us by the example of Tolstoy, an author creates his own Jesus – if not in that author's own image, then in answer to his own yearnings.[5] Tolstoy, rejecting all supernatural mumbo jumbo and brooking no narrative (or philosophical) contradictions, sought to rewrite the Gospels, harmonizing all the contradictory versions of what Jesus said and did into one Tolstoyan text. *The Idiot* provides ample evidence of how Dostoevsky's Jesus was radically different from Tolstoy's. Dostoevsky most cherishes the very aspects of Jesus denied by Tolstoy: his divinity and the contradictions.[6]

The whole narrative of *The Idiot* is in a sense constructed in imitation of the New Testament. Although it may be tempting to say that Dostoevsky's Jesus is the Jesus of John the Evangelist,[7] or that Dostoevsky's Jesus is primarily the Jesus of the Last Supper who in the face of death preaches love, Dostoevsky in *The Idiot* draws on *all* the New Testament sources, and the narrative borrows from the very multiplicity of witnesses.

With this in mind, we should perhaps approach this "fantastic" novel not in order to judge whether Myshkin is an effective savior, but instead to understand, if only through a glass darkly, how Dostoevsky presents his imitation of Christ.

In Myshkin, who arrives in Saint Petersburg in part 1 of the novel, may be seen reflections (of reflections) of Christ: he has traits that remind us of the early Christians who modeled their lives on Jesus', breaking with family and living at odds with the state. Myshkin has incorporated the attitudes that Paul tried to cajole the Philippians, Romans, and Corinthians into adopting. (Dostoevsky would later in his life declare Paul's Epistles to be an excellent source on faith: "There quite a bit is said specifically about faith and it cannot be said better" [30.1:10, February 1878].) In the Myshkin who arrives in Saint Petersburg on November 27, 1867, Dostoevsky has presented what Paul had in mind when he said: "For I think that God has exhibited us apostles as last of all, like men sentenced to death. We are fools for Christ's sake, but you are wise in Christ. We are weak, but you are strong. You are held in honor, but we are in disrepute" (1 Cor. 4:9–10).[8] Myshkin, called a "holy fool" by Rogozhin on the train when they first meet, then greets the Epanchin household with stories of executions, reminding his listeners that Jesus himself was sentenced to death and lived his life in the face of this agony and horror. Listening to Myshkin's stories, members of the Epanchin household, through a murky glass, guessingly, behold an imitation of Jesus.

"Imagine a number of men in chains and all condemned to death," writes Blaise Pascal. Of these some "are slaughtered each day in sight of the others, those remaining see their own fate in that of their fellows, and, looking at each other with pain and without hope, they wait their turn. Such is the image of the condition of men."[9] In the next paragraph, Pascal depicts human life as that of a convict in a *cachot* (cell) awaiting execution and not knowing whether or not he will be reprieved. Pascal's image of the human condition recalls Paul's shifts in his epistles between discussing the actual imprisonment of early Christians and creating images of all men being condemned to death (as a result of human mortality). Both the Pascalian and Pauline images of condemnation to death are reflected in Victor Hugo's *Last Day of a Condemned Man*, which, in turn, influenced Dostoevsky's *The Idiot.* Thus *The Idiot* presupposes that living with a death sentence – living with the Pascalian "image of the condition of men" – can make you a holy fool or it can drive you mad.

For Dostoevsky, "imagining" "the condition of men" was not hard; he had lived through Pascal's *Gedankenexperiment* when, condemned to death in 1849 along with other members of the Petrashevsky Circle, he watched as three of his fellow members were readied for slaughter, knowing that his turn came next. Moreover, Dostoevsky watched his loved ones die of "natural" causes (as Ippolit himself declares, illnesses such as consumption are simply another kind of "death sentence," pronounced by nature rather than temporal authority). And, to add to the above, Dostoevsky underwent epileptic attacks that, aside from the physical suffering they involved, brought to him a "mystical" suffering associated with fear of death.[10] His wife's diary for the period when he was at work on *The Idiot* (during the planning stages) records his fear that he would end up in an insane asylum and his pleas that, were this to happen, she should not leave him abroad but at least take him back to Russia to be committed.[11]

Myshkin tells of having inspired through his own example the children of his Swiss village to love, during her last days, Marie, a young woman, seduced and abandoned, and suffering from consumption. An important component of Myshkin's story is that the love he imparted was subversive to the status quo of the village: initially, the parents of the children felt that Myshkin, Pied Piper–like, was leading their children astray. Especially disconcerting for the adults was that Myshkin did not judge Marie. Here Myshkin imitates Jesus in his refusal to judge a fallen woman. He loves in a seditious way that threatens authority and divides families. The tale of Marie – where Myshkin shows his Christlike love in action – is part dreamy Swiss miracle and part a warning of a socially subversive force that can create chaos.

On arriving at the Epanchins', Myshkin speaks man-to-man about questions of life and death with the Epanchins' servant, leaving the servant himself befuddled. (The servant wonders, Is the visitor "a poor little fool" without social ambition or is he a social climber with some scheme up his sleeve?) In humbling himself to the servant, Myshkin was imitating Jesus and thus following Paul's advice to the Philippians: "Do nothing from selfishness or conceit, but in humility count others better than yourselves. Let each of you look not only to his own interests, but also to the interests of others. Have this mind among yourselves, which you have in Christ Jesus, who, though he was in the form of God, did not count equality with God a thing to be grasped, but emptied himself, taking the form of a servant, being born in the likeness of men. And being found in human form he humbled himself and became obedient unto death, even death on a cross" (Phil. 2:3–8). But imitation of Christ can easily be misunderstood and misinterpreted, as the response of the Epanchins' servant reveals. Myshkin has so naturally taken "the form of a servant" that Nastasya Filippovna mistakes him for one when she first meets him at the Ivolgin apartment. This possible confusion and multiplicity is part of Dostoevsky's intention here.

Although contemporary views are at times critical of the way Christianity has responded to the "woman question," some interpreters of the Church have suggested that one of the radical aspects of Jesus's ministry was his inclusion of women as followers, whether or not their role was adequately chronicled in the official "good news" of the Church. For Mary Magdalene, Joanna, and others, following Jesus was an escape from convention.[12]

Nastasya Filippovna and the Epanchin women, especially Aglaya, are drawn to Myshkin and to what he embodies. (Being distant cousins, the Epanchin women may see something of themselves reflected in Myshkin.) Nastasya Filippovna is prepared to allow Myshkin to decide her fate at her birthday party and sees him as someone who will liberate her from domination by another person: she will belong to no one and experience new independence. Aglaya, fed up with going to "their balls" and with everyone's attempts to marry her off, refuses to remain or become the dutiful daughter or wife she is expected to. And Myshkin seems to be her advocate in this rebellion. In citing her reasons for not wanting simply to be married off, she expresses her yearning to see a Gothic cathedral; at a certain point, her mother wonders whether she has not been infected by nihilism. But here Dostoevsky leaves the reader wondering whether her behavior is not also an attempt at imitation of the angels of God, residents of heaven who "neither marry nor are given in marriage" (Matt. 22:30). Here again Dostoevsky presents behavior that may be interpreted one way (Aglaya's behavior looks fishily like woman's emancipation), and yet, if one looks through a murky glass, guessingly, one sees glimmers of some otherworldly reality in these same actions.

When he is asked by the men he meets in the train whether he is a "great connoisseur of the female sex," Myshkin replies that because of his illness he has not known women. His response prompts Rogozhin to liken him to a God's fool, noting that God loves people like him. From the outset, Myshkin's virginal lack of erotic love seems part of his Christlike nature. His Christlike love is incompatible with marriage, as becomes apparent when Aglaya demands of Myshkin, "Why do you debase yourself?" and then in the next breath declares, "I wouldn't marry you for anything in the world" (8:283). At the very least, Aglaya presumes that an eligible suitor and successful husband should not behave humbly and meekly but rather should be more of a peacock. More than that, however, her hesitation also points to some deeper sense in which Myshkin is, in fact, not a fitting husband because marriage is predicated on certain selfish, un-Christlike qualities he seems to lack.

Throughout *The Idiot* Dostoevsky explores the question of whether imitation of Christ can occur within marriage and family or not. Here again, Jesus and his spokesmen gave mixed messages on the subject. For example, Jesus tells his followers to hate and/or leave behind their families, letting the dead bury the dead (Luke 14:26; Matt. 8:22); he denies his own biological family in favor of the faithful (Matt. 12:46; Mark 3:31–32; Luke 8:19); he turns family members against each other (Matt. 10:35; Luke 12:53); and in the face of the Apocalypse, he blesses "the wombs that never bear, and the paps which never gave suck" (Luke 23:39), and he announces that in the Resurrection, "they neither marry, nor are given in marriage but live like angels of God" (Matt. 22:30). And yet Paul says, "It is better to marry than to burn" (1 Cor. 7:9); the Church eventually made a sacrament out of marriage. What is to be done?

In a diary entry that begins "Masha is lying on the table. Will I see Masha again?" (20:172), written on Holy Thursday, 1864, in the presence of his wife's corpse, as Dostoevsky attempts to imagine eternal life, he refers to how hard it is for the human earthly mind to envision it.[13] One piece of evidence we have about it, he notes, recalling Matthew, is that there "they neither marry, nor are given in marriage but live like angels of God" (20:173). In trying to envision the afterlife (without which earthly life makes no sense to him), including this aspect of heavenly life, Dostoevsky added that marrying and giving in marriage are "the most extreme rejection of humanism, the complete isolation of the couple from *all others* (little is left over for everyone else)." But having recorded this brutal truth about the selfish nature of marriage, Dostoevsky continues, "The family is the greatest holy of man on earth." Dostoevsky's diary entry records the thought that Christlike love is an ideal that men and women strive for on earth, in time, and within the family.

> And so, man strives on earth toward an ideal, *counter* to his nature. When man has not fulfilled the law of striving toward this ideal, that is, has not through *love* sacrificed his *I* to people or to another being (I and Masha), then he experiences suffering and has called his state sin. And so, man must constantly experience suffering that is counterbalanced by the heavenly delight of fulfilling the law, that is, through sacrifice. Herein lies the earthly balance. Otherwise earth would be without meaning. (20:175)

Only after the Second Coming will men and women live like angels of God and there will be time no more.

Dostoevsky's "fantastic" Myshkin, as he fondly called him later, through his epilepsy knew something of what it is like for there to be time no more, and also something of what it means to live like an angel of God. He rebels against isolating himself with one wife and having nothing left over for others. The "earthly balance," or compromise, Dostoevsky described to himself in his diary (and which Dostoevsky himself attempted in his life) eludes Myshkin, who, rather, attempts to have it both ways: he returns to Russia in search of family and sets himself up as a potential groom; yet, at the same time, he still wants to love others humbly, without isolating himself and without having "nothing left for everyone else."

For some of his critics, within the novel and without, Myshkin's whole problem, it would seem, is his inability to choose *either* Aglaya *or* Nastasya Filippovna. Radomsky, speaking for the social order, criticizes Myshkin for acting as bridegroom almost simultaneously to two women. "You want to love them both, is that it?" says Radomsky. To which Myshkin replies, "O, yes, yes!" (8:484). Once again, just as when he conversed with the servant, Myshkin's behavior can be interpreted in more than one way: either he's an ineffectual lover, unwilling or unable to make up his mind; or he's a modal bigamist, a selfish Don Juan, or worse. Or, looking guessingly through murky glass, perhaps one can see a reflection of Christ and of all the contradictions he represented. And indeed in Myshkin's leaving Aglaya and Nastasya Filippovna in the lurch, there is even some similarity to Jesus' treatment of Mary Magdalene, whom he allowed to wash and kiss his feet, to leave everything and follow him, only to abandon her a bit caddishly at the last moment, according to some apocryphal or blasphemous interpretations.[14]

Tiutchev's "O, my knowing soul!" (1855) depicts much the same conflict as that felt by Dostoevsky's characters.[15] According to Tiutchev (under the influence of Pascal), the soul, "a resident of two worlds," lives in a constant state of conflict, suffering, and passion, resulting from its condition of "dual existence." Tiutchev finds the answer to this duality in the image of Mary Magdalene throwing herself at Christ's feet: "The soul is ready, like Mary, / To cling forever to the feet of Christ." Dostoevsky's novel explores the effects of this kind of desire when put into action.

As the novel draws to a close, the fear that Christlike behavior is ineffectual and that it propels others to destruction (rather than the reverse) enters the hearts and minds of many of the characters of the novel, its narrator (who becomes increasingly critical of what Myshkin embodies), and its readers.[16] Rogozhin may have been right when he remarked to Myshkin that Myshkin's pity perhaps does more damage than Rogozhin's unambiguous eros (8:191). Nastasya Filippovna's act of running away from Myshkin to Rogozhin, and her eventual death, may further condemn what Myshkin represents.

In the novel, characters such as Radomsky and Prince Shch. cast aspersions on Myshkin and his love. Radomsky reduces Myshkin's Christlike charity to "philanthropy" as he undermines the whole venture: "You see, Prince, being a philanthropist is pleasant, but not very" (8:261–62). At another point, Prince Shch. informs Myshkin that enacting heaven on earth is harder than he thinks. Whatever specific form the criticisms leveled at Myshkin take, they essentially ask why things get worse rather than better in the presence of Myshkin's love.

Similar concerns have arisen among readers of *The Idiot*, who perceive failure in Myshkin, or in the novel, or in Dostoevsky's attempt to imitate Christ. This critical response to his novel might not have surprised Dostoevsky, for he was familiar with this sort of attitude at least from the 1840s, the period of his friendship with Belinsky. (As Joseph Frank has suggested, Dostoevsky, who, prior to writing *The Idiot*, had been working on an article on Belinsky, may well have had Belinsky's views on Christ in mind as he set about to depict a Christlike man in *The Idiot*.)[17] In an entry in his *Diary of a Writer* in 1873, Dostoevsky noted that Belinsky, unlike other atheists such as Renan, rejected not only Christ's divinity but even the very notion that Christ was an ideal to be emulated. In Belinsky's view (or Dostoevsky's view of Belinsky's view), Jesus would not have had much of an effect had he lived in their present day (he probably would have joined forces with the socialist movement), and the imitation of Christ should not be set forth as man's goal because "it is absurd and even cruel to demand from man that which he, by the very laws of nature, could not live up to even if he wanted to" (21:11). As understood by Dostoevsky, the Belinskian viewpoint was that Christlike tactics fail to produce the desired effects (peace and justice for all), whereas a more savvy Realpolitik that expects less of men and women would be more successful.

Radomsky's criticism of Myshkin concerning the lack of positive results produced by his Christlike love (with the implication that his love in fact does more harm than good) harks back to Belinsky's views on Jesus. At the same time, these moments in *The Idiot* where Myshkin's *imitatio Christi* is condemned also look forward to Ivan Karamazov's "Legend of the Grand Inquisitor." In both the denouement of *The Idiot* and that "legend," an advocate of good points out to (a) Christ (figure) his multiple failures to effect any good; in each case the Inquisitor suggests concrete steps that would, he argues, result in greater welfare. Jesus, the argument runs, seems to expect too much of men and women: they are not up to the challenge; hence chaos continues to reign. With a bit more authority, miracle, and bread, a better world would result. (Ultimately, these Inquisitors are of the "bread-to-stones" materialist mentality Dostoevsky was to decry in his last decade of writing.) In each case, (the) Christ (figure) turns the dialectic cheek and fails to argue back: Jesus kisses the Grand Inquisitor; Myshkin is silent and becomes a mute idiot.[18]

Radomsky, accusing Myshkin of applying democratic, pro-woman-question tactics in his behavior toward Aglaya and Nastasya Filippovna, blames him for creating an impossible muddle and ruining their lives. When, a bit later, Nastasya Filippovna is murdered and Aglaya ends up married to a charlatan and converted to Catholicism, it would seem that Radomsky was right: Myshkin has only made everyone's lot worse.

Readers of the novel and residents of Pavlovsk object, Why all the chaos and destruction in the wake of Myshkin? Many suggestions have surfaced to explain what goes wrong here. For example, in a recent dissertation,[19] Marina Woronzoff-Dashkoff suggests that because Myshkin is a quixotic hero, his "moral understanding is thwarted by the failure to sympathize." While she may be right in her argument about Myshkin's failure to *understand* others, further "understanding" might not have altered the tragic denouement.

(What possibilities for a happier ending are there, anyway? For a double wedding? For a socialist ménage à quatre?)

Again, Dostoevsky in his writings appears to have anticipated some of the criticism leveled at the Idiot and *The Idiot.* For Dostoevsky, the fact that, alas, chaos, suffering, and destruction persist is not justification for denying Christ or Christianity. In his diary entry of Holy Thursday, 1864 ("Masha is lying on the table"), Dostoevsky contemplates the meaning for man of Christ's life and death, and declares Christlike love of another as oneself as the ideal toward which man strives. But then he adds:

> NB. The Antichrists are mistaken in trying to refute Christianity by means of the following major objections: 1) "Why is it that if Christianity is true it does not reign on earth; why do men continue to suffer, why have they not become brothers to each other?"
>
> In fact it is quite obvious why: because it is an ideal for the future, ultimate life of man, whereas on earth man is in a transitional state. It will come into being but only after the goal has been achieved, when man has by the laws of nature been definitively reborn as another nature that does not marry and is not given in marriage and, second, Christ Himself preached his teaching only as an ideal, He Himself foretold that until the end of the world there would be struggle and development (the teaching about the sword), for this is a law of nature, because on earth life is in the process of developing, whereas there [what awaits is] an existence that is one of total synthesis, eternally delightful and full, for which, therefore, "there will be time no more."

The above passage is relevant to *The Idiot* in more ways than one. Dostoevsky makes it clear that his Jesus comes wielding a sword,[20] and that the strife will continue, literally, until kingdom come. Even if Easter and resurrection promise that in the long run the strife may be over and the battle won, in the short run, until the Second Coming, the struggle continues, despite mankind's efforts to love. Further, this ongoing strife, in Dostoevsky's view, does not nullify Christ or his teaching.

Central both to Dostoevsky's conception of Myshkin as a Christlike figure and to the objections to Myshkin in the novel is the way Myshkin imitated Jesus' treatment of the sinning woman brought to him by the scribes and Pharisees for judgment (John 8:3–11).[21] They lead her in, announcing: "Now in the law Moses commanded us to stone such. What do you say about her?" Several entries in Dostoevsky's notebooks for the novel suggest that this passage was very much on his mind as he wrote *The Idiot* and that Myshkin's treatment of Nastasya Filippovna was, indeed, in imitation of Jesus' behavior here. In the novel itself, Myshkin, referring to Nastasya Filippovna, tells Aglaya not to throw a stone at her (8:361). But Radomsky, the raisonneur of the novel,[22] chides Myshkin for having carried forgiveness of Nastasya Filippovna too far and turned it into approval of her behavior. Radomsky believes that a tougher love would yield better results. Radomsky argues that Myshkin's imitation of how Jesus acted in John 8 is flawed. He tells Myshkin: "But, you know, of course, she [the woman taken in adultery] was not told that she was doing the right thing, that it was worthy of all sorts of honors and respect" (8:482). Radomsky essentially feels that Myshkin has taken a dangerous step in turning sympathy and forgiveness into approval and praise, whereas Christ, Radomsky implies, stopped short of this. Is Radomsky right or is Radomsky a bit of a scribe and a Pharisee in wanting the sinning woman not to get off too easily?

It should be noted that, while John has Jesus conclude by saying "Go and sin no more" to the adulterous woman, Jesus explicitly does not judge her. Having challenged whoever of the scribes and Pharisees was "without sin" to cast the first stone, Jesus waits while they file out one by one, "convicted by their own conscience." Then he asks the woman: "Where are those thine accusers? Hath no man condemned thee?" When she answers, "No man, Lord," he tells her, "Neither do I condemn thee: go and sin no more."

In the tradition of Russian Orthodoxy, a noncondemning love of the sinner was the ideal. "He who has achieved true prayer and love is incapable of making distinctions; he does not distinguish the righteous from the sinner, but loves all equally and does not judge, like God himself; the sun shines and rain falls on the just and on the unjust," declares the narrator of *Tales of a Pilgrim Told to His Spiritual Father*, weaving in paraphrases from the Philokalia.[23] This type of love – love that "does not make a distinction of things" – runs counter to earthly, worldly notions of justice, bred in the bone. Myshkin exemplifies this type of love in that he refuses to distinguish between sinner and righteous woman. In so doing, however, he violates people's sense of order and form and promotes earthly chaos.

In *Adultery in the Novel*, Tony Tanner discusses the tension in novels of adultery between the Christlike forgiveness of the sinning woman, as described in John 8, and the scribe-like and Pharisee-like desire to stone her.[24] Tanner argues that the bourgeois novel of adultery depends largely on the tension that develops as the novel seeks to incorporate both responses to adultery: "a strictness that works to maintain the law, and a sympathy and understanding with the adulterous violator that works to undermine it" (14). And indeed, "it is arguable that it is just such a tension between law and sympathy that holds the great bourgeois novel together, and a severe imbalance in either direction must destroy the form" (14). If Tanner's assumptions about "the great bourgeois novel" are applied to *The Idiot*, then it just may be that the formal problems many critics have seen in *The Idiot* result from "severe imbalance" between sympathy and law.[25]

But perhaps it is an error to judge *The Idiot* by the standards of the bourgeois novel of adultery. *The Idiot* presents a main hero and, I would argue, an author, who both tip the scale toward compassion and a refusal to condemn, no matter what the destruction all this brings to traditional forms. This suggests that this novel is, indeed, different from the "great bourgeois" novels Tanner discusses. (According to Tanner, lack of the prescribed tension between sympathy and law results in a degeneration into sexuality or "linguicity,"[26] – but this does not quite fit Dostoevsky, although there may be elements of each.) Rather, in *The Idiot*, Dostoevsky sets forth a new type of novel, the novel of the *accidental* family, a family he himself in

*Diary of a Writer* opposed to the *genetic* family, whose chronicler was Tolstoy.

The novel of the accidental family, as Dostoevsky understood it, had its own poetics, which Dostoevsky commented on, directly and indirectly, in his works.[27] In Dostoevsky's view, new artistic forms had to be created to represent disorder and decay. In order to arrive at these, however, the writer had to "guess and . . . make mistakes" (13:455).[28] In *The Idiot*, a novel with a Christlike hero, Dostoevsky works out these new forms, new forms that happen to bear some resemblance to the chronicle of Christ's life: the New Testament.

Much of the end of *The Idiot* is devoted to the narrator's throwing up his hands at the task of chronicling the last days of the action. Rather than go in search of the historical events or attempt to create a coherent narrative, the narrator chooses to give us several different reports, based on different accounts, and with various inconsistencies and contradictions.[29] Is this not a bit like the narratives of Jesus's life?

Many readers, including Tolstoy and Strakhov, have been frustrated and have wanted one harmonious version of what happened in and about Pavlovsk during the White Nights of 1868 and of what happened in and around Jerusalem in 33. But, for Dostoevsky, if you choose Christ or an imitation of Christ, you must be willing to forgo having one "true" version. And you will spend your time "looking through a murky glass, guessingly," until there is time no more, when you will "see face to face."

The accidental family, whose chronicle, by necessity, needed new forms and new poetics, differs from the "genetic" family, where genealogy and patrimony drive the narrative. The accidental family is a family born out of the decomposition of the genetic family and one that is bound together by love rather than blood and genes. Perhaps Dostoevsky even regarded Jesus as the founder of the accidental family: according to John's Gospel, Jesus' last act before dying on the cross is to bind his grieving loved ones, who have to watch him die, all the while knowing, like Pascal's convicts, that their turn will come. Jesus tells his mother, "Woman, behold your son!" referring to John ( "the disciple standing by whom he loved") and he tells John, "Behold, your mother!" – from which point on John "took her into his own home" (John 19:26–27). Here perhaps is Jesus' most pro-family act of all: here he counterbalances the damage that he had done to families throughout his ministry when he announced that he had come to wield his sword and set families against each other (Matt. 10:34–35).

The "family" Jesus creates provides a model for the accidental family whose poet-chronicler Dostoevsky saw himself becoming. In his *Diary of a Writer* Dostoevsky notes that the "old form" of the Russian family is gone, and he asks: "Does the family have the strength to form a new and desirable form that satisfies the Russian heart?" (25:173). For Dostoevsky, such a family would be a family where the balance is tipped toward compassion and forgiveness, and the disorder that results. The "Russian heart," in Dostoevsky's view, had a strong capacity for these things. Dostoevsky, in the end of *The Idiot*, depicts the Epanchin family, as well as the Lebedev family, as just such families. Although shaken by all the "terror" it has lived through, the Epanchin family has survived in a new form and seems to count as one of its members their distant relative and the former fiancé of Aglaya, the "idiot" Myshkin, of whom we are told: "Apparently, he was forgiven for everything." By prefacing the news of this forgiveness with "apparently," the narrator makes some judgment about what he conveys, and he betrays his own possibly less forgiving heart. (This "apparently" has much the same effect as Radomsky's complaints that Myshkin overdid his imitation of Jesus' forgiving the sinning woman.)

In *Dostoevsky and "The Idiot,"* Robin Feuer Miller discusses the effects resulting from the division Dostoevsky creates between the author (who has a more forgiving heart) and the narrator (who is more prone to judgment). She argues that the reader is, to some degree, left to choose sides.

In this respect *The Idiot* is much like *Madame Bovary*, another novel where John 8 is a subtext and readers find themselves, willy-nilly, in the position of scribes and Pharisees, who must decide whether to condemn or not condemn Emma. Flaubert achieves this effect of drawing the reader into this role by opening his novel in the French schoolroom where the new pupil Charles Bovary (who arrives on the scene as a definite outsider, wearing a funny hat, rather like the way Myshkin will arrive in Saint Petersburg) is met with the derision and cruelty of his scribe-like classmates who pelt Charles with spitballs. Throughout the novel, Flaubert forces his readers to decide whether to throw stones at Emma, to throw spitballs at Charles Bovary, to join in the cries of "charivari" that both his name and the action of the novel seem to invite – or to look into their own conscience and refrain from punishing others.[30]

Dostoevsky challenges his reader no less than does Flaubert. Dostoevsky seems to have understood the second layer to the story of John 8: whereas it seems initially that the drama (or miracle) is what transpires between Jesus and the sinning woman, the essence of what Jesus has done in this scene is ultimately the change undergone in the consciences of the scribes and Pharisees, who "convicted by their own conscience, went out one by one," without casting a stone.[31]

Certainly Dostoevsky makes it tempting for readers to join those residents of Pavlovsk, including the novel's narrator, who are ready to join in the charivari if Myshkin marries (8:491) or to cast spitballs and stones when he does not. But Dostoevsky, imitating Jesus in John 8, challenges us to convict ourselves in our own consciences. At this point, we land ourselves in the Pascalian *cachot* Dostoevsky's novel so convincingly re-creates, and we risk becoming idiots. In this *cachot*, Dostoevsky wants us to realize that love is the only possible response to death and that this love can make us behold our mother, or our son.

## Afterword: From *The Idiot* to *The Brothers Karamazov*

Dostoevsky remained loyal to his beloved "fantastic idiot" in the face of the criticism heaped on his novel and his own doubts about its success, but he would also go on in *The Adolescent* and *The Brothers*

*Karamazov* to explore other ways to be "positively beautiful" and Christlike: ones perhaps less true to the spirit of the whole New Testament (which Myshkin embodies) and more in the spirit of the religious tradition developed by the Russian people, whom Dostoevsky (and Myshkin) prized so highly. In *The Adolescent*, in the pilgrim Makar Dolgoruky, Dostoevsky presents a positively beautiful man, whose meek, all-forgiving, nonconvicting love miraculously comforts and inspires his (accidental) family, when he comes "home" to them to die. And in *The Brothers Karamazov*, Dostoevsky presents other versions of a positively beautiful man in the elder Zosima and in the novice Alyosha Karamazov, who leaves the monastery at his elder's behest in order better to love his brothers. In "The Aesthetics of Russian Folk Religion and *The Brothers Karamazov*," Shanti Elliott identifies and discusses the difference between the elder (the bearer of Dostoevsky's religious vision in *The Brothers Karamazov*) and the holy fool (whom Myshkin resembles): the holy fool, as an idiot, stands apart, outside of the community, and challenges it in a static way, but the elder, still using elements of holy foolery, builds community and responds to suffering in a more overtly constructive way.[32]

Like *The Idiot*, *The Brothers Karamazov* was written as Dostoevsky grieved over the death of a child.[33] When Dostoevsky's three-year-old son, Alyosha, died (of what was believed to be epilepsy), Dostoevsky went with Vladimir Solovyov on a pilgrimage to the monastery of Optina Pustyn. There he was comforted in his grief by the elder Amvrosy, in much the same way as Zosima comforts the peasant woman who comes to him grieving over the loss of her three-year-old son. Whereas the sting of death is felt brutally throughout *The Idiot*, in *The Brothers Karamazov* there are moments when the novel seems to echo Paul in asking, "O Death, where is thy sting? O grave, where is thy victory?" (1 Cor. 15:55).

*The Idiot* boldly asks whether facing death (one's own or that of a loved one) does not make one lose one's faith in God (without which any imitation of Christ is meaningless, for Dostoevsky). In this regard, Dostoevsky echoes Hugo's *Notre Dame de Paris*, where Esméralda's mother, who believes Esméralda has been murdered, declares that "a mother who has lost a child no longer believes in God" in her prayer to Mary, whom she addresses because Mary, too, has been a grieving mother. But in Hugo's *Notre Dame de Paris*, this mother miraculously gets her child back; further, Hugo presents the cathedral, where the action of the novel takes place, as a symbol of faith in 1482, a faith maintained even in the face of dying children. Admittedly, Hugo's concern in *Notre Dame de Paris* is that the printing press, the "Mother-Revolution" will (in his words) "kill" the cathedral and all it represents. The printing press, by allowing any individual to reproduce and disseminate his word, will "kill" the collective faith and spirit that built cathedrals such as Notre Dame.

In *The Idiot*, Dostoevsky picks up where Hugo left off, asking whether faith is possible in the postrevolutionary world of the printing press. In modern Europe and even in the Russia he depicts, Hans Holbein's 1521 painting *Christ in the Tomb* and – even worse, but exactly proving Hugo's point – *copies* of this painting seem to have replaced the Cathedral of Notre Dame as an expression of man's artistic response to death. For Ippolit, this painting makes the universe into a machine that swallows Christ; Myshkin, however, finds in the Russian people a capacity for faith that transcends even Holbein's Christ.[34]

In *The Brothers Karamazov*, Dostoevsky presents the icon of the Mother of God as an emblem of the Russian people's faith (the faith that Myshkin attempted to describe in words to Rogozhin). The Mother of God comforts those grieving over dead children and those fearing death, in general. The devotion of the Russian people to the Mother of God is proverbial and, as Shanti Elliott discusses in her work, the use Dostoevsky makes of this aspect of Russian spirituality determines the aesthetics and ethics of *The Brothers Karamazov*. Here again we see Dostoevsky availing himself of other, perhaps more comforting, ways, of imitating Christ than those set forth in *The Idiot*.

Recent studies have argued, following Dostoevsky's wife's observations, that the Gospel of John was Dostoevsky's favorite and the most influential.[35] While it may have been his favorite all along, perhaps only in *The Brothers Karamazov* (and *Crime and Punishment*, earlier) did he allow its good news to be heard loud and clear. In this regard, his choice of John 12:24 as an epigraph to *The Brothers Karamazov* is significant; it proclaims the fruitfulness of death: "Verily, verily, I say unto you, except a corn of wheat fall into the ground and die, it abideth alone: but if it die, it bringeth forth much fruit." *The Brothers Karamazov* ends with a funeral feast that recalls the celebration of the Eucharist at the Last Supper (as recorded by John), at which Alyosha attempts to convince Kolya Krasotkin (in the role of John's materialist doubting Thomas) that they will indeed see their dead friend Ilyushechka again in heaven. In contrast, Dostoevsky ends *The Idiot* with a murkier message, not wholly comforting, one that preserves all the complexity and disturbing ambiguity of the New Testament: one that combines John 19:26–27, where Mary is told "Behold thy son" and John is told "Behold thy mother," with Mark 16:8, where the Marys find the empty tomb and flee, "for trembling and astonishment had come upon them; and they said nothing to any one, for they were afraid."

## NOTES

1. Friedrich Nietzsche, according to Walter Kaufman, "conceived of Jesus in the image of Dostoevsky's *Idiot.*" In his repudiation of Christ, *Der Antichrist* (The Antichrist) of 1895, Nietzsche elaborated on what he falsely (in my view) perceived as Dostoevsky's criticism of Jesus in *The Idiot.* For more on Nietzsche's response to *The Idiot,* see Walter Kaufman, *Nietzsche: Philosopher, Psychologist, Antichrist,* 3d ed. (New York: Vintage, 1968), 338–42.

2. Robin Feuer Miller, *Dostoevsky and "The Idiot." Author, Narrator, and Reader* (Cambridge: Harvard University Press, 1981), 84. This quote is from the chapter reprinted in this volume, which gives the argument in fuller form.

My reading of *The Idiot* also extends some of the insights provided in Roger Cox's *Between Earth and Heaven: Shakespeare, Dostoevsky and the Meaning of Christian Tragedy* (New York: Holt, Rinehart and Winston, 1969).

3. Aristotle, "Rhetoric," *On Poetry and Style*, trans. and introd. G. M. A. Grube (Indianapolis, Ind.: Bobbs-Merrill, 1958), 1410b–1413a.

4. A translation into English of the Russian 1 Cor. 13:12.

5. Hugh McLean, "Tolstoy and Jesus," in *Christianity and the Eastern Slavs*, Vol. 2, *Russian Culture in Modern Times*, ed. Robert P. Hughes and Irina Paperno (Berkeley and Los Angeles: University of California Press, 1994), 103–23.

6. In a now famous statement (in a letter to N. D. Fonvizina, one of the Decembrists' wives Dostoevsky met in exile [28.1:176; January–February 1854]), Dostoevsky wrote that he would choose Jesus over truth, if forced to make that choice. In writing *The Idiot*, Dostoevsky showed himself, on a novelistic level, making this choice. As he wrote *The Idiot*, he chose Jesus over "truth," a choice that makes the reader's job particularly difficult. The novel contains no easy answers (no answers that can be termed "true"). If it gives us a sense of who Dostoevsky's Jesus was, it does so by indirection. His novel depicts a certain chaos in which it is hard to discern the truth, indeed, in which no particular truth seems to exist, but the essence of Dostoevsky's Jesus is there.

7. G. G. Ermilova makes a beautiful case for this argument in her recent monograph *Taina kniazia Myshkina: O romane Dostoevskogo "Idiot"* (Ivanovo: Ivanovskii gosudarstvennyi universitet, 1993). Natalie Nikolaevna Minihan, "O vliianii Evangeliia na zamysel i na osnovnye literaturnye istochniki romana 'Idiot,'" Ph.D. diss., Brown University, 1989), sees John as the most important (though not exclusive) New Testament source. Minihan (18) cites the interesting statistic that 80 of 180 notations Dostoevsky made in his copy of the New Testament are in John's writings; for that text, see Geir Kjetsaa, *Dostoevsky and His New Testament* (Oslo: Solum, 1984).

8. Cox, *Between Earth and Heaven*, 167.

9. "Qu'on s'imagine un nombre d'hommes dans les chaines, et tous condamnés à mort, dont les uns étant chaque jour égorgés à la vue des autres, ceux qui restent voient leur propre condition dans celle de leurs semblables, et, se regardant les uns et les autres avec douleur et sans espérance, attendent à leur tour. C'est l'image de la condition des hommes." Blaise Pascal, *Pensées*, ed. Ch.-M. des Granges (Paris: Garnier, 1964), no. 199, p. 130.

10. On Dostoevsky and his epilepsy, see the comprehensive study by James Rice, *Dostoevsky and the Healing Art: An Essay in Literary and Medical*

*History* (Ann Arbor, Mich.: Ardis, 1985); on the creative representation of epilepsy in *The Idiot*, see Minihan, "O vliianii," chap. 3, 1–4.

Evidence that Dostoevsky felt a connection between condemnation to death and epilepsy can be seen in his recording that he experienced an epileptic attack at what he calculated was the moment of Tropmann's execution in Paris in 1870. This "coincidence" for Dostoevsky appears to have some inner logic: the spiritual suffering brought about by an epileptic attack and that undergone by a condemned man – and to some degree by the bystanders – are similar, he seems to have felt (and here one could argue that his experience of December 22, 1849, made him something of an authority).

11. *Literaturnoe nasledstvo*, 86: *F. M. Dostoevskii. Novye materialy i issledovaniia*, ed. V. G. Bazanov et al. (Moscow: Nauka, 1973), 169.

12. Susan Haskins, *Mary Magdalen: Myth and Metaphor* (New York: Riverhead Books, 1993), 11–12.

13. The full text is given below in Primary Sources as "Notebook: April 16/28, 1864."

14. As, for example, in a curious Jesuit sermon "L'amour de Madeleine" by Joseph Bonnet (or Jacques Bénigne Bossuet?), discovered and translated by Rainer Maria Rilke (*Die Liebe der Magdalena* [Leipzig: Insel, 1922]) that offers this comment on Jesus and Mary Magdalene: "What do you mean, Jesus Christ, when you pull so strongly at the hearts and draw them so firmly to you, and then go away when they do not in the least expect it? How cruel you are! What a strange game you play with the hearts that love you!" When the women complain: "Jesus laughs at their plaints; He lets it happen that they exhaust and consume themselves in inexpressible desire. He even undertakes to kindle the flame of their passion and watches them from a distance, and it does not move Him; He makes fun, as it were, of their imagination and rage. That is how He treated Mary Magdalen also. At first, nothing is too much for Him. She desires His feet, He gives them; she wants to kiss them, He lets her; she wants to anoint His head, He endures it; the Pharisees grumble, He defends her; Judas is scandalized, He praises her; Martha complains and Jesus champions Mary." But, "Jesus, as soon as He has made the bond tight enough, cautiously withdraws His hand [from Mary]." "He gives nothing more to her; but that is not enough; he even by and by takes back what He had given" (27–29).

15. F. I. Tiutchev, *Izbrannye stikhotvoreniia* (New York: Chekhov, 1952), 154. Tiutchev was, during the period of Dostoevsky's exile, Maikov's supe-

rior in the censorship office where Maikov worked. His name crops up in the Dostoevsky–Maikov correspondence.

16. As Robin Feuer Miller has shown us in her *Dostoevsky and "The Idiot."*

17. Joseph Frank, *Dostoevsky: The Miraculous Years, 1865–1871* (Princeton: Princeton University Press, 1995), 229–30.

18. Possibly related is that in his 1873 description of the discussion forty years before in which Belinsky criticized Christ for his failings, Dostoevsky notes the tears in his own eyes but does not report his retorts. Perhaps he too responded with silence – or perhaps his response is the novels he wrote years later.

19. Marina Woronzoff-Dashkoff, "The Sympathetic Vision: Ethical and Aesthetic Patterns in Dostoevsky's *The Idiot*" (Ph.D. diss., Yale University, 1995).

20. "Do not think that I have come to bring peace on earth; I have not come to bring peace, but a sword. For I have come to set a man against his father, and a daughter against her mother, and a daughter-in-law against her mother-in-law; and a man's foes will be those of his own household. He who loves father or mother more than me is not worthy of me; and he who loves son or daughter more than me is not worthy of me; and he who does not take his cross and follow me is not worthy of me. He who finds his life will lose it, and he who loses his life for my sake will find it" (Matt. 10:34–39).

21. See also the discussions of this in the dissertations of Natalie Minihan ("O vliianii," pp. 34–38) and Marina Woronzoff-Dashkoff ("Sympathetic Vision," 180–84). Woronzoff-Dashkov, likewise citing Tanner's interpretation of John 8, goes on to criticize Myshkin's forgiveness of Nastasya Filippovna: "By acting like Christ, a benefactor who would save with his compassion, . . . he exhibits the extraordinary man's possession of the 'right in himself, to permit his conscience to overstep,'" much like Raskolnikov.

22. Konstantin Mochulsky, *Dostoevsky: His Life and Work*, trans. and introd. Michael A. Minihan (Princeton: Princeton University Press, 1967), 367.

23. *Otkrovennye rasskazy strannika dukhovnomu svoemu ottsu*, 4th ed. (Paris: YMCA Press), 100.

24. "According to Old Testament Law, the adulterous man and woman are almost without exception to be excluded from society, canceled even to the point of execution. In the New Testament, Christ confronted with the

woman taken in adultery makes the would-be lawgivers aware of her problematical reality, calling into question both the impersonal application of the law and the justification and rights of the would-be legislators. Effectively this implies the disintegration of society-as-constituted." Tony Tanner, *Adultery in the Novel: Contract and Transgression* (Baltimore: Johns Hopkins University Press, 1979), 14.

25. Although not a novel of adultery as such, *The Idiot* has many of the same concerns as the traditional novel of adultery. Or perhaps the presence in the novel of Radomsky, Prince Shch., and even the narrator (as Robin Feuer Miller's work suggests) assures that the scribes and Pharisees are properly represented and that enough of Tanner's tension exists?

26. Tanner's term for an indulgence in words analogous to sexual indulgence.

27. Robert Louis Jackson has made this argument in his discussion of how Dostoevsky "undertook in his art to express the new social chaos," a prime manifestation of which was the "disintegrating family." This required a new form and a new type of realism. See *Dostoevsky's Quest for Form: A Study of His Philosophy of Art* (New Haven: Yale University Press, 1966), 110–18.

Gary Rosenshield comments on how the chaos of the Russian family (and of the individual) depicted within the novel is also a part of its structure: "Chaos seems to affect and infect every aspect of the novel, from the daily lives of the characters to the narrative structure itself. Partly because *Idiot* was conceived as a family novel, the ravages of this disorder are most evident in the dissolution of the Russian family" (880). See "Chaos, Apocalypse, the Laws of Nature: Autonomy and 'Unity' in Dostoevskii's *Idiot*," *Slavic Review* 50 (1991): 879–89.

28. Jackson, in reference to this quote, notes that "all art – we must remember – from one point of view for Dostoevsky is a guessing, a divining of the 'subsurface unexpressed future Word'" (Jackson, *Quest*, 116–17).

For discussion of the poetics of the accidental family as it relates to Dostoevsky's *The Adolescent*, see my *The Annihilation of Inertia: Dostoevsky and Metaphysics* (Evanston: Northwestern University Press, 1996), 131–71.

29. And, in the same vein, what occurs between part 1 and part 2 of the novel is left a mystery.

30. When Charles Bovary is asked his name by the teacher, he has trouble articulating it, is asked to repeat it, and finally "hurls out one word:

*Charbovari.*" "Charbovari" evokes, as commentary on the novel has noted, the word "charivari": the term for the mocking ritual celebration of "serenading" newlyweds on their wedding night by making a loud racket (banging on pots and pans and so forth) under their windows. Couples considered to be incongruous were especially likely targets of charivari. Flaubert thus imparts a kind of onomastic destiny to Charles's name – or at least to the way he pronounces it. The fact that Charles's schoolmates then begin to taunt him by crying "Charbovari! Charbovari!" enacts a kind of charivari. The scene suggests that it is Charles's destiny to be cuckolded and mocked.

31. Tony Tanner (*Adultery*, 21–22) writes of this passage, which is one of the cornerstones of his interpretation of the "novel of adultery": "Christ refuses to look and, initially, refuses to talk. That is, he refuses to participate in his purely specular attitude to the woman and to discuss her as a category. By doing this he restores the full existential reality to the situation that society seeks to deny. By treating the woman as spectacle and category, the representatives of society attempt to alienate her from her own being and to separate themselves from her by adopting the role of being the community from which the woman by her offense has isolated herself. Christ refuses to participate in their discourse, and when he does speak it is to them directly. This has two effects. It thrusts them back into their own interiority (they are 'convicted by their own *conscience*'), and it dissolves the group identity within which they have concealed themselves (they go out 'one by one' as individuals, having arrived as 'scribes and Pharisees')."

32. (Ph.D. diss., University of California at Berkeley, 1997). Holy fools are also discussed in Walter Nigg, *Der christliche Narr* (Zurich: Artemis, 1956); Margaret Ziolkowski, *Hagiography and Modern Russian Literature* (Princeton: Princeton University Press, 1988); and Harriet Murav, *Holy Foolishness: Dostoevsky's Novels and the Poetics of Cultural Critque* (Stanford: Stanford University Press, 1992).

33. On the ways in which this novel responds to this death, see Robin Feuer Miller, "*The Brothers Karamazov*": *Worlds of the Novel* (New York: Twayne, 1992).

34. See 8:183–84. In this scene, Myshkin and Rogozhin discuss Holbein's painting. Myshkin grants that this painting *could* make some lose their faith but then launches into tales from his travels in the heart of Russia. He tells stories that express to him the Russian people's capacity for religious feeling, even in the face of sin. In one, a peasant woman likens God's joy at a sinner

praying to that of a mother witnessing the first smile of her baby. For discussion of Myshkin's response to Holbein's Christ and how it counters Ippolit's, see Joseph Frank, *Miraculous Years*, 327–28, 332–33.

35. See Minihan, "O vliianii Evangeliia," and Ermilova, *Taina kniazia Myshkina*.

# III PRIMARY SOURCES

# Primary Sources

## 1. Notebook: April 16/28, 1864

*The passage below was written by Dostoevsky on Holy Thursday, 1864, as his first wife awaited burial. The ideas about love, death, and eternal life are given artistic expression and novelistic form in* The Idiot. *All four of the articles in the Criticism section of this volume refer to this seminal passage from Dostoevsky's notebook.*

F. M. Dostoevskii, *Polnoe sobranie sochinenii v tridtsati tomakh*, ed. V. G. Bazanov et al. (Leningrad: Nauka, 1973), 20:172–75.

*April 16.* Masha is lying on the table. Will I see Masha again?

To love a person, *as oneself*, according to Christ's commandment, is impossible. The law of the self is binding on earth. The *I* stands in the way. Only Christ was able to, but Christ was the eternal ideal of ages, toward which man strives and must strive, according to the law of nature. Further, after the appearance of Christ, *the ideal of man in flesh*, it became as clear as day that the highest, the final development of the self must exactly (at the end of development, at the very moment of achieving the goal) get to the point when man will find, recognize, and with all the strength of his nature become convinced that the highest use to which man could put his self and the full development of his *I* – that is to destroy that *I*, to give it away in its entirety to each and everyone, completely and unconditionally. And that is the greatest happiness. In this way, the law of *I* merges with the law of humanism, and in that merger, both the *I* and *the all* (evidently two extreme opposites), are mutually destroyed for each other, while at the same time they achieve, each in its own way, the highest goal of individual development.

And that is what the paradise of Christ is. All of history, whether of mankind or even to some extent of each person separately, is just a process, a struggle, a striving for and approach to this goal.

But if this [is the] ultimate goal of mankind (once it is attained, mankind will not have to develop, that is, to strive, to struggle, in the face of all his failures to glimpse the ideal and eternally to strive for it; that is, there'll be no need to live), then, consequently, man, by striving, defines his earthly existence. Thus, man on earth is a being necessarily developing, accordingly, not finished, but transitional.

But to strive for such a great goal, to my way of thinking, would be utterly senseless if, upon reaching the goal, all is extinguished and disappears; that is, if man does not also have life after he reaches the goal. Consequently, there is a future, heavenly life.

What it is like, where it is, on what planet, in what center, in the ultimate center, that is in bosom of the universal synthesis, that is, of God? – we don't know. We know only one feature of the future nature of the future being, which will hardly be called man (accordingly, we don't have a clue what kind of beings we will be). This feature has been foretold and guessed by Christ – the great and ultimate ideal of the development of all mankind – who appeared to us, in accordance with the law of our history, in flesh;

that feature:

"They neither marry nor are given in marriage but live as angels of God" – this is a deeply meaningful feature.

1) They do not *marry* and are not *given in marriage* – because there's no reason; to develop, to strive for the goal whereby one generation succeeds another is no longer necessary and

2) Marriage and giving a woman in marriage is the most extreme rejection of humanism, the complete isolation of the couple from *everyone* (little is left over for everyone else). The family – that's the law of nature, but it is nevertheless an abnormal, egoistic (in every sense of the word) condition of man. The family – that is the greatest holy of man on earth, for by means of this law of nature, man strives for the development of his goal (that is, by means of the succession of generations). But at the same time man must, by the same law of nature, in the name of the ultimate ideal of his goal, constantly deny it. (Duality).

NB. The Antichrists are mistaken in trying to refute Christianity by means of the following major objections: 1) "Why is it that if

Christianity is true it does not reign on earth; why do men continue to suffer, why have they not become brothers to each other?"

In fact it is quite obvious why: because it is an ideal for the future, ultimate life of man, whereas on earth man is in a transitional state. It will come into being but only after the goal has been achieved, when man has by the laws of nature been definitively reborn as another nature that does not marry and is not given in marriage and, second, Christ Himself preached His teaching only as an ideal, He Himself foretold that until the end of the world there would be struggle and development (the teaching about the sword), for this is a law of nature, because on earth life is in the process of developing, whereas there [what awaits is] an existence that is one of total synthesis, eternally delightful and full, for which, therefore, "there will be time no more."

$NB_2$. The atheists, in rejecting God and the future life, are horribly inclined to present it all in human terms, and that is how they err. The nature of God is diametrically opposed to the nature of man. As a result of science man is going from multiplicity to the Synthesis, from facts to generalization and comprehension. But the nature of God is different. It is the complete synthesis of all being, self-contemplating itself in multiplicity, in Analysis.

But if man is not man – what will his nature be?

It is impossible to understand that on earth, but its law can be sensed both by all of mankind through its indirect manifestations (Prudhomme, the origin of God), and by each individual person.

It is the merger of the full *I*, that is, of knowledge and synthesis *with all.* "Love all like oneself." That is impossible on earth, for it contradicts the law of the development of the self and the striving for the final goal, by which man is bound. Accordingly, it is not an ideal law, as the Antichrists say, but the law of our ideal.

NB. Thus, it all hinges on this: Christ is taken as the ultimate ideal on earth; that is, it all depends on Christian faith. Should you believe in Christ, then you believe that you will live forever. Is there future life for any *I* in that case? They say that man disintegrates and dies *entirely.*

We already know that it can't be entirely, because man, just as when he gives birth physically to a son, he transfers to him some part of his self, so also morally he leaves a memory of himself to people (NB. *The wish for eternal memory* at memorials is significant); that is, man, through a part of his former self that lived on earth, enters into the future development of mankind. We can see clearly that the memory of great teachers of man lives among people (as does the development of villains), and even for man it is the greatest happiness to follow after them. That means that part of their natures goes by flesh and spirit into other people. Christ has entirely gone into mankind, and man strives to transform into the *I* of Christ as his ideal. If he should achieve that, he would clearly see that everyone who has this goal on earth has come to participate in the makeup of his final nature, that is, in Christ. (The synthetic nature of Christ is astounding. After all that is the nature of God, so, Christ is the reflection of God on earth.) Just how each *I* will be resurrected then – in the universal Synthesis – is difficult to imagine. But what is living, what has not died even before the final attainment and what is reflected in the final ideal – that must revive in the life that is final, synthetic, eternal. We will be people, constantly merging with everything, not giving in marriage and not marrying, in various arrangements (in my father's house are many mansions). All will then perceive and know itself for all time. But how that will be, in what form, in what nature – it is difficult for man to formulate for himself definitively.

And so, man strives on earth toward an ideal *counter* to his nature. When man has not fulfilled the law of striving toward this ideal, that is, has not through *love* sacrificed his *I* to other people (I and Masha), then he experiences suffering and has called this state sin. And so, man must constantly experience suffering, which is counterbalanced by the heavenly delight of fulfilling the law, that is, through sacrifice. Herein lies the earthly balance. Otherwise the earth would be without meaning.

The teaching of the materialists – universal inertia and the mechanics of matter – is death. The teaching of the true philosophy is the annihilation of inertia, it is the thought, it is the center and Synthesis of the universe and its external form, matter, it is God, it is eternal life.

## 2. Anna Dostoevsky, "Geneva (1868)"

*In the passage below Dostoevsky's wife describes Dostoevsky as father to their first child and his response to her death.*

A. G. Dostoevskaia, *Vospominaniia A. G. Dostoevskoi,* ed. L. P. Grossman (Moscow and Leningrad: Gosdarstvennoe izd., 1925. Reprint: [n.p.]: Gregory Lounz Books, 1969), 121–22.

When a certain order had been established, there began a life that left fond memories forever. To my great happiness, Fyodor Mikhailovich turned out to be a very tender father: he always was there during her bath helping me, he himself wrapped her up in his arms in a little blanket and pinned her up with English pins, carried her and rocked her and, stopping work, would hurry to her as soon as he heard her cry. His first question on awakening or returning home was, "How's Sonya? Healthy? Did she sleep well? Eat?" Fyodor Mikhailovich would sit for hours on end at her bed, singing her songs or talking with her. In fact, by the third month he was convinced that she recognized him. Here is what he wrote to Maikov on May 18/May 29, 1868: "This little, three-month-old being, so helpless, so tiny – for me was already a face and a character. She had begun to recognize me, and love me, and she would smile when I came near. When I would sing her songs in my funny voice, she loved to listen to them. She did not cry and make a face when I kissed her. She stopped crying when I came near."

But it was not to be for long that we would enjoy this cloudless happiness. In the first days of May the weather was glorious, and we, on the insistent advice of the doctor, would take our precious baby to the Jardin des Anglais, where she would sleep two or three hours in her carriage. On one fateful day during one of these walks, the weather changed suddenly, and a wind (*bise*) came up, and evidently our girl caught cold, because that same night she began to run a fever and developed a cough. We immediately consulted the best pediatrician in Geneva, and he saw her every day, assuring us that she would recover. Even just three hours before she died, he said that she was noticeably better. Despite his reassurances, Fyodor Mikhailovich could not concentrate on anything, and hardly left the side of her cradle. We both were in a horrible state of anxiety, and our gloomy forebodings proved justified: on the afternoon of May 12/24, our beloved Sonya died. It is beyond me to describe the despair that took hold of us when we saw our dear daughter dead. While I was deeply shaken and saddened by her death, I was terribly afraid for my unhappy husband: his despair was stormy, he sobbed and cried like a woman standing in front of the cold body of his beloved child, and covered her pale little face and hands with burning kisses. Such stormy despair I have never ever seen. It seemed to both of us that we would not survive our grief. For two days we went together, not parting for a moment, around to various institutions to get the permission to bury our little baby, together we ordered everything for her burial, together we dressed her in a white velvet dress, together we put her in a small white coffin lined with velvet, and we cried, cried without restraint. It was horrible to look at Fyodor Mikhailovich, in the week of Sonya's illness he had grown so thin. On the third day we took our little treasure to the Russian church for services, and from there to the cemetery in Plainpalais, where she was buried in a separate section for children. After several days her grave was planted around with cypress trees and in their midst a white marble cross was placed. Every day my husband and I would go to the cemetery, take flowers, and cry. It was just too painful for us to part with our priceless baby, so genuinely and deeply had we come to love her, so many hopes and dreams were tied with her very existence.

## 3. Letters

*Isolated from homeland, friends, family, and his reading public, Dostoevsky relied heavily on his correspondence during the period he was writing* The

Idiot. *The letters below have been selected for the insights they provide into the writing of* The Idiot *and the life of the man who wrote it.*

*The translations and notes are from volumes 2 and 3 of David Lowe's edition of the* Complete Letters *of Dostoevsky (Ann Arbor, Mich.: Ardis, 1989–90). The letter numbers in parentheses are the same as those used in the Russian edition of Dostoevsky's collected works. Lowe's notes are included, with slight alterations.*

## AUGUST 16/28, 1867: APOLLON MAIKOV (NO. 317)

*This letter to Dostoevsky's close friend Apollon Maikov provides an excellent picture of Dostoevsky's state of mind as he settled down in Geneva to write* The Idiot. *It also describes the circumstances and conditions of the Dostoevskys' "exile" from Russia, Dostoevsky's feelings about his second wife, and his ruminations over the fate of Russia and contemporary ideological trends. It gives an entertaining account of his meeting with Turgenev. Like many of Dostoevsky's letters, it details his desperate finances and ends with a plea for a loan.*

For what a long time I've been silent and not answered your dear letter, dear and unforgettable friend Apollon Nikolaevich.[1] I call you *unforgettable friend* and feel in my heart that the title is correct: you and I *go back so far and are so used to each other* that life, which has sometimes separated and even *pulled us apart,* not only has failed in fact to pull us apart, but may even have brought us together permanently. If you write that you have rather felt my absence, then how much more have I yours. In addition to the conviction about the similarity and agreement in our views and feelings, which has been confirmed in me daily, consider as well that having lost you, I have landed, in addition, in an alien land, where not only is there not a Russian face, Russian books, or Russian thoughts and cares to be found, but not even a friendly face![2] Really, I can't even understand how a Russian abroad, if only he has feelings and sense, can fail to notice this and feel it painfully. Perhaps those faces are in fact friendly for themselves, but to us it seems that they aren't for us. It really is that way! And how can one spend one's life abroad? Without one's native land it's suffering, honest to God! To go even for half a year, even for a year, is all right. But to go the way I have, without knowing and without foreseeing when I'll return, is very bad and distressing. The idea is distressing. And I need Russia, need it for my *writing* and work (not to mention the rest of life), and how badly I need it! It's just like a fish out of water; you lose your strength and means. In general we'll have a talk about this. I need to talk to you about a lot of things and ask your advice and help. You are the *only* person with whom I can speak from here. NB. By the way, read this letter off on your own and don't tell anyone about me who doesn't need to know. You'll see for yourself. One more word: why haven't I written to you in such a long time? I don't have the energy to answer you about that in detail. I felt myself to be too unstable and was waiting for the slightest settled way of life in order to begin a correspondence with you. I rely on you, on you alone. Write me more often; don't abandon me, my friend! And I'll be writing you very often and regularly now. Let's start up a constant correspondence, please! That will take the place of Russia for me and will give me energy.

I'll tell you about these four months tant bien que mal [so-so] and frankly.

You know how I left and for what reasons. The two main reasons: (1) to save not only my health, but even my life. The attacks had begun to repeat themselves every week, and clearly *sensing* and recognizing that nervous and *cerebral* disorder was unbearable. My reason really was coming unhinged – that's the truth. I sensed that, and the derangement of my nerves sometimes led to moments of frenzy. The second reason is my circumstances: the creditors could not wait any longer, and at the time I left, Latkin and Pechatkin had already initiated proceedings against me for recovery of their money,[3] and I just barely avoided being seized. Let's suppose (and I'm not saying this for the sake of ornament and not for the sake of effect) *debtors' prison*, on the one hand, would have been even useful for me: the reality, the material, a second House of the Dead, in a word, there would have been enough material for four or five thousand rubles, but after all, I had just gotten married and, in addition, would I have survived that stifling summer in Tarasov's building?[4] That made an insoluble question. If it were impossible for me to write in Tarasov's building, because of increased attacks, what would I pay off my debts with? And a terrible burden had accumulated. I set off, but I left back then with death in my heart: I didn't believe in abroad, that is, I believed that the psychic influence of abroad would be very bad: alone, *without material*, with a young person who with naive joy strove to share my peripatetic life with me; but after all, I saw that there was a great deal of inexperience and first ardor in that naive joy, and that disturbed me and worried me. I was afraid that Anna Grigoryevna[5] would be bored with me. And after all, we really have been alone together until now. I wasn't relying on myself: I have a morbid personality, and I foresaw that she would be tormented to death with me. (NB. True, Anna Grigoryevna has turned out to be stronger and deeper than I knew her to be and imagined, and in many cases she has simply been a guardian angel for me; but at the same time there is much of the child and the twenty-year-old in her, which is wonderful and naturally essential, but to which I doubt that I have the energy and capacity to respond. All of that occurred to me during the departure, and although, I repeat, Anna Grigoryevna has turned out to be both stronger and better than I thought, I'm still not at ease yet.) Finally, our limited means worried me: we had left with quite small means and *had borrowed an advance of* THREE (!) thousand from Katkov. True, I planned to get down to work right away after leaving for abroad. What has turned out to be the case? I have not done anything or hardly anything yet and am only beginning to do serious, finished work now. True, I'm still in doubt with regard to my not having done *anything;* but lots of various things have been felt sharply and *thought up;* but there is still only a little down *in black and white*,[6] and after all, what's *in black and white* is in fact what's final; that's the only thing they pay for.

After quickly leaving boring Berlin (where I stayed for one day, where the boring Germans nonetheless had time to unsettle my nerves to the point of fury and where I went to a Russian bathhouse), we moved on to Dresden, rented an apartment, and settled in for a while.

A strange impression resulted; right away the question occurred to me of why I was in Dresden, precisely in Dresden, and not somewhere in another place, and for what precisely had it been worth dropping everything in one place and moving to another. The answer was clear (health, debts, and so on), but what was also bad was that I sensed very clearly that no matter where I live now, it turns out to be *all the same*, in Dresden or anywhere, anywhere abroad, everywhere a loner. I had wanted to set immediately to work and sensed that I absolutely couldn't work, that the impression was absolutely the wrong one. What did I do? Led a vegetable existence. I read, wrote a bit, suffered from ennui, and then from the heat. The days passed monotonously. Anya and I regularly took walks after dinner in the Grand Garden, listened to cheap music, then read, and then went to sleep. In Anna Grigoryevna's personality there has turned out to be absolute antiquarianism (and that's even pleasant and amusing for me). For her, for example, it's a thoroughly satisfying undertaking to go examine some silly town hall, make notes about it, describe it (which she does with her own stenographic marks and has filled up seven tablets), but more than anything else she has been taken and struck by the Gallery, and I was very glad for that, because too many impressions were revived in her soul for her to get bored. She went to the Gallery every day. How much have she and I talked about and discussed all our friends, Petersburgers, Muscovites, you and Anna Ivanovna;[7] it was rather sad.

I'm not describing my thoughts to you. Many impressions have accumulated. I read Russian newspapers and unburdened my heart. I sensed in myself at last that enough material had accumulated for a whole piece about Russia's relations to Europe and about the Russian upper stratum.[8] But what's the point of talking about that! The Germans upset my nerves, and the life of our Russian upper stratum and its faith in Europe and *civilization* did too. The incident in Paris shook me horribly.[9] The Paris lawyers who shouted "Vive la Pologne" [Long live Poland] are fine ones too. Ugh, what vileness, and most importantly – stupidity and conventionalism. I also became even more convinced of my former idea that it's even rather to our advantage that Europe doesn't know us and knows us in such a foul way. And the details of the trial of that shitty Beryozovsky![10] How much vile conventionalism; but most importantly, most importantly – how is it they haven't run out of things to say, how is it they're still stuck in the same spot, the very same spot!

From here Russia also seems more distinct to people like me. The extraordinary fact of the stability and unexpected maturity of the Russian people in encountering all our reforms (if only the legal one alone) and at the same time the news about the merchant of the first guild of Orenburg Province flogged by the chief of police.[11] One thing can be felt: that the Russian people, thanks to its benefactor and his reforms,[12] has finally been put little by little into such a position that it is being forced to become accustomed to efficiency and self-observation, and that's the whole point. Honest to God, because of the great break and the reforms, the time now is nearly more important than Peter the Great's. And how about the railroads? Let's have some to the south soon, as soon as possible; that's the whole point. By that time there will be *correct judgment* everywhere, and then what a great renewal! (All of that is being thought about, dreamed of, and wished for with all one's heart here.)

Here, although I've hardly seen anyone, it's impossible not to run into people by accident. In Germany I ran into a Russian who lives abroad permanently, goes to Russia every year for three weeks or so to receive his income, and returns to Germany again, where his wife and children are; they've all become Germanized.

By the way, I asked him why exactly he had become an expatriate. He answered literally (and with irritated impudence): "There is civilization here, while we have barbarism. In addition, there aren't any nationalities here; I rode the train yesterday and couldn't tell a Frenchman from an Englishman or from a German."

"So in *your* opinion, that means that's progress?"

"But of course."

"But you know, that's absolutely not so. A Frenchman is above all a Frenchman, and an Englishman an Englishman, and being themselves is their highest goal. Moreover, that is in fact their strength."

"Absolutely untrue. Civilization ought to level everything, and we won't be happy until we forget that we're Russians, and everyone looks like everyone else. We shouldn't listen to Katkov, after all!"[13]

"You don't like Katkov?"

"He's a scoundrel."

"Why?"

"Because he doesn't like Poles."

"And do you read his journal?"

"No, I never read it."

I'm conveying that conversation literally. This person belongs to the young progressives, although he seems to steer clear of everyone. They all turn into peevish and squeamish spitzes abroad.

Finally, in Dresden ennui wore Anna Grigoryevna and me out. And most importantly, the following facts presented themselves: (1) according to the letters that Pasha[14] forwarded me (he in fact only wrote me once), it turned out that my creditors had instituted proceedings against me for recovery of the money (that means *that I cannot return to Russian until the money is paid).* (2) My wife felt herself to be pregnant *(that is, please,* between us. Nine months will be up in February: that means there's all the more reason I cannot return.). (3) The question arose of what would happen to my people in Petersburg, Emilia Fyodorovna[15] and Pasha and certain others. Money, money, and I didn't have any! (4) If we were to spend the winter, then we should winter somewhere in the south. Moreover, I wanted to show Anna Grigoryevna at least something, to amuse her, to travel a bit with her. We decided to winter somewhere in Switzerland or in Italy. But no money. The money we'd borrowed had already been spent. I wrote to Katkov, described my situation, and asked for *an advance* of another 500 rubles. And what do you think: it was sent! What a wonderful person he is! What a heart the man has! We set off for Switzerland. But here I'll begin describing for you my vile and shameful deeds.

Dear Apollon Nikolaevich, I sense that I could have considered you as my judge. You're a person and a citizen; you're a person with a heart, of which fact you have long since persuaded me; you're a model husband and father; finally, I have always valued your judgment. It's not painful for me to confess to you. But I'm writing this only for you, just you. Don't turn me over to the tongues of idle gossips.

Passing not far from Baden, it occurred to me to drop in there. I was tormented by a tempting idea: of sacrificing 10 louis d'ors and maybe winning 2000 extra francs; after all, that is living expenses for four months, with everything, with the Petersburg people. Most awful of all is that previously I had had occasion to win sometimes. And worst of all is that my nature is vile and very passionate: everywhere and in everything I go to the last limit; I've been going over the line my whole life.

The devil immediately played a prank on me: in some three days I won 4000 francs, with extraordinary ease. Now I'll depict for your how all of this presented itself to me: on the one hand, that easy win – in three days I had made four thousand francs out of a hundred. On the other hand, the debts, the legal proceedings, the spiritual alarm, the impossibility of returning to Russia. Finally, third and most important – the gambling itself. You know how that draws you in. No, I swear to you, it's not just self-interest, although above all I needed the money as money. Anna Grigoryevna implored me to be satisfied with the 4000 francs and leave immediately. But after all, such an easy and possible chance to fix everything! And examples? In addition to my own winnings you see people getting 20,000 or 30,000 francs daily. (You don't see losers.) What makes them sacred? I need money more then they do. I took a further risk and lost. I began losing *the last* of my money, getting feverishly irritated, and lost. I started pawning my clothing. Anna Grigoryevna pawned *everything* of hers, her last things (What an angel! How she tried to comfort me, how she languished in thrice-cursed Baden, in our two rooms over a blacksmith shop, where we had moved.). Finally, it was enough, everything was lost. (Oh, how vile the Germans are at the same time. What usurers, scoundrels, and cheats they all are, every last one of them. The landlady for our apartment, realizing that for the time being, until we got money, we had no place to go, increased the price!) Finally, we had to save ourselves, to leave Baden. I wrote Katkov again, asked for 500 rubles again (without mentioning the circumstances, but the letter was from Baden, and he probably understood a thing or two). Well, sir, he sent it! He sent it! I have now taken a total *advance* of 4000 from *The Russian Herald.* But here's what's the matter: out of that 500, more than half went for the payment of the interest and the re-pawning of our furniture in Petersburg, which Anna Grigoryevna's mother did. At my request, the money from *The R[ussian] Herald* was addressed to her. Then 100 rubles went to pay off debts in Baden; we're still waiting for 50 rubles: Anna Grigoryevna's mother will send it (out of the same 500 rubles. That's the remainder that's not yet been received); and finally, about two hundred francs were left for the move to Geneva (Why to Geneva? How should I know? Isn't it all the same?). We moved to Geneva, rented a chambre garnie [furnished room] from two old women, and now, that is, on the fourth day, *all the money we have left* is 18 francs. Except for the 50 rubles that we expect any day from Anna Nikolavna, there is no prospect of receiving any money for a couple of months.

But to finish with Baden, we suffered through seven weeks in that hell. At the very beginning, when I had just arrived in Baden, I met Goncharov at the train station. How embarrassed Ivan Alexandrovich was by me at first. That deputy counselor of state or counselor of state was also losing. But since it turned out that it was impossible to hide, and that in addition I myself was gambling with very crude candor, he stopped hiding from me too. He gambled with a feverish ardor (for small stakes, silver), gambled for the 2 weeks that he stayed in Baden and, I think, lost a significant amount. But God grant him health, the nice man; when I had lost my shirt (and he had seen a lot of gold in my hands), he gave me a loan of 60 francs, at my request. He must have reproached me horribly for losing everything, and not half, as he had done.

Goncharov kept talking to me about Turgenev, so that although I had put off going to see Turgenev, I finally ventured to pay him a visit. I went at 12:00 noon and found him having breakfast. I'll tell you candidly: even before that I disliked the man personally. Worst of all is that since 1867, since Wiesbaden, I have owed him 50 thalers (and haven't yet paid them back!). I also dislike the aristocratically farcical embrace of his with which he starts to kiss you but offers you his cheek. The horrible airs of a general; but most important, his book *Smoke* had put me out. He himself told me that the main idea, the main point of his book was contained in the phrase "If Russia disappeared, *there would not be* any loss or any agitation among mankind." He told me that was his fundamental conviction about Russia. I found him terribly put out by the failure of *Smoke*. And I confess that I did not know all the details of the failure. You had written me about Strakhov's article in *Notes of the Fa[therland]*, but I didn't know that he had been given a lashing everywhere and that in Moscow, at a club, I think, people were collecting names in order to protest his *Smoke*. He told me that himself. I confess to you that I could never have imagined that one could expose the wounds to one's vanity as naively and awkwardly as Turgenev does. And those people boast of the fact, by the way, that they are *atheists!* He declared to me that he is an atheist through and through. But my God, deism gave us Christ, that is, such a lofty notion of man that it cannot be comprehended without reverence, and one cannot help believing that this ideal of humanity is everlasting! And what have they, the Turgenevs, Herzens, Utins,[16] and Chernyshevkys presented us with? Instead of the loftiest divine beauty, which they spit on, they are all so disgustingly selfish, so shamelessly irritable, flippantly proud, that it's simply incomprehensible what they're hoping for and who will follow them. He criticized Russia and Russians monstrously, horribly. But here's what I've noticed: all these trashy little liberals and progressives, primarily still of Belinsky's school, find their greatest pleasure and satisfaction in criticizing Russia.[17] The difference is that

Chernyshevsky's followers simply criticize Russia and openly wish for its collapse (primarily for its collapse!). Those people, Belinsky's offspring, add that they *love Russia*. But meanwhile not only is everything of the slightest originality in Russia hateful to them, so that they deny it and immediately take enjoyment in turning it into a caricature, but that if one really were to present them finally with a fact that they could not overturn or ruin in a caricature, but to which they definitely would have to be reconciled, I think that they would be unhappy to the point of torture, *to the point of pain*, to the point of despair. (2) I noticed that Turgenev, for instance (just like everyone who has not been to Russia in a long time), are absolutely ignorant of the facts (although they do read newspapers) and have so crudely lost every bit of feeling for Russia, fail to understand such ordinary facts, which even our Russian nihilist no longer denies, but simply caricatures in his own way. By the way, Turgenev said that we ought to crawl before the Germans, that there is one path common to everyone and unavoidable – civilization, and that all attempts at Russianism and independence are swinishness and stupidity. He said that he was writing a long article against Russophiles and Slavophiles.[18] I advised him, for the sake of convenience, to order a telescope from Paris. "What for?" he asked. "It's far from here," I replied, "Train your telescope on Russia and examine us, because otherwise it really is hard to make us out." He got horribly angry. Seeing him so irritated, I really said to him with extraordinarily successful naiveté: "But I really didn't expect that all this criticism of you and the failure of *Smoke* would irritate you so much; honest to God, *it isn't worth it*, forget about it all." "But I'm not at all irritated. What do you mean?" he said, turning red. I interrupted the conversation; we began talking about domestic and personal affairs. I took my hat and somehow, absolutely without intention, by the way, said what had accumulated in my soul from the Germans in three months:

"Do you know what rogues and swindlers one comes across here. Really, the common people here are much worse and more dishonest then ours, and what is sillier, there's no doubt of that. Well, here you go on talking about civilization; well, what has civilization done for them and what can they boast of so very much before us?"

He turned pale (literally; I'm not exaggerating a bit, not a bit!) and said to me: "In talking like that you offend me *personally.* You should know that I have settled in here permanently, that I consider myself a German, not a Russian, and I'm proud of that!" I replied: "Although I have read *Smoke* and have been speaking with you now for a whole hour, I couldn't at all have expected that you would say that, and therefore please forgive me for having offended you." Then we parted quite politely, and I vowed to myself never again to set foot at Turgenev's. On the following day Turgenev, at exactly *10 o'clock* in the morning, came by to see me and left the landlords his calling card, to have it given to me. But since I myself had told him the day before that I could not receive him earlier than *twelve o'clock* and that we slept until *eleven,* I took his arrival at *10 o'clock* in the morning as a clear hint that he didn't want to meet me and had paid a visit to me at 10 o'clock precisely so that I would realize that. During the whole seven weeks I met him one time only, at the train station. We looked at each other, but neither he nor I wished to exchange greetings.

It may be, dear Apollon Nikolaevich, that the malicious pleasure with which I have been describing Turgenev to you and how we offended each other will seem unpleasant to you. But honest to God, I can't help it; he offended me too much with his convictions. Personally I don't care, although with his airs of a general he is not very attractive; but one can't listen to such criticism of Russia from a Russian turncoat who could have been useful. I noticed his crawling before the Germans and his hatred of Russia a long time ago, as early as four years ago.[19] But the present irritation and anger at Russia, to the point of foaming at the mouth, comes exclusively from the failure of *Smoke* and the fact that Russia has dared not to recognize him as a genius. It is pure vanity at work here, and that is all the more disgusting.

But to hell with all of them!

Now listen, my friend, to my intentions: I of course did a foul thing in losing. But relatively speaking, I lost only a little of my money. Nonetheless that money could have served me for two months of living expenses, even for four, judging by the way we live. I've already told you: I couldn't stand up against the winning. If I had originally lost ten louis d'ors, as I had decided for myself, I would have immediately given it all up and left. But winning 4000 francs was my undoing! There was no chance of resisting the temptation of winning more (when that had turned out to be so easy) and at one fell swoop to get out of all these proceedings, provide for myself for a time and for all my family: Emilia Fyodorovna,[20] Pasha,[21] and the others. However, none of that justifies me in the least, because I wasn't alone. I was with a young, kind, and wonderful creature who believes in me entirely, of whom I am the defender and protector, and cons[equently], whom I could not bring to ruination and thus risk everything, even if by risking only a little.

My future seems very depressing to me: most importantly, I can't return to Russia, for the above-mentioned reasons, and worst of all is the question of what will happen to the people who depend on me for help. All these thoughts are killing me. But one way or another, sooner of later, I have to get out of this situation. I can only rely on myself, of course, because there is nothing else in sight.

In 1865, after returning from Wiesbaden, in October, I barely managed to persuade my creditors to wait a bit, concentrated, and set to work.[22] I was successful, and the creditors were paid back decently. Now I've arrived in Geneva with ideas in my head. I have a novel, and if God helps, it will turn out to be a long thing and, perhaps, not a bad one. I like it terribly much and will be working on it with pleasure and anxiety.

Katkov himself told me in April that they would like to and that it would be best to begin publishing my novel in January 1868. That's the way it will be, although I'll start sending the novel in parts earlier.[23]

Even though there aren't any creditors here, my situation is worse than in 1865.[24] At least Pasha and Emilia Fyodorovna were before my eyes. Moreover, I was single. True, Anna Grigoryevna is an angel, and if you only knew what she means to me now. I love her, and she says that she is happy, quite happy, and that she doesn't need any amusements or people, and that she's quite satisfied with just the two of us alone in the room.

All right. Now that means I have six months of uninterrupted work ahead. But by then it will be time for my wife to give birth.[25] Geneva is a good city: there are both doctors and the French language here. But the climate is very bad, gloomy, and the fall and winter are vile. Perhaps, if we have the means, we can still move to Italy in two-and-a-half months. In general we should winter either in Italy or in Paris. In general, I don't know where it's more advantageous and comfortable. But perhaps we'll stay in Geneva clear through to the spring.

The financial calculations are the following: if the novel is published, Katkov won't refuse another advance of three thousand or so next year. That means there would be some for us as well as for Pasha and Em[ilia] Fyod[orovna], and even a little for the creditors too (to buck them up). The novel can be either sold or sold in advance, from any time after the middle of the year, in a second edition.[26]

You are all I have, my dear friend, my Providence. Please help me in the future. Because I'll be imploring you to assist in all these major and minor affairs of mine.

The idea is probably clear to you, the basic idea of all these hopes of mine: it's clear that this can all have time to happen and to bring its results on ONLY ONE condition, namely: THAT THE NOVEL BE GOOD. That means I need now to see to that for all I'm worth.

(O my dear friend, it was burdensome, too burdensome to take that arrogant idea upon myself three years ago that I would repay all those debts, and foolishly give out all those promissory notes! And if experience has already shown that a success can occur, then only on what condition: only on the condition that any work of mine must definitely be so successful as to arouse sufficiently great interest among the public; otherwise everything is lost. But is that really possible, can that really enter into an arithmetical calculation!)

Now is my last word to you. Hear me out, think it over, and help me!

We now have 18 francs. Tomorrow or the day after the 50 rubles that she still has to send us from Katkov's money will come from Anna Grigoryevna's mother. And that's *everything*, all our means, until a new payment from Katkov. (Anna Grigoryevna's mother right now, at this moment, is in such circumstances that she can't help us out with even a single kopeck.)

But I absolutely cannot ask Katkov for anything *now*. In 2 months it will be another matter: then I'll send him about *1500 rubles'* worth of a novel and describe my situation. He'll count 1,000 rubles toward my debt and send me 500. I'm relying on that *absolutely:* he's kind and noble.

But how am I to live for these two months of work? Don't judge me, and be my guardian angel! I know, Apollon Nikolaevich, that you yourself don't have any *extra* money. I would never have appealed to you for help. But really, I'm drowning, have utterly drowned. In two or three weeks I'll be absolutely without a kopeck, and a drowning man extends a hand without consulting reason. That's what I'm doing. I know that you are well-disposed to me; but I also know that it's almost impossible for you to give me financial help. And nonetheless, knowing that, I'm asking you for help, because besides you – I don't have *anyone*, and if you don't help me, I'll perish, utterly perish!

Here's my request:

I'm asking you for *150 rubles.* Send it to me in Geneva, poste restante. In 2 months the editorial office of *The Russian Herald* will send you 500 rubles addressed to me. I'll ask them to do that myself. (And *there's no doubt* that they'll send it, as long as I send the novel. And *I'll send it.* That's also without doubt.)

And so, I'm asking you for money *for 2 months.* Dear friend, save me! I'll repay you with eternal friendship and attachment. If you don't have any, borrow from someone for me. Forgive me for writing like *this:* but after all, I'm a drowning man![27]

Beginning in September Pasha will be left without any money.

(I'm not even mentioning Emilia Fyodorovna!) And therefore, out of the 150 rubles allot 25 to him and give it to him, telling him to tighten his belt and cut back for a couple of months. Later I'll write you how much to set aside for him for the time being out of Katkov's 500. (It's for that reason I in fact intend to ask the editorial office of *The Russian Herald* to send the advance money care of you; because I implore you to be my assistant for a while in some of my Petersburg business; that is, I'll conduct certain payments and repayments through you. Don't worry, there won't be anything here that would put you in an *ambiguous* position. I ask you only for your cordial interest, I implore you, because I have *no one, no one* in Petersburg besides you that I could rely on!)

I also ask you to write me as soon as possible. Don't leave me alone! God will reward you for this.

Tell Pasha to write me here, in Geneva, about everything that has happened to him, and if he has letters for me, to forward them to me here the same way as last time. I've received only one letter from him this whole time. I don't think he likes me, at all. And that's really hard for me to take.

My address:

Mr. Theodore Dostoiewsky, Suisse, Genève, poste restante.

Write me your address too. Since I don't know your building, I'm sending this letter via Anna Nikolavna Snitkina (Anna Grigoryevna's mother). She'll have it delivered to you.

*In any case*, I beg you most earnestly to write me, dear friend, as soon as possible and let me know all the news about all of our people, about what's going on, what's current, what you yourselves are doing. In a word, water my soul, which has become dried out in the desert, with a drop of water. Please!

Regards to all of *your* folks, your parents, and Anna Ivanovna.[28] From Anna Grigoryevna especially. How much we've reminisced about you, how much we've talked about you.

When will we see each other!

*Advise me* something too. Tell me your view of my situation. And have you by any chance heard anything about my Petersburg affairs, at least from Pasha?

In the next letter I'll write you about some other things.

I'm completely isolated in Geneva and haven't seen any of the Russians.

Not a Russian sound, not a Russian face! Good-bye. I hug you very, very tightly and kiss you.

Entirely yours, Fyodor Dostoevsky

### JANUARY 1/13, 1868: SOFIA IVANOVA (NO. 332)

*The addressee of this letter was Dostoevsky's beloved niece Sonya, to whom, as he informs her here, he dedicated* The Idiot. *In this letter, Dostoevsky records his intent in* The Idiot *to "depict a positively beautiful person." Further, aside from attesting Dostoevsky's warm feelings for his sister's family, and especially for the addressee, this letter shows that as he wrote* The Idiot, *he was pondering the "woman question" in general as well as the choices faced by his niece in particular.*

My dear, priceless friend Sonechka, in spite of your insistent request to write you, I've been silent. And meanwhile, in addition to the fact that I experienced a strong and special need to talk to *you,* if for no other reason than that I *definitely* ought to have replied to a point in your letter[29] and replied right away, as soon as possible – I should have replied. Tell me: how could it have occurred to you, dear and eternal friend, that I left Moscow after becoming angry with you and didn't offer you my hand! But could that have happened? Of course, my memory is weak, and I don't remember details, but I assert positively that *none* of that could have happened, and that it just seemed that way to you. In the first place, there could not have been any reason; I know that as well as I do that twice two is four; and secondly, and most importantly, could I really break off with my friends so easily? So that's how you know me, my dear! How painful it was for me to read that. You *ought* to have realized, Sonya, how I appreciate and respect you, and how I value your heart. I've met few people in my life like you. You'll ask how, for what reasons I've become so attached to you. (You'll ask if you don't believe me.) But my dear, it's awfully hard to answer these questions; I remember you as practically a little girl, but I didn't begin peering into you and recognizing in you a rare, special person and a rare, wonderful heart until four years ago or so, and most importantly, I came to know you the winter that the late Marya Dmitrievna died.[30] Do you remember when I came to see you after a whole month of my illness, when I hadn't seen you for a very long time? I love you all, and you especially. I love Mashenka,[31] for example, for her charm, grace, naïveté, charming manner; but I only very recently came to know the seriousness of her heart (oh, you are all talented and marked by God) – but I'm especially attached to you, and the attachment is based on a special impression that is difficult to dissect and explain. I like your restraint, your inborn and elevated feeling of your own worth, and I like the consciousness of that feeling. (Oh, don't ever betray it in any way; take the straight path, without compromises in life. Fortify your good feelings in yourself, because you need to fortify everything, and you need only make a compromise with your honor and conscience once in order to have a weak spot remain in your soul, so that just as soon as something difficult, but on the other hand, advantageous, presents itself in your life, you'll immediately retreat before the difficult and head toward the advantageous. I'm not stating a commonplace now; what I'm saying is something that afflicts me myself; and I spoke of a weak spot perhaps out of personal experience. I may love in you precisely what leaves much to be desired in me.) I especially love in you that firm edifice of honor, view, and convictions, which, of course, is absolutely natural and not yet much realized by you, because you couldn't even have recognized all of it, by reason of your extraordinary youth. I also love your mind, which is calm and discriminates clearly and distinctly, and sees truly. My friend, I agree with you about everything you've been writing me in your letters, but that I should ever agree about your accusation – that even the slightest fluctuation in my friendship for your has occurred – never! It's simply that perhaps everything should be explained through some minor matter, as some irritability of the moment in my vile character – but even that could *never* have been directed at you personally, but at someone else. Don't ever wound me with such accusations.

But for the fact that I didn't answer for so long, in spite of your request to write you soon, I give you my *word of honor* that I'll send you a letter a month regularly. In my letter to Alexander Pavlovich and Verochka I explained, as much as I could, the reason for my silence. I was in such a bad psychic mood and under such tension the whole time that I felt the need to lock myself up inside myself and grieve on my own. It would have been depressing for me to take up a letter, and besides, what would I have written? About my melancholy? (It would surely have shown through in my letter.) But that's bad material. And besides, my situation was bothersome. My entire fate depends on my work. On top of that, I have taken an advance of around 4500 rubles from *The Russian Herald*, and I gave them my word of honor, and repeated it the whole year long in every letter to the journal, that there would be a novel. And then, almost just before sending the novel off to the journal, I had to throw it out, because it had ceased to please me. (And if it had ceased to please, I couldn't have done a good job of finishing it.) I destroyed much of what I had written. Meanwhile, both the repayment of my debt, and my daily life, as well as the whole future, were contained in the novel. Then, about three weeks ago (18 December, New Style), I tackled another novel[32] and began working day and night. The idea of the novel is an old and favorite one of mine, but such a hard one that for a long time I didn't dare to take it up, and if I have taken it up now, then absolutely because I was in a nearly desperate situation. The main idea of the novel is to portray a positively beautiful person. There's nothing more difficult than that in the whole world, and especially now. All the writers, and not just ours, but even all the European ones, who ever undertook the depiction of a *positively* beautiful person, always had to pass. Because it's a measureless task. The beautiful is an ideal, and the ideal – both ours and that of civilized Europe – is far from having been achieved. There's only one positively beautiful person in the world – Christ, so that the appearance of this measurelessly, infinitely beautiful person is in fact of course an infinite miracle. (The whole Gospel of John is in this sense; he finds the whole miracle in the incarnation alone, in the appearance of the beautiful alone.) But I've gone too far. I'll just mention that of the beautiful people in Christian literature Don Quixote stands as the most complete. But he is only beautiful because he's ridiculous at the same time. Dickens' Pickwick (an infinitely weaker idea than Don Quixote, but still an enormous one) is also ridiculous, and effective in fact because of that. Compassion appears for the beautiful that is mocked and does not know its own value, and therefore, sympathy appears in the reader too. That arousal of compassion is in fact the secret of humor. Jean Valjean[33] is also a strong attempt, but he arouses sympathy by virtue of his misfortune and society's injustice to him. I have nothing like that, absolutely nothing, and therefore I'm terribly afraid that it will be an absolute failure. Certain details, perhaps, will be decent. I'm afraid it will be boring. The novel is long. I wrote the whole *first part* in twenty-three days and sent it off a few days ago. It will definitely not be striking. Of course, that's just the introduction, and it's good that nothing yet has been compromised; but hardly anything has been explained, hardly anything laid out yet. My only wish is that it arouse at least some curiosity in the reader, so that he'll take up the second part. I'll finish the second, which I'm beginning tomorrow, in a month (I've in fact worked like this my whole life).[34] I think it will be stronger and better than the first. Wish me at least some success, my dear friend! The novel is called *The Idiot* and is dedicated to you, that is, to Sofia Alexandrovna Ivanova. My dear friend, how I would wish that the novel turn out to be at least somewhat worthy of the dedication. In any case, I'm no judge of myself, especially not when so much in the heat of the moment as now.

My health is absolutely satisfactory, and I can bear difficult work, although a difficult time is ahead for me, because of Anna Grigoryevna's delicate condition.[35] I'll put in another four months or so at work, and then I dream of moving on to Italy. Solitude is essential for me. I'm distressed about Fedya[36] and about Pasha.[37] I'm also writing to Fedya with this mail. It's very depressing for me abroad, however; I want terribly to go to Russia. Anna Grigoryevna and I are all alone. My life: I get up late, fuel the fireplace (it's terribly cold), drink coffee, then get down to work. Then at four o'clock I go have dinner at a restaurant and dine for two francs with wine. Anna Grigoryevna prefers to dine at home. Then I go to a café, drink coffee, and read *The Moscow News* and *The Voice* and reread them to the last letter. Then I walk through the streets a half an hour, for exercise, and then home and to work. Then I again fuel the fireplace, we drink tea, and again to work. Anna Grigoryevna says that she's terribly happy.

Geneva is boring, gloomy, a stupid Protestant city, with a vile climate, but so much the better for work. Alas, my friend, I may not return to Russia before September. As soon as I do, I'll immediately rush to embrace you. I have the idea of starting, after arriving in Russia, a new publication.[38] But everything depends, of course, on the success of my current novel. And just imagine – I'm working like this, and I don't yet know whether I was too late for the January issue. That will be a problem!

I'll see you somehow, get together with you somehow, meet you somehow! I often daydream about all of you. A few days ago I dreamed of you and Masenka[39] – I dreamed a whole novella; Masenka was the heroine. Give her a sound kiss from me. But what's this with your health? You frightened me. Don't grieve, my friend, that's the main thing, and the main thing is not to hurry, not to worry very much; everything will come in its own time and will come fine, all on its own. There is an infinite number of chances in life; worrying too much means losing time. I wish you energy and firmness of character; I'm certain of them, however. My dear, look after your education and don't neglect even a profession, but the main thing is not to rush; you are still very young; everything will come in its own time, but you should know that the woman question, and especially that of the Russian woman, will definitely make several great and wonderful strides even within your lifetime. I'm not speaking of our precocious ladies – you know how I view them.[40] But a few days ago I read in the papers that a former friend of mine, Nadezhda Suslova (Apollinaria Suslova's sister), passed the examination for doctor of medicine at the University of Zurich and defended her dissertation brilliantly. She's a very young woman; she's twenty-three now, a rare personality, noble, honest, lofty!

I had planned to write you a lot, too much, but here I've covered over so many pages and not written even one-tenth of it. Until the next letter, my friend!

I would like to have a talk with you about one very interesting subject concerning you.[41] Don't forget me, and write. Take care of your health most of all. Embrace Masenka one more time. I've heard that ———[42] has been promoted to the rank of lieutenant general in the Papal Army and will be playing on his pipe a polka of his own composition on the destruction of Garibaldi, and Cardinal Antonelli[43] and the chancellor-general (for the woman) will dance in the Pope's presence, and Yulenka[44] will watch and be angry. Kiss her too, if she'll allow a kiss (from me); kiss Vitya[45] for me too, as well as the *much praised* Lyolya.[46] Then everyone, and give your brother Alexander Alexandrovich[47] a firm handshake from me.

I embrace you and kiss you. Your friend *always*,

Fyodor Dostoevsky

I'll keep my word about writing you every month. But you please write to me too!

## MARCH 21–22/APRIL 2–3, 1868: APOLLON MAIKOV (NO. 341)

*This letter to Maikov shows Dostoevsky in his new role of very proud and joyful father of a newborn daughter and in his habitual role of concerned and frustrated stepfather to Pasha Isaev and brother-in-law to Mikhail Dostoevsky's widow, Emilia. He expresses optimistic views about Russia's future and his perpetual concern about his progress with the novel and its success with readers.*

Dear and kind friend Apollon Nikolaevich, first, thank you very much, dear fellow, for carrying out all my errands, which turn out to be very troublesome and for which you have had to run around so much. Forgive me for tormenting you, but really, you're the only person I can rely on (which does not at all constitute a reason for tormenting you). Second, thank you for the greeting, congratulations, and best wishes for the three of us. You are right, my kind friend, you have described this feeling of being a father from nature and you have taken your wonderful words from nature: everything is absolutely right. I have been feeling, for almost a month now, terribly much that is new and that until now has been unfamiliar to me, from exactly that moment that I first saw my Sonya,[48] up to that moment when, through joint efforts, we had just bathed her in a basin. Yes, an angelic soul has in fact flown in to be with us. But I won't describe my feelings to you. They are growing and developing with every day. Here's what, my dear fellow, the last time, when I wrote you in such alarm, I *forgot* (!) to write to you what Anya[49] and I had agreed on while *still in Dresden* last year (and what she reproached me horribly about for having forgotten now) – *is that you're the godfather for my Sonya.* Dear fellow, please agree! We've had it decided for almost ten months. If you refuse, that will be a misfortune for Sonya. Even her first godfather refused! But you won't refuse, my friend. I'll add that this won't cause even the slightest trouble for you, and that you'll become a godfather for us is so much the better. The godmother is Anna Nikolavna[50] – has she told you? Please tell me your answer soon – because we need it for the christening.[51] It's been a month now, and she's still not christened! (Does that happen in Russia?) But your goddaughter (I'm sure that she's your goddaughter) – I'm telling you – is very cute – in spite of the fact that she looks impossibly, even ridiculously, like me. Even to the point of strangeness. I wouldn't believe it if I hadn't seen it. The child is only just a month old, but she already even has absolutely my facial expression, my whole face, including the wrinkles on the brow – she lies there and looks as though she's writing a novel! I won't even mention the features. Her brow resembles mine even to the point of strangeness. From that, of course, it should follow that she's not especially pretty (because I'm a *good-looking* man only in Anna

Grigoryevna's eyes – and that's serious, I'll tell you!). But you, yourself an artist, know perfectly well that it's possible to resemble even an unattractive face and at the same time be very nice itself. Anna Grigoryevna begs you very much to be the godfather. She loves you and Anna Ivanovna[52] terribly much and respects you infinitely.

You are too great a prophet: you have been prophesying for me that I have new cares now and will become an *egoist*, and that, unfortunately, because of impossibility, has come true quite otherwise: just imagine: I have not gotten *a single line* written this whole month! My God, what I'm doing to Katkov, to my promises, word of honor, obligations! I was unbelievably glad when, following my notification that I would be late, because of the birth, *The Russian Herald* printed at the end of the first part of the novel that the continuation would be in the April issue rather than the one for March. But unfortunately, I have no more than *twenty* days left for the April one, too (having been terribly late), and not a line has been written! I'm writing to Katkov tomorrow and apologizing, but really, my apologies are worthless to them. And nonetheless I have to be in time for the April issue, even though it is late. And meanwhile, in addition to everything else, my whole existence (financial means) depends on them. A truly desperate situation. But what can be done: the whole month passed in extraordinary worries, troubles, and cares. I sometimes didn't sleep for nights on end, and not just because of psychic uneasiness, but because that really was necessary. And for falling sickness that's terrible. My nerves are now on edge to the highest degree. We had a hideously vile March here – with snow and freezing temperatures, almost like in Petersburg. Anna Grigoryevna was horribly out of sorts physically. (Don't tell Anna Nikolavna that FOR ANYTHING, because she'll imagine God only knows what. It's just that it's taking Anya a long time to recover, and, in addition, she's feeding the baby herself.) There's little milk, of course. We use a bottle as well. The baby, however, is fine. (Knock on wood!) Anya is finally beginning to go out for walks. We've had amazing sunny days for three days now, and the greenery is already starting to sprout. I can hardly come to from all this. Money is also a terrible worry. Three hundred rubles was sent to us. That's 1025 francs after the exchange. But we already have hardly anything. Expenses have increased, we had to pay off our earlier debts, redeem our pawned things, and exactly three weeks from today there are large expenditures in store, in connection with changing our apartment (we're being thrown out of this one for the baby's crying), and, in addition, there are some payments ahead – it's horrible. And in addition we have to live, beginning today, for at least two months or so until there's the hope of getting some more from *The Russian Herald.* But in any case I can't get anything from *The Russian Herald* without sending them the second part – and when will I get it written? Surely not again in eighteen days, like what was published in the January issue?

Your handling of the money was very good. And painful as it is for me to trouble you, send me the 25 rubles you have left here, to Geneva, *immediately, if possible.* That's how urgent the need is! (NB. Just put a 25-ruble note in a letter, register it, so that it doesn't get lost at the post office, and send it here, to my address. They change our Russian paper money here as well. But here's what: we now have new twenty-five ruble notes, I think. I'm afraid they don't know them here yet. So it's better to send old bills.)

I'm very glad that you gave Pasha[53] 50 rubles instead of 25. That's all right. I'm awfully glad that he's working.[54] Dear fellow, check up on him occasionally, at least from time to time! If I write him, I'll write that after finding out that you had given him 25 rubles as a loan, I have already repaid you. But here's what: can it really be that Pasha isn't going to write me anything and isn't going to congratulate me on the birth of Sonya? Other people have congratulated me: you, Strakhov, from Moscow, Anna Grigoryevna's friends from Petersburg,[55] but not only has there not been anything from Pasha even now, but I haven't even received an answer to a letter of mine that I wrote him about a month and a half ago, addressing it care of you. (Did you get it? For some reason you *don't* mention it.) And he could answer that one. By the way, there's also something *extremely important:* after all, I still don't know whether he went to Moscow or not. Did he go to see Katkov? That's terribly important for me to know.[56] Just imagine – I sent Katkov a long letter of apology exclusively apropos of that! I need to know extremely badly. Can't you please find out, dear fellow?

(I informed Emilia Fyodorovna officially, solemnly, that I have a new daughter – nothing, no response from her! And earlier, too, there was no reply from her to an extremely important question of mine regarding their apartment and the landlord, Alonkin. That even surprises me. After all, that's even outrageously rude!)

Regarding a will and other such advice of yours I have always, always been of your opinion myself.[57] But my friend, my sincere and devoted friend (perhaps the only one!), why do you consider me so kind and generous? No, my friend, no, I'm not particularly kind, and that saddens me. But poor Marya Dmitrievna[58] left me Pasha on her deathbed. How can I completely abandon him? (But you don't even advise that.) At least from time to time I have to help him, the more so as I sincerely love him; after all, I raised him in my home from the age of ten! He's the same as a son. He and I lived together. And at such a young age, and alone, to leave him on his own – is that really possible? At least sometimes, poor as I may be, I have to help him. He's a horribly frivolous person, that's true; but after all, at his age I may have been even worse than he (I remember). He needs to be supported just now. If a good, kind impression is left in his heart now, it will be of use to him in his further development. And that he's in service and himself now earning – I'm terribly, terribly glad about that – let him work a bit. And you I hug and kiss fraternally for having gone to see Razin and taking care of him there.[5]

As for Em[ilia] Fyodorovna, after all, the point again is my deceased brother Misha. And really, you don't know what that man was for me my whole life, from the first moment of consciousness on! No, you don't know that! Fedya[60] is my godson and also a young man who earns his keep through hard work. Here too, *if it's at all possible,* I need to support him sometimes (because he's a young man, he can't have everything around his neck, it's too heavy, sir). But why do you, my dear fellow, make yourself out to be such a practical person and an egoist? Aren't you the one who gave me a loan of 200 rubles and who with the death of my brother Misha and the collapse of the journal lost almost 2000 rubles? But I was wrong to start up about all this. I consider your advice, in any case, absolutely correct. And actually, with regard to me, there is a proverb: don't boast when you're headed into battle. I write that apropos of needing to help them, and so on. But how do I know what's going to happen to me?

No matter how hideous, no matter how vile life abroad has become for me, I sometimes think with horror about what will happen to my health when I manage to return to Petersburg. After all, if I have attacks here, what about there? My mental capacities, memory, for instance, are absolutely lost.

Everything that you write about Russia, and most importantly, your mood (the rosy color), makes me very happy.

It's absolutely true that there's no point in paying attention to various individual cases;[61] as long as there is an integral whole and an impetus and a goal for that whole, and everything else cannot be any other way in view of such an enormous regeneration as under our present great sovereign.[62] My friend, you view things absolutely the same way I do, and you have finally said what I even said aloud three years ago, at the time I was still publishing the journal, and what people misunderstood me about, namely: that our constitution is in fact the reciprocal love of the monarch for the people and of the people for the monarch.[63] Yes, our state's basis of love, rather than of conquest (which the Slavophiles were first to discover, I think), is a very great idea, on which much will be built. We'll tell this idea to Europe, which doesn't understand anything at all about it. Our misfortunate class of clever fellows,[64] who have lost touch with the soil, had to end up like that, alas. They'll die like that; you can't remake them! (Turgenev!) But the new generation – that's where you have to look. (A classical education could help very much. What is Katkov's lyceum?)[65] Here abroad I have definitely become an absolute monarchist for Russia. If anyone among us has done anything, then, of course, it is only he (and not just because of that, but simply because he's tsar, loved by the Russian people, and personally because he's tsar. Our people has always given and continues to give its love to every tsar and ultimately believes only in him. For the people that's a mystery, a priesthood, an unction). The Westernizers don't understand anything about this, and they, boasting of their basis in facts, have overlooked the main and greatest fact of our history. I like your idea about Peter's pan-Slavic significance. I've heard that idea for the first time in my life, and it's absolutely true.[66]

But here's what: I read *The Voice* here. Terribly sad facts are sometimes presented in it. For instance, about the disarray of our railroads (the newly-built ones), about zemstvo affairs, about the sad state of the colonies.[67] It's a horrible misfortune that we still have few people, doers. There are talkers, but when it comes down to business, you can count them on the fingers of one hand. Of course I don't mean people who get things done in lofty matters, but simply the petty bureaucrats of whom we need many, and who are lacking. Let's assume that there have been enough people for judges and jurors. But on the railroads? And several other places too. A terrible confrontation of new people and new needs with the old order. I'm not talking about bringing their ideas to life: there are lots of freethinkers, but no Russians. Most importantly, the consciousness of a Russian person in oneself – that's what's needed. But how openness helps the tsar and all Russians – oh, Lord, it's inimical, Westernizing.

I would terribly much like our political railroads to get established quickly (Smolensk, Kiev, but quickly, and new rifles quickly too!).[68]

Why has Napoleon increased his forces and risked a thing so unpleasant for his people, at such a critical moment for himself? The D[evil] only knows. But it won't lead to anything good for Europe. (I somehow believe that terribly much.) It's bad if they drag us in too. If only it can be after a couple of years. And not just Napoleon. Besides Napoleon the future is frightening, and we need to prepare for it. Turkey is hanging by a thread, Austria is in too abnormal a situation[69] (I'm just analyzing the elements and not judging about anything), the cursed Western proletarian question that has become terribly developed (which is hardly mentioned in daily politics!), and lastly, Napoleon is an old man and in poor health. He won't live long. During that time he'll create even more failures, and the Bonapartes will sicken France even more – and what will happen then? Russia definitely must prepare, and quickly, because this may happen terribly soon.

How glad I am that the heir apparent has shown himself to Russia in such a good and majestic way and that Russia is giving such evidence of its hopes for him and its love of him.[70] Yes, let there be even only half the love that there is for his father, and that would be enough. But may God grant that our Alexander live another forty years. He has done for Russia practically more than all his predecessors taken together.[71] But the most important thing is that he is so loved. All Russian movement now, all regeneration, is based on that *support* and only on it. Oh, my friend, how I would like to return, how sickening my life here is. An awful life. And most importantly, work is not going well. If only I could do a decent job of finishing the novel,[72] how good that would be! That's the basis of my whole future. Anna Grigoryevna doesn't pine and says sincerely that she's happy. But I'm miserable. I don't go anywhere and don't see anyone. But even if there were friends I don't think I'd go visit. I've gone completely to seed, but the work still isn't moving. I only leave the apartment for two hours a day, at five o'clock, and go to a café to read Russian papers. I don't know anyone here and am glad for that. It's disgusting even to meet our *clever fellows.* Oh, poor people, oh, worthless people, oh, trash, swollen from vanity, oh, shit! It's disgusting![73] H[erzen] and I met by chance on the street, talked ten minutes in a hostilely polite tone, with little gibes, and went our separate ways. No, sir, I won't go, sir. How they, oh, how they have fallen behind, to what an extent they fail to understand anything. And they've swollen up, how they've swollen up!

I read here thirstily the newspaper announcements of the appearance of issues of journals and the titles. Strange names and contents of issues, for instance, *Notes of the Father[land],* yes, rags instead of banners, that's true! Dear fellow, don't give them anything, wait a bit. But the question of where to publish obviously even troubles you. Don't worry, my friend. I'm writing you in a hurry right now, otherwise I'd have a talk with you. I have an idea for you, but it requires special exposition, in a whole letter, and I don't have the time right now. I'll write soon. This idea occurred to me apropos of your "Sofia Alexeevna." And believe me, it's serious, don't laugh. You'll see for yourself what sort of an idea it is! I'll lay it out. It's not a novel and not a narrative poem. But it's so needed, will be so essential, and will be so original and new and with such an essential, Russian tendency that you yourself will gasp! I'll lay out the program for you. It's too bad that it will be in writing, rather than in a live conversation. You'll be able to become famous with this, and most important, it will *have* to be issued in a separate book, after printing several excerpts beforehand, and the book will *have* to sell a huge number of copies.

So have you finished *Revelations?*[74] I had imagined that you had abandoned it. There's no way of avoiding the ecclesiastical censorship, of course, and it's impossible any other way, but if you have been translating it absolutely accurately, they'll permit it. I received a letter from Strakhov. It made me happy. I want to write him soon, but since he didn't write me his address (he forgot!), I'll answer him via you. And I'll ask you to deliver it. Dear fellow, write me more often. You wouldn't believe what your letters mean for me! It's already April 3, local style, and the 25th is the last deadline (minimum!) for sending off the novel, and *I don't have a single line*, not a single line written! Lord, what's going to happen to me! Well, goodbye. I kiss you and embrace you, Anya sends her regards, and we both send our regards to Anna Ivanovna. Entirely yours,

Fyodor Dostoevsky

P.S. Please write me everything you hear (if only you hear anything) about *The Idiot.* I need that, need it, definitely need it! Please! The finale of the second part, about which you wrote, is the same that is published at the end of the first part. I was relying on that! I still believe in the absolute truth of Nastasya Filippovna's character, however. By the way: many little things at the end of the first part are taken from nature, and certain characters are simply portraits, for instance, General Ivolgin, Kolya. But your judgment may in fact be very accurate.[75]

## MAY 18/30 MAY, 1868: APOLLON MAIKOV (NO. 346)

*A heartbroken Dostoevsky writes of his baby daughter Sonya's death. His question "But where is Sonya?" will be raised in different guises in* The Idiot *and other subsequent works.*

Thank you for your letter, my dear Apollon Nikolaevich, and for the fact that after getting angry at me, you didn't cease corresponding with me. I always, at the bottom of my heart, was certain that *Apollon Maikov* wouldn't do that.

My Sonya[76] has died; we buried her three days ago. Two hours before her death I didn't know that she would die. Three hours before her death the doctor said she was better and that she would live. She was sick for only a week; she died of pneumonia. Oh, Apollon Nikolaevich, my love for my first child may have been ridiculous; I may have spoken of it ridiculously in many letters of mine to people congratulating me. The only person ridiculous for them was me alone, but I'm not afraid to write to you, *to you.* That little three-month-old creature, so poor, so tiny, was already a personality and a character for me. She was beginning to know and love me and to smile when I approached. When I sang songs to her with my funny voice she loved to listen to them. She didn't cry and frown when I kissed her; she would stop crying when I approached. And now people tell me by way of consolation that I'll have more children. But where is Sonya? Where is that little person for whom I state boldly that I would accept crucifixion if only she could be alive? But let's stop this; my wife is crying. We'll finally take our leave of our little grave the day after tomorrow and go away somewhere. Anna Nikolavna[77] is with us: she arrived just a week before her death.

The last two weeks, beginning with the onset of Sonya's illness, I haven't been able to work. I sent an apology to Katkov again, and again only three chapters will appear in *The Russian Herald*, in the May issue.[78] But I hope that now I'll be working day and night, without a break, and beginning with the June issue the novel will come out at least decently.

Thank you for agreeing to be the godfather. She was christened eight days before her death.

I know, my friend, that I'm very guilty before you for not yet having returned the money borrowed from you and, in addition, for giving part of the money that I only recently received from Katkov to Emilia Fyodorovna[79] and Pasha[80] and not yet to you, when you must now be in very great need.[81] But you can't repair anything with regrets, and therefore I'll tell you straight out everything I can tell you *for certain:* at the present moment I can't give back anything; I myself have *almost* nothing, and in leaving Geneva, I even pawned my clothes and my wife's (I'm only telling you this). I don't dare ask Katkov for anything right now, since I've been deceiving him for three months now. But in a month and a half and *at the most* in two (*that's for certain*) – I'll ask Katkov to send you 200 rubles from me. That's for certain. As for the fact that I have not yet thought of you, that's unfair, *honest to God.* It bothered me a lot; but what can I tell you? I can't tell you anything. Just remember one thing, Apollon Nikolaevich, that when I borrowed that 200 rubles from you back then, even then I was borrowing almost half for them, for my relatives, and 75 of the 200 rubles went to them via you. I think that's how it was, as far as I recall. I thank you very much for having saved me then, and I very much appreciate your tact with me until now, in spite of the fact that your situation was a difficult one, about which I have now learned.

By the way, one *great request:* don't pass on the news about my Sonya dying to any of my *relatives* if you see them. At least I wouldn't like them to know about this for a while, including, of course, Pasha. I think that not only will none of them feel bad about my child, but perhaps even the contrary, and the thought of that alone enrages me. In what way is that poor creature to blame before them? Let them hate me, let them laugh at me and at my love – I don't care.

Forgive me for Pasha's bothering you so. I don't understand what's going to become of him. What's he leading up to?[82] The two positions that he had could have made him honest and independent. What a tendency, what views, what ideas, what bragging! It's typical.

But once again, on the other hand, how can I leave him like that? After all, a little bit more and such ideas will result in a Gorsky or a Raskolnikov.[83] After all, they're all madmen and fools. I don't know what's to become of him. I just *pray* to God for him. Also by the way: he has not replied *a thing* to my letter three months ago. I couldn't have written him more gently. He *to such an extent* regards me exclusively as someone obliged to send him money that he didn't even write me a couple of lines, even if only as a postscript to someone's letter, to congratulate me when Sonya was born. I would rather he not learn of her death.

I have also learned that he has in his hands some extraordinarily important letters that have come for me this year. (One of them from my earlier friend Krukovskaya.) How could I get them forwarded to me here. That's very, very important for me.[84] He may have other letters as well.

Good-bye, my friend. I'll try to write you from the new place. *Montreux*, which you write about, is one of the most *expensive* and fashionable places in all of Europe. I'll look for a little village near Vevey. Your translation of *Revelations* is magnificent, but it's too bad that's it isn't all of it. I read it yesterday.

Entirely yours, Fyodor Dostoevsky

My wife thanks you for everything and asks you to keep Sonya's little icon for her.[85]

### NOTES BY DAVID LOWE

1. Dostoevsky had received the letter May 29, 1867.

2. A reference to Chatsky's monologue in act 3, scene 21, of Griboyedov's *Woe from Wit.*

3. Dostoevsky's promissory note to Vyacheslav Petrovich Pechatkin had fallen due in November 1864.

4. Saint Petersburg's debtors' prison was located in one Tarasov's building.

5. Anna Dostoevskaya.

6. Dostoevsky did not make the first notes for *The Idiot* until September 1867.

7. Anna Maikova, Maikov's wife.

8. Dostoevsky treated those topics in *The Possessed*, *A Raw Youth*, and *The Diary of a Writer.*

9. On May 25, 1867, a Polish émigré, A. Beryozovsky, made an attempt on the life of Alexander II in Paris. Unharmed, Alexander left Paris for Berlin. Soon thereafter, Paris lawyers staged a demonstration to show their support of the Poles in general and Beryozovsky in particular.

10. Beryozovsky was sentenced to hard labor rather than to death.

11. The merchant had been flogged when he refused to give the chief of police a bribe of five thousand rubles. The incident had been exposed in the Russian press.

12. Reference to the extensive reforms carried out by Alexander II in the 1860s. The most significant, no doubt, was the abolition of serfdom.

13. Katkov's political views were those of a conservative Russian nationalist.

14. Pavel Isaev, the son of Dostoevsky's first wife.

15. Emilia Dostoevskaya, the widow of Dostoevsky's brother Mikhail.

16. Reference to Nikolay Isaakovich Utin (1841–1883), revolutionary, member of the Central Committee of the "Land and Freedom" Party, member of Marx's First International.

17. The attitude that Dostoevsky expresses toward Westernizers here prefigures the sentiments later dramatized in *The Possessed.*

18. Reference to Turgenev's lost article "The Aksakov Family and the Slavophiles."

19. Dostoevsky has in mind his meetings with Turgenev in Baden in September 1863.

20. Emilia Dostoevskaya.

21. Pavel Isaev.

22. Dostoevsky refers to work on *Crime and Punishment.*

23. *The Idiot.*

24. See Letters 233 and 253.

25. The Dostoevskys' daughter Sofya Fyodorovna was born March 5, 1868. She died less than three months later.

26. A second edition of *The Idiot* was not published until 1874.

27. Maikov sent the money.

28. Anna Maikova, Maikov's wife.

29. Sofya Ivanova had written Dostoevsky to ask for advice about her

mother's insistence that she rescue the family financially by marrying a man whom she did not love.

30. Dostoevsky's first wife died in April 1864.

31. Maria Ivanova, daughter of Dostoevsky's sister Vera and her husband, Alexander Ivanov.

32. *The Idiot.*

33. The hero of Victor Hugo's *Les Misérables* (1862).

34. Dostoevsky did not in fact send off the second part for another month and a half.

35. Anna Dostoevskaya was pregnant.

36. Dostoevsky's nephew Fyodor Dostoevsky.

37. Pavel Isaev.

38. Dostoevsky refers to an almanac, an early version of *The Diary of a Writer.*

39. Maria Ivanova.

40. Reference to the so-called nihilists of the 1860s.

41. Dostoevsky was hoping to persuade Ivanova to take part in the almanac he was planning.

42. In the original letter the name here has been completely inked out.

43. Giacomo Antonelli (1806–76), head of the State Council of the Papacy beginning in 1850.

44. Yulia Ivanova, daughter of Vera and Alexander Ivanov.

45. Viktor Ivanov, son of Vera and Alexander Ivanov.

46. Alexey Ivanov, son of Vera and Alexander Ivanov.

47. Alexander Ivanov, Dostoevsky's brother-in-law.

48. The Dostoevskys' daughter Sofya.

49. Anna Dostoevskaya.

50. Anna Snitkina, Dostoevsky's mother-in-law.

51. Maikov agreed to be the godfather.

52. Anna Maikova.

53. Pavel Isaev.

54. Pavel Isaev had been transferred from the Address Bureau to the Archive of the Kingdom of Poland.

55. N. M. and V. Ya. Stoyunin.

56. Pavel Isaev had not gone to Moscow.

57. Maikov had advised Dostoevsky to draw up a will, lest Emilia Dostoevskaya and her family automatically inherit the right to Dostoevsky's works.

58. Marya Dostoevskaya, Dostoevsky's first wife.

59. Razin served in the Chancellery for Affairs of the Kingdom of Poland.

60. Dostoevsky's nephew Fyodor Dostoevsky.

61. Maikov had written Dostoevsky about his sense that things were improving in Russia dramatically and would soon get even better.

62. Maikov had written of the Russian people's love for Alexander II and of the importance of Russia for the world.

63. Dostoevsky does not in fact seem to have published any remarks to this effect in *The Epoch*.

64. Dostoevsky apparently means Russia's Westernizers.

65. The Moscow Lyceum in Memory of Tsarevich Nikolay Alexandrovich was founded in 1868 on funds donated by Katkov and others. The curriculum was virtually the same as for the so-called classical gymnasiums.

66. Maikov had written Dostoevsky about Peter the Great's pan-Slavic significance vis-à-vis the East (i.e., Turkey).

67. Dostoevsky apparently means the non-Russian areas of the Russian Empire.

68. Dostoevsky is reacting to Maikov's statement that in a year the Russian Army would be rearmed.

69. Dostoevsky refers to the large Slavic population under the rule of Germans and Magyars.

70. Reference to the tsarevich's role in soliciting contributions for victims of famine in Russia.

71. Reference to the reforms undertaken by Alexander II.

72. *The Idiot.*

73. Dostoevsky apparently refers to Westernizers abroad such as Turgenev and Herzen.

74. An excerpt from Maikov's *From Revelations* was published in 1868.

75. Maikov had written that the characters in part 1 of the novel seemed to inhabit a fantastic world, and that one did not believe in them.

76. Dostoevsky's daughter Sofya.

77. Anna Snitkina.

78. Chapters 3, 4, and 5 of part 2 of *The Idiot* came out in the May issue.

79. Emilia Dostoevskaya.

80. Pavel Isaev.

81. Maikov had written Dostoevsky about his father's illness and his own complete lack of money.

82. Pavel Isaev had quit his job and asked Maikov to vouch for him for a loan.

83. Vitold Gorsky, an eighteen-year-old student, had murdered six people. Dostoevsky saw Gorsky's actions as the natural consequence of the sort of "nihilistic" ideas sometimes entertained by Raskolnikov in *Crime and Punishment.*

84. Dostoevsky was making use of his experiences with Krukovskaya and her family in *The Idiot.*

85. The Maikovs had planned to send the Dostoevskys an icon for Sonya.

# IV SELECT BIBLIOGRAPHY

The list below contains works relevant to *The Idiot* in particular. For a full bibliography of recent works on Dostoevsky, see: W. J. Leatherbarrow, *Fedor Dostoevsky: A Reference Guide* (Boston: G. K. Hall, 1990) and the bibliographical listings in the "Current Bibliography" section of each issue of *Dostoevsky Studies* (*Journal of the International Dostoevsky Society*).

## Editions, Translations, Sources

### COLLECTED WORKS

Dostoevskii, F. M. *Polnoe sobranie sochinenii v tridtsati tomakh* (Complete collection of works in thirty volumes). 30 vols. Edited by V. G. Bazanov et al. Leningrad: Nauka, 1972–90.

This definitive edition of Dostoevsky's works and letters includes superb detailed commentary about all the works.

### *THE IDIOT* (TRANSLATIONS)

*The Idiot* was first translated into English in 1887 by Frederick Whishaw. Constance Garnett translated the novel in 1913. (She translated all of Dostoevsky's works; for decades Dostoevsky was known to the English-speaking world largely through her translations.) Her translation of *The Idiot* is still in print (New York: Bantam).

Of the translations available, probably the best to use are those of Henry and Olga Carlisle (New York: New American Library, 1969) and of Alan Myers (Oxford: Oxford University Press, 1992), both because of the quality of the translations and because of the explanatory notes. The translation by David Magarshack (London: Penguin, 1955) lacks notes.

### NOTEBOOKS

For help in deciphering these notebooks and in understanding their relationship to the finished novel, readers should consult Robin Feuer Miller's article in this volume. The Russian text of the notebooks in which Dostoevsky recorded plans and ideas for *The Idiot* and helpful commentary on these notebooks are found in volume 9 of his collected works. These notebooks have also been published in the following editions:

Dostoevskii, F. M. *Iz arkhiva F. M. Dostoevskogo. Idiot: neizdannye materialy. P. N. Sakulina i N. F. Bel'chikova.* Moscow:

Khudozhestvennaia literatura, 1931.
An early edition of the notebooks for *The Idiot.*
Dostoevsky, Fyodor. *The Notebooks for* The Idiot *[by] Fyoydor Dostoevsky.* Edited and with an introduction by Edward Wasiolek. Translated by Katharine Strelsky. Chicago: University of Chicago Press, 1967.

### LETTERS

Dostoevsky's letters and commentary on them are found in are found in volumes 28, 29, and 30, each of which consists of two books. The letters relevant to *The Idiot* are found in book 2 of volume 28 and book 1 of volume 29. Dostoevsky's letters are also available in the following editions:

Dostoevskii, F. M. *Pis'ma* (Letters). 4 vols. Edited by A. S. Dolinin. Moscow and Leningrad: Gosudarstvennoe. izd., 1928–59.
Superseded by the *Polnoe sobranie sochinenii,* but often referred to.
Dostoevsky, Fyodor. *Complete Letters.* Edited and translated by David Lowe. Vol. 2, *1860–1867.* Vol. 3, *1868–1871.* Ann Arbor, Mich.: Ardis, 1989–90.
This complete English edition of Dostoevsky's letters follows the numbering system of *Polnoe sobranie sochinenii.*
Dostoevsky, Fyodor. *Selected Letters of Fyodor Dostoyevsky.* Edited by Joseph Frank and David I. Goldstein. Translated by Andrew R. MacAndrew. New Brunswick: Rutgers University Press, 1987.

### OTHER SOURCES

Dostoevskaia, A. G. *Dnevnik 1867 goda* [Diary for 1867]. Edited by S. V. Zhitomirskaia. Moscow: Nauka, 1993.
During the early part of their stay abroad, Dostoevsky's wife kept a diary in shorthand, which she later transcribed and published. This edition, which made use of an exact transcription of Dostoevsky's wife's original shorthand, presents her transcription along with notation about the changes she made.
———. *Vospominaniia A. G. Dostoevskoi* [Memoirs of A. G. Dostoevskaia]. Edited by L. P. Grossman. Moscow/Leningrad: Gosdarstvennoe izd., 1925. Reprint; [n.p.]: Gregory Lounz Books, 1969.
Based on her diary, letters, and memory of their years together, this informative document has at times been criticized for presenting a hagiographic account of Dostoevsky.

Dostoevsky, Anna. *Reminiscences.* Translated and with an introduction by Helen Muchnic. New York: Liveright, 1975.

Translation of above.

A. N. Maikov. "Pis'ma k F. M. Dostoevskomu. 1867–1878" (Letters to F. M. Dostoevsky. 1867–1878). Edited, with commentary, by N. T. Ashimbaeva. In *Pamiatniki kul'tury. Novye otkrytiia. 1982.* Leningrad: Nauka, 1984.

These letters provide the other half of the Dostoevsky-Maikov correspondence, which is a very important source of information about Dostoevsky's life and thoughts during the period he spent abroad at work on *The Idiot.*

CRITICISM

Al'tman, M. S. "Iz arsenala imen i prototipov literaturnykh geroev Dostoevskogo" (From the arsenal of names and prototypes of Dostoevskii's literary heroes). In *Dostoevskii i ego vremia,* edited by V. G. Bazanov and G. M. Fridlender, 196–216. Leningrad: Nauka, 1971.

Anderson, Roger. "*The Idiot* and the Subtext of Modern Materialism." *Dostoevsky Studies* 9 (1988): 77–90.

Arbery, Glenn. "The Violated Ikon: Dostoevsky and the Riddle of Beauty." *Renascence: Essays on Value in Literature* 36 (1984): 182–202.

Bakhtin, Mikhail. *Problems of Dostoevsky's Poetics.* Translated and edited by Caryl Emerson. With an Introduction by Wayne Booth. Theory and History of Literature 8. Minneapolis: University of Minnesota Press, 1984.

Very influential in the way Dostoevsky has been read in recent decades, this work has promoted an understanding of the "dialogical nature of artistic creation" and offers discussion of *The Idiot* in regard to "carnivalization." The chapter "Toward a Reworking of the Dostoevsky Book" deepens understanding of Bakhtin's thought.

Bem, A. L. "Pered litsom smerti" (In the face of death). In *O Dostojevském. Sborník statí a materiálů,* edited by Julius Dolanský and Radegast Parolek, 150–82. Prague: Slovenská knihovna, 1972.

Discusses the influence of Victor Hugo's works, especially *The Last Day of a Condemned Man,* on Dostoevsky's oeuvre.

Bethea, David M. *The Shape of Apocalypse in Modern Russian Fiction.* Princeton: Princeton University Press, 1989.

An examination, beginning with *The Idiot* (see Bethea's chapter in this volume), of the apocalyptic tradition in Russia, tying together the nineteenth and twentieth centuries (Bely, Platonov, Bulgakov, and Pasternak).

Blackmur, R. P. "A Rage of Goodness. *The Idiot* of Dostoevsky." In *The Critical Performance.* Edited by Stanley Edgar Hyman, 235–57. New York: Vantage, 1956.

Børtnes, Jostein. "Dostoevskij's Idiot or the Poetics of Emptiness." *Scando-Slavica* 40 (1994): 5–14.

Burgin, Diana. "Prince Myshkin, the True Lover and Impossible Bridegroom: A Problem in Dostoevskian Narrative." *Slavic and East European Journal* 27 (1983): 158–84.

———. "The Reprieve of Nastasja: A Reading of a Dreamer's Authored Life." *Slavic and East European Journal* 29 (1985): 258–68.

Cascardi, Anthony J. *The Bounds of Reason: Cervantes, Dostoevsky, Flaubert.* New York: Columbia University Press, 1986.

Discussion of epistemology (and its limits) as related to *The Idiot, Madame Bovary,* and *Don Quixote,* presenting the argument that these works (often linked together on thematic grounds) share philosophical underpinnings, specifically the concern with going beyond "the bounds of reason" without falling victim to skepticism.

Catteau, Jacques. *Dostoyevsky and the Process of Literary Creation.* Translated by Audrey Littlewood. Cambridge Studies in Russian Literature. Cambridge: Cambridge University Press, 1989.

A behind-the-scenes guide to how Dostoevsky wrote his novels, examining the role played by the notebooks and other sources and factors in the novels as written. Offers discussion of Dostoevsky's epilepsy as it relates to his process of literary creation, and the demonstration of Dostoevsky's authority and control over his literary creation.

Comer, William J. "Rogozhin and the 'Castrates': Russian Religious Traditions in Dostoevsky's *The Idiot.*" *Slavic and East European Journal* 40 (1996): 85–99.

On possible links of Rogozhin to the radical sect that denied sexuality through castration.

Cox, Roger. "Myshkin's Apocalyptic Vision." In *Between Earth and Heaven: Shakespeare, Dostoevsky and the Meaning of Christian Tragedy,* 164–91. New York: Holt, Rinehart and Winston, 1969.

A discussion of the influence of the Revelation of John and the Epistles of Paul, reminding readers that although "Dostoevsky had no illusions about the immediate social efficacy of the Christian witness," he rejects the notion that "goodness is inadequate" because "Myshkin does not succeed in changing Petersburg into heaven on earth in any objective, measurable way."

Curtis, James M. "Spatial Form as the Intrinsic Genre of Dostoevsky's Novels." *Modern Fiction Studies* 18 (1972): 135–54.

Dalton, Elizabeth, *Unconscious Structure in The Idiot: A Study in Literature and Psychoanalysis.* Princeton: Princeton University Press, 1979.

The Freudian interpretation of the novel (including a chapter, "The Epileptic Mode of Being") and analysis of other aspects of Myshkin's character. Offers the argument that Dostoevsky's moral intentions were subverted by the creative process and that the novel demonstrates "the dangers of 'goodness.'"

Ermilova, G. G. *Taina kniazia Myshkina: O romane Dostoevskogo "Idiot"* (The mystery of Prince Myshkin: on Dostoevsky's novel *The Idiot*]. Ivanovo: Ivanovskii gos. un-tet, 1993.

A sympathetic view of Myshkin (with reservations about his apparent "failures") in the context of Russian Orthodox thinking, with an argument for the centrality of the Gospel of John to Dostoevsky's vision and a view of *The Brothers Karamazov* as a reworking of issues raised in *The Idiot.*

Fiene, D. M. "Dostoevsky's 'Poor Knight': The Key to Perceiving Dostoevsky's *Idiot* as Allegory." *Bulletin of the International Dostoevsky Society* 8 (1978): 10–21.

Frank, Joseph. *Dostoevsky: The Miraculous Years, 1865–1871.* Princeton: Princeton University Press, 1995.

This, the fourth volume of Frank's extraordinary biography of Dostoevsky, covers the years of *The Idiot,* combining an account of Dostoevsky's life and a portrait of his mind with a reading of *The Idiot.*

———. "A Reading of *The Idiot.*" *Southern Review* 5 (1969): 303–31.

On how the novel presents the "eschatological tension" resulting when the "totally selfless *agape*" of early Christianity (for which the end of time was imminent) is embedded in modern life.

Goerner, Tatiana. "The Theme of Art and Aesthetics in Dostoevsky's *The Idiot.*" *Ulbandus Review* 2 (1982): 79–95.

Guardini, Romano. "Dostoevsky's Idiot: A Symbol of Christ." *Cross Currents* 6 (1956): 359–82.

Guerard, Albert J. "On the Composition of Dostoevsky's *The Idiot.*" *Mosaic* 8 (1974/75): 201–15.

Hingley, Ronald. *The Undiscovered Dostoevsky.* London: Hamish Hamilton, 1962.

Myshkin as a "comic" figure. "As for the suggestion sometimes made that he represents a serious ethical ideal, this is perhaps the richest piece of comedy about him."

Hollander, Robert. "The Apocalyptic Framework of Dostoevsky's *The Idiot.*" *Mosaic* 6 (1974): 123–39.

Holquist, Michael. "The Gaps in Christology: *The Idiot.*" In *Dostoevsky and the Novel.* Princeton: Princeton University Press, 1977. Reprinted in *Dostoevsky: New Perspectives,* edited by Robert Louis Jackson, 126–44. Englewood Cliffs, N.J.: Prentice-Hall, 1984.

Offers the argument that "the major symbol clusters of the novel – execution, the Holbein Christ, epilepsy, Don Quixote, money" deny "the promise of Christ's life."

Ivanov, Vyacheslav. *Freedom and the Tragic Life: A Study in Dostoevsky.* Translated by Norman Cameron. New York: Noonday, 1960.

A symbolist interpretation of Dostoevsky; discussion of metaphysical, mythic, and mystical aspects of Dostoevsky's work with intriguing views of characters: Myshkin and Rogozhin as a "duality-in-unity" representing the "synthesis of the Russian soul," Aglaya as "the Feast of life on earth" enfolding Myshkin in her "primitive darkness," Nastasya Filippovna as the potential of resurrection.

Jackson, Robert Louis. *Dostoevsky's Quest for Form: A Study of His Philosophy of Art.* New Haven: Yale University Press, 1966.

A detailed study of Dostoevsky's aesthetics (a topic at the heart of *The Idiot*), arguing that Dostoevsky's "quest for form" was where he worked out his deeply held spiritual beliefs. Topics of particular relevance to *The Idiot:* the fantastic, types of beauty, the "poet" versus the "artist," Holbein's Christ, the aesthetics of depicting the disintegrating family.

———. "The Ethics of Vision I: Turgenev's 'Execution of Tropmann' and Dostoevsky's View of the Matter." In *Dialogues with Dostoevsky: The Overwhelming Questions,* 29–54. Stanford: Stanford University Press, 1993.

The aesthetics and ethics of violence and execution in *The Idiot*, including discussion of Holbein's Christ.

Johnson, Leslie A. "The Face of the Other in *Idiot.*" *Slavic Review* 50 (1991): 867–78.

Jones, John. *Dostoevsky.* Oxford: Clarendon Press, 1983.

*The Idiot* as failure.

Jones, Malcolm V. *Dostoyevsky after Bakhtin: Readings in Dostoyevsky's Fantastic Realism.* Cambridge: Cambridge University Press, 1990.

The chapter "*The Idiot:* Driving the Reader Crazy" explores the strategies used by the narrator "for creating emotional confusion," such as shifts of voice, changes of tempo, "switches from one topic to another while maintaining the same emotional wavelength," all, possibly, to a cathartic effect on the driven-crazy reader.

———. "K ponimaniiu obraza kniazia Myshkina" (Understanding the image of Prince Myshkin). *Dostoevskii: Materialy i issledovaniia* 2 (1976): 106–12.

Draws attention to what Jones calls the "dark side" of Myshkin.

Kimmey, John. "James and Dostoevsky: The Heiress and the Idiot." *Henry James Review* 13 (1992): 67–77.

Kjetsaa, Geir. *Dostoevsky and His New Testament.* Slavica Norvegica 3. Oslo: Solum, 1984.

Makes available in English translation the marginalia Dostoevsky made in his copy of the New Testament, with an introductory essay.

———. *Fyodor Dostoyevsky. A Writer's Life.* Translated by Siri Hustvedt and David McDuff. New York: Viking (Elisabeth Sipton), 1987.

A lively and informative account of Dostoevsky's life and works, emphasizing ways in which Dostoevsky's life is reflected in his works.

Knapp, Liza. *The Annihilation of Inertia: Dostoevsky and Metaphysics.* Evanston: Northwestern University Press, 1996.

Kovacs, Arpad. "The Poetics of *The Idiot:* On the Problem of Dostoevsky's Thinking about Genre." In *Critical Essays on Dostoevsky,* edited by Robin Feuer Miller, 116–26. Boston: G. K. Hall, 1986.

An exploration of the problems that result when Myshkin attempts to apply his ideal of "passionate participation in the suffering of others"; partly a response to Bakhtin.

Krieger, Murray. "The Curse of Saintliness." In *The Tragic Vision,*

209–27. New York: Holt, Rinehart and Winston, 1960. Reprinted in *Dostoevsky: A Collection of Critical Essays*, edited by René Wellek. Englewood Cliffs, N.J.: Prentice-Hall, 1962.

The damaging effects of Myshkin's "psychosis of humility," with Radomsky as the positive hero and/or Dostoevsky's spokesman in the novel.

Kristeva, Julia. "Holbein's Dead Christ." *Zone* 3 (1989): 238–69.

Lary, N. M. *Dostoevsky and Dickens: A Study of Literary Influence.* London: Routledge and Kegan Paul, 1973.

Leatherbarrow, W. J. "Apocalyptic Imagery in Dostoevsky's *The Idiot* and *The Devils.*" *Dostoevsky Studies* 3 (1982): 43–51.

Lesser, Simon O. "Saint and Sinner: Dostoevsky's Idiot." *Modern Fiction Studies* 4 (1958): 211–24.

Lord, Robert. *Dostoevsky: Essays and Perspectives.* Berkeley and Los Angeles: University of California Press, 1970.

———. "Dostoevsky's Novel *The Idiot.*" *Slavonic and East European Review* 45 (1967): 30–45.

Martinsen, Deborah. "The Cover-Up: General Ivolgin and Private Kolpakov." *Slavic and East European Journal* 39 (1995): 184–99.

On the untrue story told by General Ivolgin as an instance of Dostoevsky's "vran'e" – a type of lying discussed in his *Diary of a Writer* – showing how shame functions for Dostoevsky's liars "both as a source of lying and as a source of healing."

Matich, Olga. "*The Idiot:* A Feminist Reading." In *Dostoevsky and the Human Condition after a Century*, edited by Alexej Ugritsky and Valija K. Ozolins, and with an Introduction by Pete Hamill, 53–60. New York: Greenwood, 1986.

The conflict of the novel viewed as one between "feminine values of selflessness and sacrifical love," with attention to how "the novel's images of women characters, sex roles, and sex role reversals" are reflected in the Epanchin women and Nastasya Filippovna, who are "nascently masculinized women" attracted to Myshkin, a "man with female attributes."

———. "What's to Be Done about Poor Nastia: Nastas'ja Filippovna's Literary Prototypes," *Wiener Slawistischer Almanach* 19 (1987): 47–64.

Discusses Nastasya Filippovna in relation to previous fallen women.

Meerson, Olga. "Ivolgin and Holbein: Non-Christ Risen vs. Christ Non-Risen." *Slavic and East European Journal* 39 (1995): 200–13.

The relationship of a story told by Ivolgin about a man coming back from the dead to the message Ippolit sees in Holbein's Christ; shows Dostoevsky making use of the apophatic method of Orthodox theology.

Miller, Robin Feuer. *Dostoevsky and "The Idiot." Author, Narrator, and Reader.* Cambridge: Harvard University Press, 1981.

The most comprehensive and detailed reading of the novel, illuminating the process whereby the reader of this novel is challenged to "choose" whom and what to believe. It examines the split of author and narrator (and, consequently, of author's reader and narrator's reader) and shows that this narrative technique stems from Dostoevsky's view that the truth of this novel must be told "slant." It includes discussion of the notebooks of the novel (excerpted for this volume) and of subtexts (especially the Gothic novel and Rousseau) of the inserted narratives.

———. "Dostoevsky and Rousseau: The Morality of Confession Reconsidered." In *Dostoevsky. New Perspectives,* edited by Robert Louis Jackson, 82–98. Englewood Cliffs, N.J.: Prentice-Hall, 1984.

Using explication of the confessional *petit-jeu* at Nastasya Filippovna's birthday party (and parts of other Dostoevskian works), shows how Dostoevsky parodies and debunks Rousseau's confession and how Dostoevsky restores to confession its meaning of providing "sacred communication" and reuniting the sinner with the community.

Minihan, Natalie Nikolaevna. "O vliianii Evangeliia na zamysel i na osnovnye literaturnye istochniki romana *Idiot.*" Ph.D. diss., Brown University, 1989.

Mochulsky, Konstantin. *Dostoevsky: His Life and Work.* Translated and with an Introduction by Michael A. Minihan. Princeton: Princeton University Press, 1967.

The chapter on *The Idiot* regards it as the "spiritual biography" of its author; whereas Myshkin believes that "beauty saves the world," the novel demonstrates that in this evil world, "beauty must be saved."

Monas, Sidney. "Across the Threshold: *The Idiot* as a Petersburg Tale." In *New Essays on Dostoyevsky,* edited by Malcolm Jones and Garth Terry, 67–93. Cambridge: Cambridge University Press, 1983.

A demonstration that the novel incorporates many of the topoi of the Petersburg tale with the suggestion that Peter the Great is an ideological villain whom Myshkin challenges.

Moser, Charles A. "Nihilism, Aesthetics, and *The Idiot*." *Russian Literature* 11 (1982): 377–88.

Murav, Harriet. *Holy Foolishness: Dostoevsky's Novels and the Poetics of Cultural Critique*. Stanford: Stanford University Press, 1992.

Chapter on *The Idiot* argues that Dostoevsky was using a "deliberate narrative strategy" to which holy foolishness is central and in which the "perceived impossibilities" associated with the novel ("the impossibility of a novelistic portrayal of an epileptic, the impossibility of a novelistic portrayal of a Christ figure, and, beyond that, the failure of that figure to transform the world around him") play a part.

Nigg, Walter. *Der christliche Narr.* Zurich: Artemis, 1956.

Myshkin as holy fool.

Passage, Charles. *Character Names in Dostoevsky's Fiction*. Ann Arbor, Mich.: Ardis, 1982.

Peace, Richard. *Dostoevsky: An Examination of the Major Novels.* Cambridge: Cambridge University Press, 1971.

Regards the novel as "an artistic success" but the "portrayal of 'the positively good man'" a failure.

Rayfield, Donald. "Dumas and Dostoevskii – Deflowering the Camellia." In *From Pushkin to Palisandriia: Essays on the Russian Novel in Honor of Richard Freeborn*, edited by Arnold McMillin, 70–82. New York: St. Martin's, 1990.

Rice, James L. *Dostoevsky and the Healing Art: An Essay in Literary and Medical History*. Ann Arbor, Mich.: Ardis, 1985.

A study of all aspects of Dostoevsky's epilepsy: the medical evidence, both general and specific to Dostoevsky; Dostoevsky's view of his epilepsy, and how he wrote it into his works.

Rosenshield, Gary. "Chaos, Apocalypse, the Laws of Nature: Autonomy and 'Unity' in Dostoevskii's *Idiot*." *Slavic Review* 50 (1991): 879–89.

Suggests chaos to be a facet both of the novel's plot (the disintegration of the family, of society) and of its structure; views *The Idiot* and *Notes from the Underground* as Dostoevsky's most "modern" and revolutionary works, because Dostoevsky challenges the reader to discern the makings of "a new, dynamic order, far more open-ended, 'unfinalizable' order."